W9-AOS-981

COMPLETE CONTEMPORARY CRAFT

embellishments

MURDOCH BOOKS

contents

beading

embroidery

crochet

knitting

beading

Introduction

Beads have been valued since ancient times for their beauty and delicacy. The earliest known examples, made of teeth and bone and designed to be worn as pendants, date back to 38,000 BC. In early times, beads would have been basic in form and fashioned from whatever materials were at hand, but as long ago as the third or fourth century BC, a method of mass-producing glass beads was developed in Southeast Asia. The resulting tiny beads were traded worldwide for 2000 years. Ancient Egypt was another centre for beads, hand-made from stone and later glass.

Throughout the ages, beads have been extensively traded, by nomadic peoples who found them a convenient way of carrying wealth, and by European traders and colonists, who used them to deal with the peoples of other continents. Beads have also been used for religious purposes; indeed, the word bead comes from the old English 'bede', meaning prayer. Rosary beads are perhaps the best-known example of this use. Beads have also had symbolic and superstitious meaning — to ward off evil or attract fertility, or to imply power, friendship or love.

The uses of beads today are primarily ornamental. Whether made from precious or semi-precious gems, shell, glass, ceramic, seeds, wood, stone, bone, plastic or other materials, they are one of the most versatile of all decorative items. They can be strung, wired, glued or sewn to make jewellery or homewares or to decorate clothing. The uses to which they can be put are limited only by your imagination.

This section presents 23 original, contemporary designs, graded roughly in order of difficulty. The tools needed for these projects can be easily found at any jewellery or bead store and at many craft stores. Although not expensive, there are different qualities of tools and therefore different prices; as with all crafts, to achieve the best possible result from your efforts, buy the best tools and materials you can afford.

For the first-time beader, the number and variety of beads and jewellery components in a craft store can be overwhelming. The trick when starting off is to decide on one or two projects and concentrate on getting the materials for those projects only. When you have familiarized yourself with the techniques and components used, you will be able to build on your knowledge and progress to more complicated designs.

Beads and findings

The following are some of the basic components used in making beaded jewellery and other items. In addition to beads of many types, there are various other components (usually metal) that are known as findings.

AB crystal This is a type of crystal with a reflective coating, giving the bead a shiny, rainbow finish. AB stands for Aurora Borealis (the Northern Lights) and the effect is similar. Crystals and beads with an AB finish are available in all sizes from seed beads to large crystals.

Artist's wire This tin-plated copper wire is available in a variety of colours and thicknesses, and used for stringing beads when a flexible but semi-rigid form is called for.

Belcher chain A style of chain that has half-round wire links.

Bell cap A decorative metal dome used to cover the ends of beads.

Bicone A type of diamond-shaped faceted crystal bead; they come in various sizes.

Clasp A component used to secure necklaces and bracelets. There are several types, including parrot clasps, magnetic clasps and screw clasps.

Eye pin A round wire post with a looped circular end (the eye). Beads can be threaded onto the post before being attached to other components.

Florist's tape Green tape used to bind flowers and cover their stems; also used in jewellery making to bind the ends of wires.

AB crystals A special reflective coating gives these beads and crystals an iridescent shimmer.

half beads Flat on one side, these can be glued; some have holes either end and can be sewn.

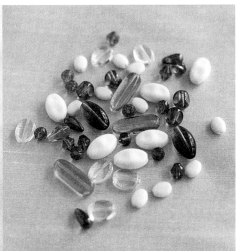

crystal beads Very precisely cut, these beads add a luxurious sparkle to special items.

glass beads A wide variety of shapes, sizes and finishes is available.

pearl beads Whether natural or artificial (glass or plastic), pearls have a lovely lustre.

seed beads These small beads are formed from a glass tube cut into smaller sections.

Head pin A round wire post with a flattened end (the head). Beads can be threaded onto the post before the end of the post is formed into an eyelet, then attached to other components.

Jump rings Wire rings that are used to link components. Open jump rings have a split allowing them to be opened so that they can be attached directly to other components. Closed jump rings have been soldered into a circle. Jump rings are available in various sizes. Depending on the size and weight of the beads used, you will need to use different thicknesses and sizes of jump ring.

Memory wire Coiled steel wire that retains its circular shape. It is available in various ring, bangle and choker diameters and can be cut to give as few or as many continuous loops as you require.

Parrot clasp Teardrop-shaped clasp with a spring opening mechanism, used for fastening necklaces and bracelets. These are available in a variety of sizes and finishes.

Pony beads This is the name given to larger seed beads.

Seed bead Tiny glass beads available in a wide variety of colours and finishes. They are made from glass rods cut into small sections.

Spacer bar A flat, elongated oval or rectangular shape with holes, used to connect multiple strands together on chokers or bracelets.

Tiger tail A type of nylon-coated metal thread onto which beads can be strung; it is a very strong and flexible material.

belcher chain A chain with circular, half-round links.

head pins Used when beads are to be attached at one end only.

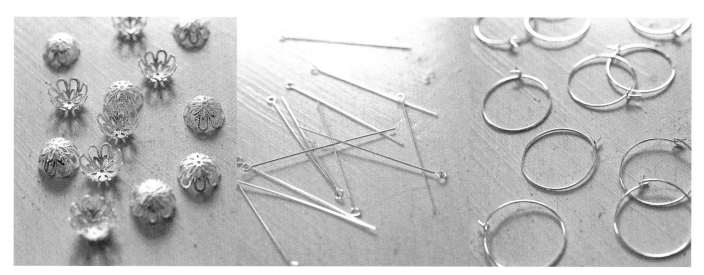

bell caps Decorative metal findings used to hold beads in place.

eye pins The eye at the end allows a bead to be linked on both sides.

findings Metal components such as these earring hoops are known as findings.

jump rings Small round rings, either open or closed, used for linking components together.

parrot clasp Metal clasp with an opening mechanism like a parrot's beak.

spacer bars Used to separate multiple strands in bracelets or chokers.

Basic tools

Below is a list of basic tools you will need when making the designs from this book. Some projects may require more specific tools. These tools can be found at jewellery suppliers, craft stores and some hardware stores.

Round-nose pliers These have two round, tapering jaws around which the posts of head and eye pins can be twisted to give oyelets of varying diameters. They should not be serrated; this applies to all types of pliers for beading work. The tapered ends allow you to hold and work with very fine components.

Snipe-nose or chain-nose pliers These are useful for gripping components while working with them. In many cases you will use a pair of pliers in each hand to open and close components such as jump rings or to attach one component to another.

Flat-nose pliers The blunt, squared-off ends of these pliers make them useful for holding components steady, but they cannot be used to bend wire into eyelets. They can, however, be used to straighten wire or eye or head posts.

Side cutters Similar in appearance to pliers but with two metal blades to cut head pins, eye pins and chains.

Ruler The metal type is preferable to plastic, as it is more durable.

Tape measure For measuring items that are longer than the ruler, or that are curved. The fibreglass type is preferable to plastic, as it is less likely to stretch and distort.

Scissors Keep separate pairs, one for paper and one for fabric; using scissors on paper blunts them, so that they will not then cut fabric easily.

Safety glasses These should be worn when cutting metal findings with side cutters so that the cut-off pieces do not fly into your eyes and cause injury.

Design fundamentals

Proportions are crucial in jewellery making, so it's important to plan your designs in their initial stages to avoid making mistakes and wasting money. When making wearable items, the following factors need to be considered.

Weight

Consider the weight of your beads when constructing your designs. Don't choose beads that are too heavy to be supported by the structure of the item or that will be uncomfortable to wear. Avoid placing beads with sharp edges on chokers and other pieces that are worn close on the body, as they will be uncomfortable.

Form

Use shapes that complement each other. If you are using organic round and oval beads, a square one will look out of place. Select the right bead for the form you are making; for example, using elongated beads on a choker will prevent the piece from sitting naturally, as it will develop kinks around the beads.

Proportions

A common mistake in beading is choosing components that don't fit together. Beads, thread, end pins and head pins are available in a variety of sizes. Make sure you select corresponding thicknesses so that the thread or post you are using will pass through the hole of your smallest bead.

Basic techniques

These techniques are employed throughout the book and, once perfected, can be adapted to a wide variety of uses.

Opening and closing jump rings

This technique is used to add beads and other components to the jump rings, or to connect a series of jump rings to form a chain to which other components are then attached.

1 Hold the jump ring on either side of its split using either snipe-nose or flat-nose pliers. Swing the jump ring open by pulling one side of the ring toward you and pushing the other side away, as shown in the photograph below.

2 To close the ring, repeat the process in the opposite direction.

3 To close a gap in a jump ring, hold either side with pliers and gently move the sides back and forth while slowly pushing them together. This technique avoids distortion of the rings and allows you to close the ring securely.

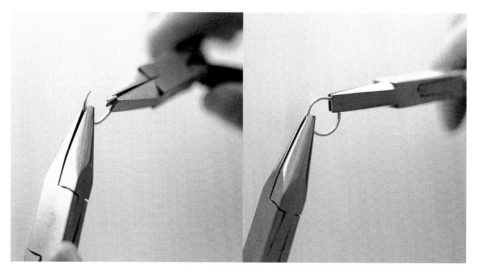

step one Pull one side of the jump ring towards you and push the other side away.

step two Close the ring by reversing the process in Step 1.

Looping head pins and eye pins

1 Thread one or more beads onto a head or eye pin, leaving at least 1 cm
(⅜ in) of post exposed.

2 Cut the post to approximately 1 cm (⅜ in) using side cutters. Wear safety
glasses when doing this as the metal offcuts may fly off and cause damage
to your eyes.

3 Hold the remaining end of the post with the top of the round-nose pliers.
Bend the wire around the pliers to create a circular loop or eyelet. You may need
to bend the wire in two movements.

4 To straighten the loop, so it sits directly on top of the post, position the round-
nose pliers inside the loop. Rest the tip of the pliers against the base of the loop
(near the post) on the closed side. Gently push down towards the post so the
loop rolls into position and rests on top of the post, as shown in the photograph.

5 If you are looping the end of an eye pin, make sure you create the second loop
in the opposite direction to the first, thus creating an 'S' shape. Straighten both
loops so they sit flat in the same direction.

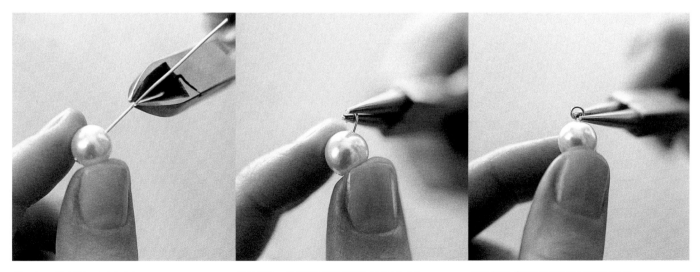

step two Cut the post, leaving
approximately 1 cm (⅜ in) exposed.

step three Roll the end of the post around
a pair of round-nose pliers.

step four Gently push the pliers down
towards the post.

Wrapping head pin posts

This technique is a more secure method of linking or attaching beads. It's best to use this technique if you are using heavy beads or fine wires, so the links will not open over time.

1 Thread a bead onto a head pin or eye pin. Make sure the post has approximately 3 cm (1¼ in) of excess wire.

2 Bend the end of the head pin around the round-nose pliers at the appropriate position, depending on the size of the loop you require; that is, use the base of the pliers to create a large loop or the tip for a smaller loop. Wrap the post 360 degrees around the pliers.

3 Open the loop with the snipe-nose pliers and thread onto the piece of jewellery or add the component to which you are linking the bead.

4 Close and hold the loop, by clamping with the round-nose pliers.

5 Hold the end of the wire with the snipe-nose pliers and wrap it 360 degrees around the post at the top of the bead in a full circle.

6 Cut off the excess wire with the side cutters.

step one Thread a bead onto a pin.

step two Bend the end of the post around the round-nose pliers.

step five Wrap the end of the wire around the post at the top of the bead.

step six Cut off the excess wire with the side cutters.

Linking head pins and eye pins

This technique is used to link beaded head pins or eye pins to other components in the design.

1 Once the pin has been beaded and an eyelet made in the end, open the end post with snipe-nose pliers.

2 Swing the loop open like a door (as for opening jump rings, page 20) so the circular shape is not distorted.

3 Attach or link to the chain or component then swing the loop closed, making sure each loop is tightly secured and there are no gaps.

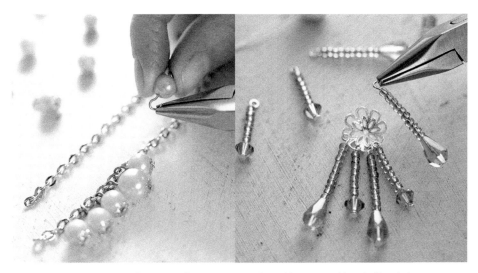

step two With snipe-nose pliers, open the eyelet at the end of the head pin.

step three Here, several beaded head pins are being attached to a bell cap.

Making clasps and earring hooks

There are many commercial clasps and earring hooks available, but you may choose to create your own as a cost-effective measure or to retain the handmade quality of your work. You can recycle excess wire that has been cut off head pins or eye pins.

Use 0.8—0.9 mm (19–20 gauge) wire. Cut the wire into a 3 cm (1¼ in) length for a clasp or 5 cm (2 in) for earring hooks.

1 To make earring hooks, create a small eyelet by looping one end of the wire into an eyelet using the tip of your round-nose pliers (see Basic techniques, page 21).

2 Position the base of the pliers approximately 1 cm (⅜ in) above the eyelet. Make sure the eyelet is facing away from the pliers. Using your fingers, push both sides of the wire around the pliers so they meet, creating a large teardrop-shaped loop.

3 Using the tip of the round-nose pliers, slightly bend the end of the post.

4 To smooth the cut ends of the hook, rub with 1000-grade emery paper, which can be bought at a hardware store.

5 You can also make clasps for bracelets and necklaces in a similar fashion; use the technique above but form the wire into an S shape in which one loop is

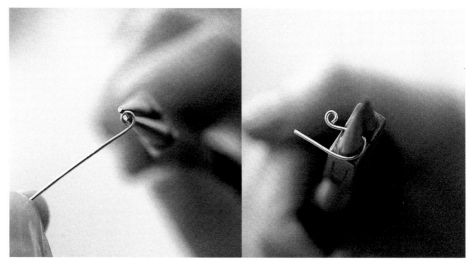

step one Create a small eyelet at one end of the wire using round-nose pliers.

step two Position the pliers and bend the wire around them.

larger than the other. You will need to leave an opening at the end of this larger loop; this gap should be big enough for the loop or jump ring to which it is to be joined to pass through it, but not so big to allow the necklace or bracelet to come loose and fall off. Close the small eyelet at the other end of the clasp completely (when later attaching it to an item of jewellery, you will need to reopen and reclose it as explained on page 23).

6 Smooth the cut ends of the clasp as explained in Step 4.

This type of clasp is useful when making jewellery for someone who finds parrot clasps too small and fiddly to manage, or to match the scale of jewellery items that use large components.

page 23

Hints

Use a fishing tackle box or ice-cube tray to organize and store your beads and findings.

Removable putty, such as Blu-Tac, is great for securing beads on half-finished projects; for example, attach a blob to the end of memory wire, tiger tail, or nylon thread to stop beads falling off while you work.

To stop beads rolling around while you're working, use a shallow tray, and cover the base with a piece of felt. Beading suppliers also stock inexpensive ready-made plastic trays. These have several compartments for storing beads as you work, as well as grooves in standard bracelet and necklace lengths, into which you can place beads and rearrange them until you have made a pleasing design.

When working with ribbons, cords or other materials that might fray, coat the cut ends with a small amount of clear nail polish.

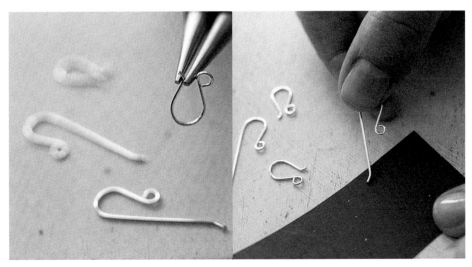

step three Slightly bend the end of the wire hook.

step four Smooth the cut ends of the wire using emery paper.

Beaded flower

This charming three-dimensional decoration

is simple to construct, and suits many purposes:

it could be worn in the hair or as a brooch, used

to decorate a gift, or attached to a hat.

Materials
204 bicone crystals, 5 mm ($\frac{3}{16}$ in) diameter
Silver artist's wire
Green florist's tape

Tools
Snipe-nose pliers
Side cutters
Safety glasses
Scissors

step two Thread crystals onto the middle of each length of wire.

step three Create a petal and twist the ends of the wire to secure it.

1 Cut the artist's wire, using the side cutters, into three 12 cm (4¾ in) lengths, four 15 cm (6 in) lengths and five 17 cm (6¾ in) lengths.

2 Thread crystals onto the middle of each length of wire: 10 crystals each on the 12 cm (4¾ in) lengths, 16 crystals each on the 15 cm (6 in) lengths and 22 crystals each on the 17 cm (6¾ in) lengths.

3 Loop the wire together and twist approximately 20 mm (¾ in) of the excess wire together to secure the beads as a petal. Gently bend the crystal petal so it sits at a slight angle to the wire stem.

4 Construct the flower from the inside out. Cut a 40 cm (15¾ in) piece of wire and bend 4 cm (1½ in) of the wire at a right angle. Hold the three smallest crystal loops in a bunch, and place the bent end of the wire on the stems. Wrap the long piece of wire around the stems three times, as shown in the photograph above.

5 Next, position the medium-sized crystal loops around the first three and secure as for Step 4, using the tail of the same long piece of wire.

6 Position the large crystal loops around the outside of the flower and secure in the

step four Construct the flower from the inside out.

step five Secure the stems together with the tail of the wire.

same manner, twisting the wire tightly so the whole form is secured. Cut the excess wire away using the side cutters.

7 For a short stem, cut the remaining wires leaving 20–30 mm (¾–1¼ in). Twist the wires together so there are no sharp edges and cover completely with green florist's tape. Wrap the tape around the wires like a bandage, making sure all of the wire is covered and any sharp ends are tucked in. Adjust the angle of the petals until you have a flower shape that you are pleased with.

Hints

Use this technique to make a decoration for a brooch or a hair comb. Complete the flower as above to Step 4. Cut the wire stems, leaving 20–30 mm (¾–1¼ in). Separate half of the stems in one direction and half in the opposite and press the wire out flat. Secure the flower to a brooch pin or comb using florist's green tape: simply wrap the tape around the wire and the brooch or comb frame.

Evening bag

A simple satin clutch purse is an evening-wear essential. Add some sparkle in the form of a satin bow encrusted with crystal flower beads.

The beads are stitched to wire-edged satin ribbon and, although it may seem like a fiddly task at first, there could be nothing quicker and easier than this stitching project once you get into the rhythm of beading.

Materials

Ribbon: wide ribbon with a tight satin weave and wire edges (these will support the beads)

Flat flower crystals with a hole through the middle

Seed beads

Clutch purse (the example shown is satin)

Tools

Needle and cotton thread (to match the colour of your ribbon)

Fabric glue (PVA), or glue to suit the material from which your bag is made; for example, leather will require a specialty glue

Scissors

Clear nail varnish

step one Tie a neat bow in the ribbon.

step two Apply a little clear nail varnish to the cut ends of the bow.

Hints

Decorate a tote bag by sewing flat embellished ribbon around the top and bottom of the bag.

You could also use this technique to attach the beaded ribbon to a cushion.

In this example the seed beads are the same colour as the flower crystals, but you could create a different effect by using contrasting colours.

1 Tie a neat bow with the ribbon, making sure it sits flat and is not too tight. The wire edges will help to hold the bow in an appealing shape. Test out the bow on the bag to determine the size of the bow — in our example, it is about half the length and two-thirds of the height of the bag.

2 Trim the ends of the ribbon and apply a little clear nail varnish to the cut edge, to prevent fraying.

3 Cut a 150 cm (60 in) length of sewing cotton, thread into the needle and knot the ends together so that you have a doubled thread 75 cm (30 in) long.

step four Sew flower crystals onto the ribbon, using seed beads to anchor the thread.

step six Apply glue to the back of the ribbon.

4 Start to bead the ribbon. Pass the thread through the ribbon and thread a flower crystal and a seed bead onto the needle. Push the beads along the thread until they sit on top of the ribbon. Thread the needle back through the flower crystal and the ribbon. Pull the thread firmly to secure the beads in place. Repeat this process, making sure the thread is pulled firmly through each bead.

5 When beading the bow's loops, pass the needle and thread through only the top layer, which will create a three-dimensional look. (If you'd like the bow to be flat, sew through both layers).

6 When the beading is complete, push the bow into the desired shape. Apply glue to the back of the ribbon at strategic points such as towards the outer ends of the loops (not too close to the ends, or the bow will be pulled flat against the bag) and behind the knot. Position the bow on the front flap of the bag and allow the glue to dry completely before using the bag.

Belt

The buckle of this belt is made from a brooch frame (available from craft and haberdashery suppliers) encrusted with pearl and crystal beads and attached to a length of ribbon. Velvet, satin and grosgrain (petersham) ribbons are all suitable.

A smaller brooch frame and narrower ribbon could be used to transform the design into a choker.

Materials
1 m (39 in) ribbon, 2.5 cm (1 in) wide
Cotton thread in a colour to match the ribbon
1 round brooch frame, 3.5 cm (1⅜ in) diameter
66 head pins, 50–60 mm (2–2⅜ in) long
33 crystal beads, 6 mm (¼ in) diameter
33 pearl beads, 6 mm (¼ in) diameter

Tools
Round-nose pliers
Snipe-nose pliers
Side cutters
Safety glasses
Needle
Scissors
Clear nail varnish

step one Thread beads onto head pins.

step two Bend head pin posts around the round-nose pliers.

1 Thread each individual bead onto a head pin (see the photograph above).

2 Bend the posts of the head pins around the base of the round-nose pliers to create a large, loose loop (see Basic techniques, page 21, and the photograph above).

3 Position the beaded head pins on the brooch frame and wrap the posts around the frame using round-nose pliers and snipe-nose pliers (see Basic techniques, page 22). Repeat this process until all of the beads are secured onto the frame. Cut off the excess posts using side cutters.

4 Measure the desired length of ribbon and cut the ends at right angles. Coat each cut end with a small amount of clear nail polish to stop the ribbon from fraying.

5 When the nail varnish is dry, thread the ribbon around the central bar of the brooch frame and fold the end back on itself. Stitch the double ribbon together using small slip stitches, to secure the ribbon to the frame. Feed the loose end of the ribbon through the frame to cinch the belt.

step three Twist the head pin posts around the brooch frame.

step five Stitch the ribbon around the frame's central bar to secure it.

Variations

Use this design to dress up an old evening
bag. Pass a length of ribbon through the
frame and stitch the ribbon to the bag.
Alternatively, make a handle of ribbon
attached to the bag at one end and passed
through a D-ring at the other end. Slide the
buckle along the ribbon to shorten or
lengthen the handle as desired.

You could also use the brooch frame and
ribbon as a curtain tie or as a pull cord for
a window blind.

Shoe jewellery

Ideal for a wedding, a formal ball or any other

special occasion, shoe jewellery is simple to

make but adds a designer touch to plain footwear.

Materials

50 cm (20 in) chain

80 head pins, 30 mm (1¼ in) long

80 bell caps, 5 mm (³⁄₁₆ in) diameter

22 pearls, 10 mm (³⁄₁₆ in) diameter

36 pearls, 7 mm (¼ in) diameter

12 round AB crystals, 6 mm (¼ in) diameter

10 round diamanté beads

Tools

Round-nose pliers

Snipe-nose pliers

Side cutters

Safety glasses

Craft glue, suitable for leather and metal

step one Thread a bell cap and a bead onto each head pin.

step four Add beads to the lengths of chain.

Hints

If you do not want to glue the chain to your shoes, take the shoes and the chain (without the beads attached) to a boot maker and have the chain sewn onto the shoes in the appropriate position at intervals. Once the chain is in place, attach all of the beads.

You may want to use plastic beads and pearls instead of glass as they weigh much less.

1 Thread a bell cap, curved side up, and a bead onto each head pin. Using side cutters, trim off the head pin post leaving 10 mm (⅜ in). Make a loop in the end of the post by wrapping it around the round-nose pliers (see Basic techniques, page 22).

2 Cut the chain into two 11 cm (4⅜ in) lengths and two 13 cm (5⅛ in) lengths, using the side cutters.

3 Sort the beads into four similar groups — one group for each chain length. Two of the groups should have a few more beads in them than the others, but all should have the same balance of colour and shape.

step five Glue the middle of the longer piece of chain to the shoe.

step six Glue the shorter piece of chain above the first.

Divide each group in half again, with one half of the beads to be applied to the chain before it is attached and the other half to be added after the chain is attached.

4 Using the snipe-nose pliers, open the loops on the beaded head pins and attach half of the beads to the lengths of chain, ensuring that the assortment is varied but similar on each chain. Make sure all the beads hang in the same direction.

5 Glue the 13 cm (5⅛ in) length of chain to the shoe first. Run a short, thin line of glue (if the glue is too thick it will block the chain links) approximately 15 mm (⅝ in)

below the front of the shoe. When the glue is tacky, position the chain across the front of the shoe. When the glue is dry, repeat the process with both sides of the chain. Gluing the middle section first will make it easier to position the rest of the chain.

6 Repeat the process, gluing the 11 cm (4⅜ in) length of chain above the first, approximately 5 mm (³⁄₁₆ in) from the front of the shoe.

7 When both of the chains are secured and the glue has dried, attach the remaining beads randomly to the chain links across the front of the shoe.

Cushion

A purchased silk cushion cover is embellished with a graduated sprinkling of half-pearls to create an inexpensive and striking designer pillow. The pearls are simply glued on using an adhesive that is designed to bond rhinestones and sequins to fabric, and which dries clear and is washable. Glues of this type are available at beading, craft and haberdashery suppliers.

Materials

1 beige silk dupion cushion cover, 45 cm (18 in) square
1 cushion insert, 45 cm (18 in) square
Clear-drying, washable fabric glue such as Gem-Tac (available from craft and beading suppliers)
45 plastic half-pearls, 16 mm (⅝ in) diameter
55 plastic half-pearls, 12 mm (½ in) diameter
90 plastic half-pearls, 10 mm (⁷⁄₁₆ in) diameter
20 plastic half pearls, 8 mm (⁵⁄₁₆ in) diameter

step two Glue large and medium beads in a random pattern.

step three Glue medium and smaller beads slightly further apart.

1 Wash, dry and iron the cushion cover, to ensure that the fabric is clean so that the glue will adhere properly.

2 Lay the cushion cover on a clean, flat surface. Start gluing all of the 16 mm (⅝ in) pearls and two-thirds of the 12 mm (½ in) pearls across the entire width of the cushion, filling the lower 8–10 cm (3¼–4 in) of the fabric. To do this, randomly place small dots of glue on the fabric at 20 mm (¾ in) intervals and gently place a pearl on top of each. Work from left to right (or the opposite direction if you are left handed), placing five dots of glue at a time then covering them with the pearls. The pearls

should be sitting closely together but not touching. Be careful not to make the glue dots too big, as the excess will ooze out, leaving visible rings around the pearls.

3 Glue the remaining 12 mm (½ in) pearls, all of the 10 mm (⁷⁄₁₆ in) pearls and two-thirds of the 8 mm (⁵⁄₁₆ in) pearls across the width of the cushion, covering the next 20 cm (8 in) of the fabric. Place dots of glue 30–40 mm (1¼–1½ in) apart to create a graduated scattering.

4 Glue the remaining 8 mm (⁵⁄₁₆ in) pearls across the last 17 cm (6½ in) of the cushion, placing them 50–60 mm (2–2½ in) apart.

option Stitch seed beads down in groups of three.

option Use beads to highlight fabric designs or stitching.

Options

Make a matching lampshade with the same effect, by following the steps above, dividing the shade into four zones from bottom (most encrusted) to top (least encrusted). Use a lampshade made of opaque fabric so that the pearls don't create strange shadows when the light is switched on.

Make other gorgeous cushion covers using luxurious striped or floral fabric and embellishing over the pattern with beads, as shown in the photographs above. To stitch seed beads onto fabric, simply double-thread a needle, knot the ends together then insert it into the fabric from back to front to emerge at the desired point on the design. Place three beads onto the needle. Lay the beads in position on the fabric and pass the needle back through the fabric, underneath and back up through the initial entry point, thus creating a circle of thread. Bring the needle back through the three beads to secure. Add another three beads and repeat the process until the design is covered sufficiently.

Stitch larger beads on separately, ensuring each one sits nicely on the fabric before passing the needle through again.

Hint

To stitch individual beads onto fabric, use a double-threaded needle and secure them as follows: bring the needle to the front of the fabric, thread on a bead and pass the needle through to the back of the fabric. Bring the needle up again through the first hole, then take it down through the second hole without stitching through the bead. As you pull the thread through, ensure that one of the threads goes on either side of the bead.

Chandelier

The glitter of light on cut glass brings a room to life. Even in daylight, sunbeams will play on the crystals suspended from this simple chandelier. At night, the electric light globe will make the clear glass droplets sparkle.

Chandelier crystals are available at craft stores and bead suppliers; vintage chandelier crystals may often be found at garage sales and antique markets. Lampshade frames can be bought at craft, haberdashery and lighting suppliers.

Materials

1 can silver spray paint
1 round lampshade frame
260 two-holed chandelier crystals,
    12 mm (½ in) in diameter
8 frilly drop chandelier crystals, 50 mm
    (2 in) long
392 silver jump rings, 10 mm (⅜ in) diameter
Fine wire

Tools

Snipe-nose pliers
Flat-nose pliers
Saw frame or fret saw (optional; available
    from hardware stores)
Flat file (optional)
Newspaper

step one If necessary, saw off unwanted parts of the lampshade frame.

step three Link two-holed crystals together with jump rings.

1 If you are unable to buy a simple round lampshade frame, buy a standard cylindrical frame and saw off the additional posts. To do this, put the frame on a flat surface with the end you want to cut off protruding over the edge of the work surface. Cut off each leg of the frame, using an up-and-down motion and keeping the blade of the saw horizontal. File the edges, if necessary, to remove burrs.

2 Lay down some newspaper in a well-ventilated area and spray the frame with silver spray paint. Leave to dry thoroughly while you proceed with the construction of the chandelier drops.

3 To create the crystal drops, link the two-holed crystals together using jump rings. Open the jump rings (see basic instructions, page 20) using the snipe-nose and flat-nose pliers, attach a crystal and close. Repeat the process to create 24 strands each containing 15 linked crystals.

4 Using jump rings (as above), link a frilly crystal drop to eight of the 24 strands.

5 When the lampshade frame is dry, begin to attach the crystal strands to the large circular rim of the frame. Place six strands in each quarter of the shade, with every third strand having a frilly crystal drop.

step four Add a frilly drop to eight of the crystal strands.

step six Attach the crystal strands to the lampshade frame.

Make sure the crystal pendants face outwards when attached.

6 Hang the chandelier on a pendant light: first, remove the light bulb and unscrew the plastic cylinder surrounding the fitting. Slide the lampshade frame on top of the fitting, screw it into place with the plastic cylinder and replace the bulb. When the chandelier is hanging in position, adjust the crystal links so they sit evenly around the frame and the frame balances evenly.

7 Secure the jump rings in position on the frame with small ties of fine wire, twisted in place using a pair of snipe-nose pliers.

Variations

You can adapt this design for a standard lampshade by using a cylindrical standard lampshade frame. Follow steps two to five above, making sure the crystal strands are the same length as the frame. Link the crystal strands to the top of the frame and again at the bottom, allowing the frilly drops to hang below the frame.

Alternatively, attach the crystal strands to the bottom edge of a plain fabric or paper lampshade. The fabric or paper covering can be pierced with an awl to accept the jump rings and will hold them in position.

Drink identifiers

Adorn the stem of elegant glassware with jewellery that serves the double purpose of decorating the glass and identifying it. This recent party phenomenon removes the problem of remembering exactly where you put your glass and whether it is the half-full one or the almost-empty one beside it.

A selection of pretty beads in colour groups is one solution — use a different colour for each guest — and the metal findings are simply small earring hoops, available from bead and craft suppliers.

Materials

3 pairs silver drop earrings with threadable hoops, 25 mm (1 in) diameter
18 jump rings, 4 mm (⅛ in) diameter
54 silver head pins, 30 mm (1¼ in) long
For each of the six colour schemes (pink, purple, silver, cream, brown and gold), you will need nine beads: 8 round beads, 5 mm (³⁄₁₆ in) diameter, and 1 oval bead, 15 mm (⅝ in) long (to make a total of 54 beads)

Tools

Round-nose pliers
Snipe-nose pliers
Flat-nose pliers
Side cutters
Safety glasses

step one Cut the post of each head pin, leaving 10 mm (⅜ in) above the bead.

1 Place each of the beads on a head pin. Cut the post of each head pin using the side cutters, leaving 10 mm (⅜ in) of post above the bead, as shown in the photograph above. Create an eyelet on the exposed end of each pin by curling the post around the shaft of the round-nose pliers (for further instructions on how to do this, see Basic techniques, page 21).

2 Using the snipe-nose and flat-nose pliers, link three jump rings together into one chain section (see Basic techniques, page 20, for further details). Repeat this process with the remaining jump rings to make a total of six chain sections.

3 Attach each group of jump rings to a hoop. To do this, open the hoop and slide the jump ring at one end of each section over the hoop, as shown in the photograph. Close the hoop again to ensure the rings don't fall off.

4 Connect the beads to the jump ring chain sections. First attach a 15 mm (⅝ in) oval bead on its pin to the end jump ring, using the snipe-nose pliers (for further instructions on how to do this, see Basic techniques, page 23). Using the same method, attach one 5 mm (³⁄₁₆ inch) bead by its pin to the end jump ring, on either side of the oval bead.

step three Attach each group of three jump rings to a hoop.

step five Attach pairs of beads to each jump ring, one on each side.

5 To the next jump ring in the chain, attach one 5 mm (³⁄₁₆ inch) bead on each side of the ring. Lastly, attach the remaining two beads on either side of the top jump ring (the one that is connected to the hoop).

6 Undo the hoop to attach it around the stem of a glass. Make sure you remove the drink identifiers before washing the glasses, and be careful to hook the hoop closed when the marker is not in use, so the beads do not slip off the hoop.

Hints

Sets of drink identifiers make great gifts, as they're so easy to construct. You can vary the colour schemes and the types of beads to make themed or seasonal attachments.

Use this technique to make keyrings or handbag charms by adding different connections. Follow the steps above and attach a keyring finding instead of an earring hoop.

Table runner

Repetition of a simple flower design unifies this piece, while the different finishes of the beads used — some opaque, some pearlescent, others mirrored — add variety and interest.

When laying out the beads, concentrate them around the edges and at the ends of the runner, so that they will not be in the way of items that you put on top of the runner.

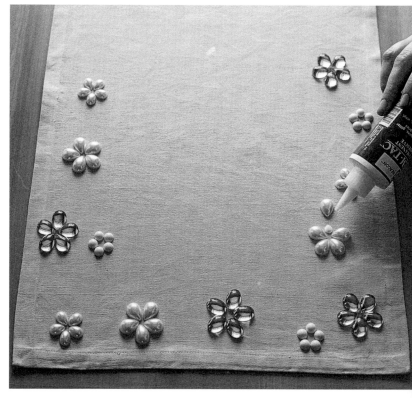

step two Glue the beads down one at a time.

Materials
1 fabric table runner; this can be hand made to match the proportions of an existing table, or bought at a homeware or craft store

Approximately 150 half-round, half-oval, and/or half-teardrop shaped plastic stones or pearls in various colours and finishes, sized from 8 mm (⁵⁄₁₆ in) to 15 mm (⅝ in)

Tools
Clear-drying, washable fabric glue such as Gem-Tac (available from craft and beading suppliers)

Large table, to lay out the design

1 Follow any preparation instructions given on the glue; you may have to wash the fabric to avoid pilling. Iron the table runner and lay it on a large, flat surface.

2 Lay out the beads and begin to arrange them in a pattern.

3 Once you have achieved a pleasing pattern, lift each bead individually and glue into position, as shown in the photograph above. Try not to use too much glue.

4 Allow to dry for 24 hours before use to make sure the glue is secure.

Hints

Use the same technique to make matching napkins. Glue a beaded flower on the corner of each napkin in similar colours.

This technique could also be used to embellish a singlet top, T-shirt or other garment.

Beaded tassel

Wear these beaded tassels as jewellery, as
a pendant or earrings; dress up your home
by using them on soft furnishings; or attach one
to a keyring or handbag and carry it with you.

Once you have mastered the basic tassel-
making process, you will be able to experiment
with variations of size, shape and materials to
create your own unique tassels.

Materials (per drop)
Silver bell cap (with 8 sections)
5 head pins, 40 mm (1⅝ in)
68 pink seed beads
1 pearl, 10 mm (⅜ in)
5 bicone crystal beads, 6 mm (¼ in)
4 teardrop crystals, 10 mm (⅜ in)

Tools
Round-nose pliers
Snipe-nose pliers
Side cutters
Safety glasses
Needle

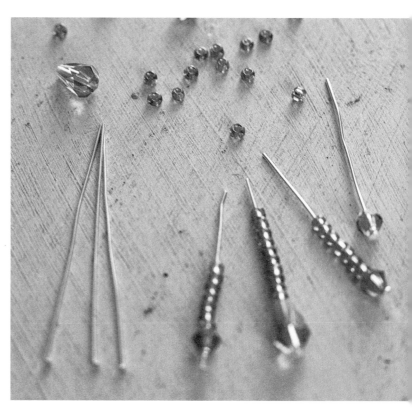

step one Thread crystals and seed beads onto head pins.

1 Thread all of the 6 mm (¼ in) bicone crystals onto head pins and top with ten seed beads to each pin. Thread all of the 10 mm (⅜ in) teardrop crystals onto head pins and top with seven seed beads to each pin. Refer to the photograph above.

2 Using side cutters, cut the excess post from the head pins, leaving a 6 mm (¼ in) length of the metal post protruding. Create an eyelet by turning the exposed metal post around a pair of round-nose pliers (see Basic techniques, page 21).

3 Attach the beaded head pins around the sections of the bell cap, alternating between the bicone crystal pins and the teardrop crystal pins. See the photograph above for details.

4 Thread the pearl onto a head pin and pass the pin through the top of the bell cap, then thread the remaining bicone crystal bead on top of the bell cap. Cut the head pin using side cutters, leaving 10 mm (⅜ in) of post protruding, then create an eyelet as described in Step 2.

5 Use the eyelet at the top of the tassel to attach it to a further fastening, such as an earring hook or a keyring, or to stitch it to ribbon or fabric as a decorative finish.

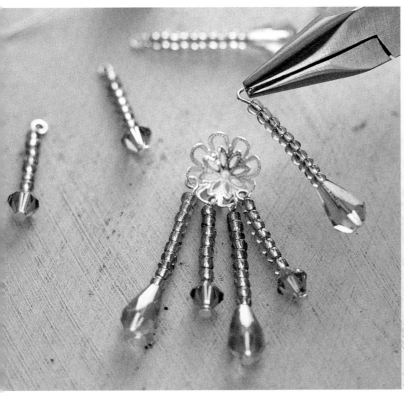

step three Alternate pins around the sections of the bell cap.

step four Pass a head pin through the pearl and the bell cap, then add a bead.

Variations

The basic tassel can be used for a variety
of purposes:

• To decorate the end of window-blind cords.

• Attach to a chain and wear as a pendant.

• Attach an earring hook to create earrings.

• Attach to silk cord and use as curtain ties.

• Attach to clip-on earrings and use as
  weights on a tablecloth.

Jewelled gift-wrapping

A beautifully wrapped present to celebrate a

special occasion or the festive season, or simply

to express love and gratitude, is always welcome.

In this case, the wrapping becomes part of the

gift, with silken cord and pretty jewels that can be

put to use after the present is opened.

Materials

Belcher chain with 3 mm (⅛ in) links
60 silver head pins, 30 mm (1³⁄₁₆ in) long
4 silver coiled end caps
4 m (13 ft) silk cord (rat's tail)
40 pearls, in various sizes from 6–12 mm
   (¼–½ in) diameter
16 bicone crystals, 6 mm (¼ in) diameter
4 oval glass beads, 17 mm (⅝ in) long

Tools

Round-nose pliers
Snipe-nose pliers
Flat-nose pliers
Side cutters
Clear nail varnish

step one Thread individual beads and pearls onto head pins.

step three Attach the beads to the lengths of chain using jump rings.

Hints

This technique can be used to make a lariat necklace, which wraps once or several times around the neck depending on the length of the cord. A lariat necklace is fastened by slipping one weighted (jewelled) end of the cord or chain through a loop at the other.

Turn this design into a pair of earrings by following Steps 2–4 and adding earring hooks to the end of the jump rings.

1 Thread individual beads and pearls onto head pins and cut off the excess metal post with side cutters, leaving 10 mm (³⁄₈ in) of post. Create eyelets in the end of the posts (see Basic techniques, page 21) with round-nose pliers.

2 Cut the belcher chain into four lengths of about 15 links (about 25 mm/1 in).

3 Divide the beads equally into four groups and attach the head pins to the chain links (see Basic techniques, page 23) so that the beads graduate along the lengths of chain, with the larger beads at one end and the smaller at the other (see photograph).

step four Coat one end of each length of silk cord with clear nail varnish.

step five Clamp the end caps on the hardened end of the silk cord.

4 Cut the silk cord into two lengths and coat 10 mm (⅜ in) at one end of each length with clear nail polish to prevent the cord unravelling as you work with it.

5 Once the nail varnish is dry on the ends of the cord, slide the open end of a coiled end cap over the hardened section of cord. Secure the cap onto the cord by clamping the last coil of wire in the end cap between the jaws of the snipe-nose pliers.

6 Wrap the cord around the gift and cut the raw ends so it sits or hangs nicely. Repeat Steps 4 and 5 with the remaining ends of the cord and the remaining end caps.

7 Attach each section of beaded chain to a coiled end cap using snipe-nose pliers.

Beaded tablecloth

A square of delicate tulle is edged with a garland of seed beads to make a table cover. Use it on its own or over the top of a fabric cloth as shown in the photograph at left.

Materials

104 cm (41 in) square of tulle
100 g (3½ oz) silver seed beads

Tools

Needle and sewing thread
Scissors
Ruler

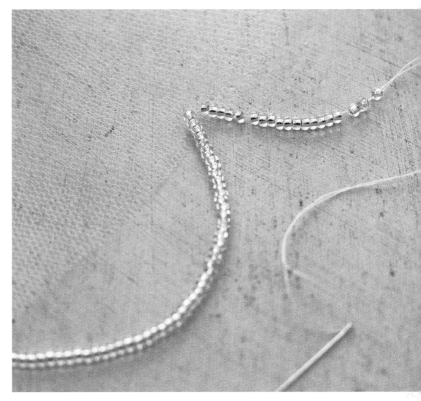

steps three and four Secure the loops at 8 cm (3⅛ in) intervals.

1 Cut the tulle to size, ensuring that it is perfectly square.

2 Thread 100 cm (40 in) of sewing thread on the needle, so the cotton is doubled and the final length is 50 cm (20 in). This will be enough thread to make five or six beaded loops. Secure the cotton to a corner of the tablecloth and thread on 10 cm (4 in) of seed beads.

3 Measure 8 cm (3⅛ in) along the tulle edge from the corner where you started and secure the cotton thread. Pass the needle though the tulle from the front to back, across three holes, then pass it through to the front. Draw through all of the remaining thread so that the loop of beads hangs in a gentle curve.

4 Thread another 10 cm (4 in) of seed beads onto the needle and secure the end of this loop at a further 8 cm (3⅛ in) interval. Repeat this process until the bead loops hang all the way around the tulle. Each side of the tablecloth should hold 13 sections of beads.

Hints

Attach beaded tassels (see pages 56–59) to the corners of this tablecloth for more glamour.

Change the proportions of the design by altering the length and width of the tulle to suit your table. Work in multiples of 8 cm (3⅛ in) to ensure that the loops of beads are shown to best effect.

Create a pretty, layered effect by making a couple of cloths in different sizes and laying one on top of the other.

Christmas decorations

Welcome the festive season by adorning

rooms and the branches of evergreen trees

with sparkling decorations in jewel colours.

These bright decorations could be modified

and used as gift-wrapping decorations and

even festive earrings, if you wish.

Materials (for each decoration)
Memory wire in large bangle shape
31 silver head pins, 20 mm (¾ in) long
2 silver eye pins, 20 mm (¾ in) long
20 cm of small belcher chain with 3 mm
    (⅛ in) links
82 silver seed beads, 3 mm (⅛ in) diameter
46 white plastic pearls, 4 mm (³⁄₁₆ in) diameter
1 Swarovski crystal drop with side holes,
    18 mm (¹¹⁄₁₆ in) long

Tools
Round-nose pliers
Snipe-nose pliers
Safety glasses

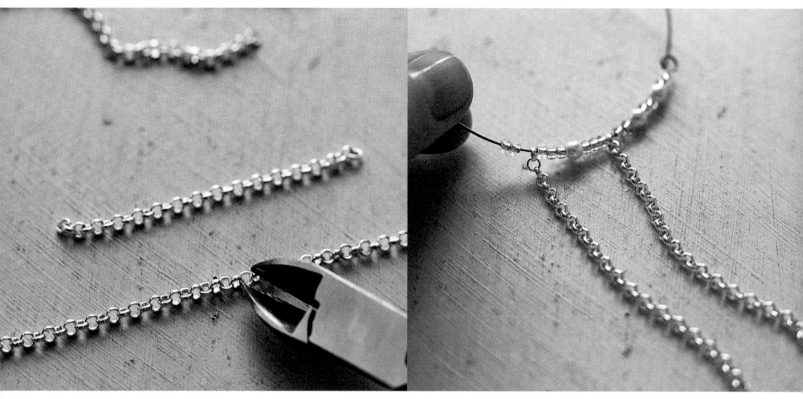

step two Cut the belcher chain to length using side cutters.

step four Begin threading beads, pearls and chain onto the memory wire.

1 Cut the memory wire into a 22 cm (8¾ in) length using side cutters and create a loop at one end using the round-nose pliers (see Basic techniques, page 21).

2 Use the side cutters to cut the belcher chain into one 55 mm (2³⁄₁₆ in) length (29 chain links) and one 68 mm (2¾ in) length (35 chain links).

3 Thread beads onto the head pins: thread 15 pins with two seed beads on each and 16 pins with a single pearl on each. Cut the head pins with side cutters, leaving 10 mm (⅜ in), and then create a loop (see Basic techniques, page 21).

step five Continue the pattern of beading to create a symmetrical arrangement.

4 Thread the beads and chain onto the memory wire in the following sequence: two seed beads, one pearl, two seed beads, one pearl, two seed beads, one end of a 55 mm (2¾ in) length of belcher chain, three seed beads, one pearl, three seed beads, one end of a 68 mm (2¾ in) chain. Next thread on two seed beads and one pearl and repeat this process 13 times.

5 Now thread on two seed beads, then the loose end of the 68 mm (2¹¹⁄₁₆ in) length of belcher chain (making sure the chain is not twisted). Repeat the same combination of beads and chain as on the opposite side of the decoration, but in reverse order to

make sure the beading is symmetrical: three seed beads, one pearl, three seed beads, the loose end of the 55 mm (2³⁄₁₆ in) length of belcher chain (making sure the chain is not twisted), two seed beads, one pearl, two seed beads, one pearl and two seed beads.

6 To complete the circular form and make sure the beads sit tightly together, cut off the excess memory wire leaving 10 mm (³⁄₈ in) and loop the cut end into an eyelet using the round-nose pliers.

step seven Attach the beaded head pins to the chains.

7 Attach the beaded head pins to the chain. Use seven pearl and seven seed bead drops for the top chain and nine pearl and eight seed bead drops for the bottom chain.

8 Attach the first post to the first loose chain link, making sure the bead is hanging straight. Repeat this process using every second link of chain, alternating pearls and seed beads (see the photographs above and on page 67 for details).

9 Cut 32 mm (1¼ in) of belcher chain (15 links) and attach either end of this length of chain to each rounded end of the memory wire using snipe-nose pliers (see

Basic techniques, page 23). Using the same technique, attach an eye pin to the middle link of the chain. Bend the post of the eye pin around the base of the round-nose pliers to create a large hook (by which you will hang the decoration).

10 Lastly, thread the 18 mm (¾ in) Swarovski crystal drop onto an eye pin and create a loop at the post end, making sure this loop is flat and sitting in the same plane as the eye. Open the loops with snipe-nose pliers and hook them into the loops on either end of the memory wire (underneath the chain). This final connection will hold the circular shape in place.

step eight Alternate beads and pearls across the chain links.

step ten Attach the Swarovski crystal droplet.

Variations

Use this design to make earrings by following the steps above and adding an earring hook to the top of the chain instead of an eye pin. You may like to use small bangle memory wire for smaller hoops, adjusting the lengths of chain and numbers of beads as appropriate.

For alternative Christmas decorations, link frilly crystal drops and two-holed crystals together with jump rings, as used in the Chandelier (pages 46–49), and hang them with earring hooks or loops of wire.

Lantern candle holder

The luminous glow of flickering candle light is

increased and refracted by rows of seed beads

in these glittering lanterns. Don't be daunted by

the number of beads used in the construction:

the method is quite simple and surprisingly

quick to complete.

Materials
For the small lantern: 864 round Indian glass
    beads, 4 mm (3/16 in) diameter
For the large lantern: 1560 round Indian glass
    beads, 4 mm (3/16 in) diameter
Artist's wire, gold 0.7 mm (21 gauge)

Tools
Round-nose pliers
Side cutters
Safety glasses
Ruler

step two Create a noose at the end of the wire, then thread on all of the beads.

step four Add the spokes of doubled wire.

1 Cut the artist's wire with the side cutters into six 70 cm (27 in) lengths. Bend each length in half and set them aside.

2 Unwind the remaining artist's wire, keeping it coiled. Create a wrapped loop in the end of the wire (see Basic techniques, page 22) with the round-nose and snipe-nose pliers. Cut off the excess wire so that only a round loop is left at the end of the wire.

3 Thread all of the beads onto the coiled wire, carefully moving them along to the end of the wire, while still keeping it coiled.

4 Thread the wires made in Step 1 onto the beaded coil, placing the first wire through the looped end of the beaded coil. Continue to thread wires 2 to 5 along the beaded coil, placing a bead in between each wire (see photograph). Secure the long wires around the coil by pulling them open in opposite directions.

5 Form the base of the lantern by continuing to wrap the beads around the initial loop, forming a flat disc. Secure each rotation of the beads with the long wires by passing them around either side of the coil. Expand the base by adding

step five Construct the flat base of the lantern.

step six Create the vertical sides of the lantern.

an extra bead in between the wires on each roation (see photograph) until there are eight beads in between each wire. Push the beads tightly together after completing each coil so that the lantern is even.

6 Construct the vertical walls of the lantern by continuing to coil and secure the beads, maintaining eight beads in each section. The first row of the wall should rest on top of the last row of the base. Continue to secure the coils until all the beads are used.

7 Once all beads are secured, twist the remaining lengths of doubled wire for

approximately 20 mm (¾ in), cut off any excess with side cutters and bend the wires so they sit inside the lantern. Push the lantern into a cylindrical shape.

Beaded curtain

Here, the hem of a plain curtain is decorated

with loops of glass seed beads to catch the

sunlight. You could use the same technique of

wire loops to decorate a pendant lampshade, or

to create a wall-hanging from a fabric panel.

Match the design by stitching beads in the same

scalloped pattern onto a cushion cover to

coordinate your soft furnishings in a room.

Materials
Memory wire in large bangle shape
100 g (3½ oz) seed beads
Netting or sheer curtain to fit the length and
    width of the window, hemmed and finished
    for hanging as you prefer
Tassel; ready-made (from haberdashery store)
    or handmade (see pages 56–59)
Ribbon, 5 mm (³⁄₁₆ in) x twice the length of
    the curtain

Tools
Round-nose pliers
Flat-nose pliers
Needle and sewing thread
Metal snips for cutting steel; these are the best
    tool to cut the memory wire as they have
    stronger blades than end or side cutters
Fabric glue

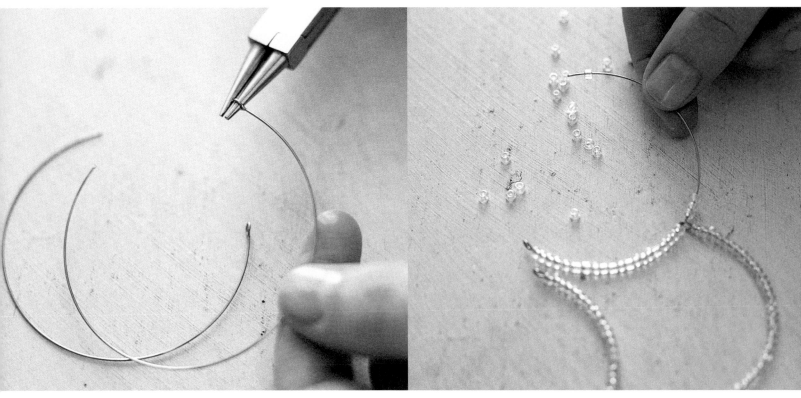

step two Create a loop in one end of the wire, so it sits flat in line with the curve.

step five Thread the loops of the previous row onto the memory wire with the beads.

1 Cut the memory wire with the metal snips into 15 cm (6 in) lengths. The memory wire will hold its 'U' shape.

2 Loop one end of the memory wire with the end of the round-nose pliers, creating a 3–4 mm (⅛ in) loop. Create the loop so it sits at a right angle but in line with the curve of the memory wire.

3 Construct the curtain in rows, working from the bottom tip of the triangle upwards. Use one 'U' shaped wire for the first row and an additional 'U' shape for every new row, up to row 11 or the desired width of the curtain.

4 Row 1: take a looped 'U' shaped memory wire and thread on 43 seed beads. Loop the end of the memory wire to hold the beads tight and to match the other side.

5 Row 2: Thread 23 seed beads onto a 'U' shape. Thread the wire through the left-hand side loop of row one. Thread another 20 seed beads on and create a loop in the end as before. Take another 'U' shape and thread 20 seed beads on, thread through the right-hand side loop of row 1, add 23 beads and create an end loop.

6 Row 3: Thread 23 seed beads onto a 'U' shape. Thread through the left-hand side

step six Add three seed beads between the loops of the memory wire.

step seven Sew the loops of the final row to the hem of the curtain.

loop of the first 'U' shape of row two. Thread another 20 seed beads on and create a loop in the end as before. Take another 'U' shape and thread 20 seed beads on, then thread through the right-hand side loop of the 'U' shape of row two. Thread on three seed beads and the loop of the left-hand side of the next 'U' below. Thread on 20 seed beads and loop the end. Repeat this process for every 'U' shape in the row, completing the last 'U' shape with 23 seed beads as before.

7 When you have constructed 11 rows (or the appropriate number for your curtain), sew the top row to the base of the curtain.

8 Glue ribbon along the side of the net curtain. When the glue is dry you may hang the curtain and complete it by adding the tassel. A purchased tassel from a haberdashery store may be used, as in the photographs, or use a beaded tassel such as the one on pages 56–59.

Hints

Choose a range of seed beads in graduated colours and use a different colour on each row.

Instead of using three beads in between each 'U' shape you could substitute a teardrop-shaped bead.

This design would work well on a frosted bathroom window or a similar window where the curtain does not need to be lifted up and down for privacy or to show a view.

Pearl choker

Pearls have a soft, rich sheen that adds a

luxurious glow to any skin tone. This stylish

choker, constructed with imitation pearl beads

on silk satin cord, gives a more casual cast

to the traditional pearl necklace.

The same simple technique would lend itself well

to other interpretations, such as leather thonging

with wooden or ceramic beads or thin cord with

crystal beads. Remember to check that your

chosen cord is thin enough to pass through the

hole in your smallest bead.

Materials
24 plastic pearl beads, 14 mm (9/16 in) diameter
  (or number required to fit neck size)
1.5 m (60 in) round silk cord
Clear nail varnish

Tools
Round-nose pliers
Scissors

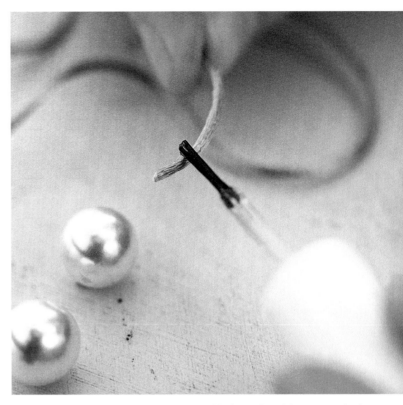

step one Paint the end of the silk cord with clear nail varnish to prevent fraying.

1 Tie a tight knot in one end of the length of silk cord. Neaten the end by cutting off the excess cord, leaving approximately 5 mm (¼ in). Dab a small amount of clear nail varnish on the end to prevent the cord from fraying. Cut the other end of the silk cord on an angle and coat the last 2.5 mm (⅛ in) of it in clear nail varnish to preserve the point (as shown in the photograph above).

2 Prepare the pearl beads by enlarging the hole in each one using small round-nose pliers. To do this, thread a bead onto the tapered shank of the pliers and push down firmly towards the handle, at the same time twisting the bead back and forth. You should notice the opening of the bead flaring out. Repeat for the other end of the hole. Enlarge the holes in all of the beads in this way, to make it easier to thread them onto the silk cord.

3 When the clear nail polish on the end of the cord is dry and firm, thread the first bead onto the cord so it is resting on the knot. Once it is in place, tie another knot in the cord to hold the pearl in place. Make sure the knot sits close to the bead: to do this, make a large, loose slip knot and, as you slowly pull the knot closed, roll it back down the cord towards the bead with fingers.

step two Enlarge the holes in the beads using a pair of round-nose pliers.

step four Knot the cord between each pearl bead.

4 Leave a 25 cm (10 in) length of silk cord and tie another knot. This is where you will begin to add the beads for the choker proper. Thread on another pearl bead (see the photograph illustrating this step above) and make a knot after it. Add another pearl bead next to this knot, then make another knot. Repeat until you have strung and knotted about 22 pearls. You may alter the number of pearls to fit your neck size.

5 Leave a 30 cm (12 in) length of cord, make another knot and finish with a pearl bead knotted in place. Cut the excess cord with scissors, leaving 5 mm (¼ in), and coat the end in nail varnish.

Variations

Tie the choker around your neck, fastening it with a bow. A choker is meant to be worn quite high on the neck, but you can make a longer necklace that can be worn wrapped as a choker or a bracelet as well as a necklace. Leave bigger gaps between the pearl beads and allow extra cord if necessary. Using smaller pearl beads will allow fluid movement in the piece and more flexibility when you wear it.

Memory wire ring

Memory wire is formed in a continuous spiral and can be cut to give as many coils as are needed. It retains its shape while also having enough flexibility to fit almost any size of finger.

In this exuberant design, seed beads cover the coils of wire, while a variety of feature beads give colour and sparkle.

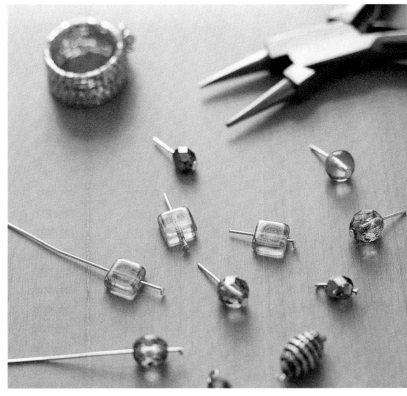

step five Place each bead onto a head pin and cut off excess wire.

Materials

1 packet ring memory wire
14 head pins, 14 mm
  (⅝ in) long
6 jump rings, 14 mm
  (⅝ in) long
10 g (⅓ oz) seed beads
14 feature beads, 5–7 mm
  (¼ in) long, in assorted
  shapes and colours

Tools

Round-nose pliers
Snipe-nose pliers
Flat-nose pliers
Side cutters
Safety glasses

1 Cut the memory wire with the side cutters, allowing for 6 coils. Curl the end of the ring wire (using round-nose pliers) to make a 3 mm (⅛ in) loop that sits on top of the ring. Straighten if needed with the snipe-nose pliers.

2 Thread seed beads onto the ring, filling all six coils. Make sure the beads end level with the same point at which you began.

3 Cut excess wire with side cutters, leaving enough to make a 3 mm (⅛ in) loop (as in Step 1). Round and loop the remaining wire with round-nose pliers, securing all of the seed beads onto the memory wire.

4 Connect the jump rings together (see basic instructions, page 20) using the snipe- and flat-nose pliers. Attach the jump rings to either side of the looped memory wire, so they rest along the top of the ring.

5 Place each bead onto a head pin and cut excess wire with side cutters, leaving about 7 mm (¼ in). Curl the end of each pin into an eyelet (see Basic techniques, page 21).

6 Attach the beaded end posts along the jump rings so the beads are distributed to give a good mix of shapes and colours. There should be some movement so the beads move around when the ring is worn.

Chandelier earrings

These spectacular earrings will glitter and glow
like chandeliers as you move. To create them,
choose drop earring hoops with an open end so
that beads and other jewellery findings can be
easily threaded onto the hoop itself.

Materials

1 pair gold threadable hoops

2 gold brass stampings, 20 mm (¾ in) long
   (these can be found at bead stores)

1 pair gold earring hooks

20 gold head pins, 30 mm (1¼ in) long

40 cm (16 in) gold oval chain

2 gold jump rings, 4 mm (⅛ in) diameter

6 gold opaque crystal beads, 6 mm
   (¼ in) diameter

6 champagne bicone beads, 5 mm
   (³⁄₁₆ in) diameter

36 round glass beads, 4 mm (⅛ in) diameter

Tools

Round-nose pliers

Snipe-nose pliers

Side cutters

Safety glasses

Earring components, clockwise from bottom left: head pins; threadable earring hoops; earring hooks; 2 lengths oval chain; gold brass stamping.

steps one and two Thread beads onto head pins, then cut and curl the posts.

Hint

If you cannot find a brass stamping, select an oval 10 mm (⅜ in) bead. Thread it onto an eye pin, then cut the remaining wire with side cutters, leaving 10 mm (⅜ in). Loop the end of the pin using round-nose pliers (see Basic techniques, page 21). One loop should be larger than the other. Attach the smaller loop to the hoop, as in Step 6. Open the larger loop with the snipe-nose pliers, thread on the five beaded head pins and close the loop again.

1 Thread a selection of beads onto the head pins as follows:
- Onto each of eight head pins, thread one round glass bead.
- Onto each of four head pins, thread one bicone bead.
- Onto each of four head pins, thread one opaque gold bead.
- Onto each of two head pins, thread one round glass bead and one bicone bead.
- Onto each of two head pins, thread one round glass bead and one opaque gold bead.

Using side cutters, cut the excess length off the posts, leaving 10 mm (⅜ in) protruding beyond the beads.

2 Using round-nose pliers, curl the post of each head pin to form an eyelet (see Basic techniques, page 21).

3 Using side cutters, cut the chain into two 80 mm (3⅛ in) and two 110 mm (4⅜ in) lengths.

4 Pull the threadable earring hoop open (one end of the loop is not secure, and can be pulled open) and thread the hoop through the last link in a 110 mm (4⅜ in) chain. Thread a 4 mm (⅛ in) round bead onto the hoop, then the last link of the 80 mm (3⅛ in) chain, as shown in the photograph above.

steps four and five Thread beads and chain onto the hoop in the order pictured.

step six Attach beaded head pins to the stamping and assemble the earrings.

5 Continue threading the hoop in sequence as follows: three round beads; one round bead on head pin; one round bead; one gold opaque crystal on head pin; one round bead; round bead and bicone bead on head pin; one round bead; one gold opaque crystal on head pin; one round bead; one round bead on head pin; three round beads; other end of the 80 mm (3⅛ in) chain; one round bead; the other end of the 110 mm (4⅜ in) chain. Refer also to the photographs for the order of components. Finish each earring by reclosing the threadable hoop.

6 Attach the remaining beaded head pins to the bottom edges of the brass stampings, referring to the photographs for the order of the pins. Attach the top of the stamping to the underside of the top of the hoop using a jump ring (see Basic techniques, page 20).

7 Using snipe-nose pliers, attach an earring hook to the top of each hoop.

Charm bracelet

A creative version of the traditional charm bracelet, this jewelled wristlet employs a variety of beads to catch the eye. Glass beads in translucent colours approximate the beauty of semi-precious gems such as amethysts, garnets, rubies and diamonds.

Mix beads of different size, shape and colours in a random pattern of repetition to ensure that you capture the eclectic look of a charm bracelet.

Materials

Approximately 15 cm (6 in) chain: the length may differ depending on your wrist size. To check the size, measure your wrist with a tape measure so the tape sits firmly around the wrist

Beads of various shapes and sizes: the number will depend on length of the chain — allow one bead per chain link, except for the two end links, plus one bead for the jump ring extension chain

Head pins, 40 mm (1½ in) long: one per bead

8 jump rings, 5 mm (⅜ in) diameter

1 parrot clasp

Tools

Round-nose pliers

Snipe-nose pliers

Flat-nose pliers

Side cutters

Safety glasses

step two Thread each bead onto a head pin and make a loop at the end of the post.

Hints

The wrist is very flexible, so select a medium-weight chain that is not too flimsy and with links large enough to thread the end posts through.

Stick to a simple colour scheme and gather six to eight different styles of bead, repeating each style and colour a few times throughout the bracelet. Choose beads of a similar size and weight to give a bracelet that is balanced in colour and style, and to avoid having one end heavier than the other.

1 Arrange your selection of beads on a tray (see Hints, page 25) in a row, paying attention to the balance and proportion of the arrangement.

2 Thread each bead onto a head pin and trim all but 10 mm (⅜ in) off the post using side cutters. Use round-nose pliers to make a loop, as shown in the photograph above.

3 Attach the beaded head pins one at a time to the chain in the desired order (see Basic techniques, page 22), leaving one link at either end to attach your clasp and jump rings. Add one beaded head pin to each link of the chain until the chain is full.

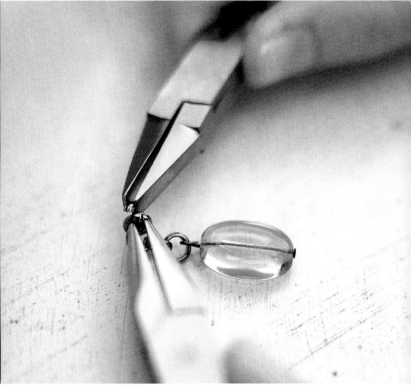

step three Attach one bead to each link of the chain.

step four Make a chain of jump rings and attach the remaining bead to the end.

4 Create the extension, which allows the bracelet to be worn at different lengths. Open the jump rings (see Basic techniques, page 20) and link seven of them together in a chain. Attach the end ring to the last link of chain in the bracelet. At the other end of the jump-ring chain, attach the remaining beaded head pin (in the same manner as for the bracelet). Attention to small details like this adds to the quality of your design.

5 Attach the parrot clasp to the empty link at the other end of the bracelet, using the remaining jump ring. Fasten the clasp to the jump ring that gives the desired size.

Hints

To make a matching necklace, extend the length of the chain (and the corresponding number of beads) to approximately 42 cm (16½ in).

For a finer look, attach beads on every second chain link.

You could also revamp an old evening bag by replacing the chain strap with a handle made using this technique. Add a clasp at each end of the handle to make it detachable.

Chain necklace

This beautiful necklace features multiple
pendants of beads on graduated chain lengths
suspended from a chain choker. The symmetry
of its structure and the triple-bead clusters at
the end of each chain create a simple yet
opulent effect.

The pictured example uses a type of blackened
silver chain and findings, but you could use other
finishes if desired.

Materials
Blackened parrot clasp
8 blackened jump rings, 4 mm (³/₁₆ in)
2 m (80 in) blackened chain with 5 mm (³/₁₆ in)
   oval links (with unsoldered links)
40 blackened head pins, 30 mm (1⅛ in) long
27 purple-grey round beads, 8 mm
   (⁵/₁₆ in) diameter
3 purple oval beads, 16 mm (⅝ in) long
10 purple flat oval beads, 11 mm (⁷/₁₆ in) long

Tools
Round-nose pliers
Snipe-nose pliers
Side cutters
Safety glasses

step one Thread beads onto head pins then make eyelets in the ends of the posts.

step two Cut the chain into graduated lengths.

1 Thread the individual beads onto head pins, cutting off all but 10 mm (⅜ in) of the exposed post with side cutters. Make an eyelet in the end of the post by bending it around a pair of round-nose pliers (see Basic techniques, page 21).

2 Cut the chain into the following lengths: one 40 cm (15¾ in) long, one 10 cm (4 in), two 8.5 cm (3⁵⁄₁₆ in), two 7 cm (2¾ in), two 5.5 cm (2⅜ in), two 4 cm (1½ in), two 2.5 cm (1 in), and two 5 mm (two links). Lay the various lengths of chain out on your work surface in the order that they will be used on the necklace. The longest (40 cm/15¾ in) piece of chain is the necklace itself. The 10 cm (4 in) length is for the central pendant and the remaining pairs of shorter lengths should graduate in size on either side of the central pendant.

3 Attach the chain lengths to the necklace by opening the top link of each chain and attaching it to a link in the necklace chain (see the instructions for opening jump rings in Basic techniques, page 20). Begin with the 10 cm (4 in) chain, linking it in the middle of the 40 cm (15¾ in) length. Continue to attach the remaining pendants to the central necklace with one empty link separating each chain from its neighbour (see the photograph).

step three Attach the chains to the necklace with one empty link between each one.

step four Attach three beads to the bottom of each pendant chain.

4 Open the eyelets of the 11 mm ($^7/_{16}$ in) and 16 mm ($^5/_8$ in) purple bead assemblies using snipe-nose pliers, and link them to the end of all 13 chain drops, using the three largest beads on the three longest pendant chains in the middle of the necklace. Attach the round beads to either side of the chain link above the purple oval bead drops. Repeat on all 13 chains. There will be one beaded head pin left over.

5 Link seven jump rings together. Attach them to one end of the necklace chain and finish by linking the remaining bead to the last ring. Link the clasp to the other end of the necklace chain, using the last jump ring.

Hint

To make a simple pair of matching earrings, use two 4 cm (1$^5/_8$ in) lengths of chain, add the same trio of beads as on the pendant chains and attach earring hooks at the other end of the chain.

Clip-on earrings

Form follows function in clip-on earrings:

because the clasp is necessarily quite large

to hold the weight of the earring on the ear in

relative comfort, clip-on earrings are often quite

extravagant in size and composition. This design

incorporates a glittering cluster of faceted

crystals and round glass beads in smoky hues.

Materials

Earring frame: 17 mm (⅝ in) silver domes and
  clip-on backs
32 silver head pins, 15 mm (⅝ in) long
8 round crystal beads, 6 mm (5⁄16 in) diameter
12 bicone crystal beads, 6 mm (¼ in) diameter
12 round beads, 6 mm (¼ in) diameter

Tools

Round-nose pliers
Snipe-nose pliers
Flat-nose pliers
Side cutters
Safety glasses

step one Thread individual beads onto head pins.

step three Secure the beads by looping the ends of the posts at the back of the dome.

Hints

This design may also be used to make shoe clips. Clip the earring on to a strappy shoe or remove the clip with end cutters and glue onto the shoe for a more permanent solution.

Make more of a statement by adding feathers to the cluster of beads. Glue a feather to the earring back before securing the dome. Make sure the feather is glued in the correct position so it sits appropriately when worn.

1 Thread individual beads onto head pins and divide them into two equal groups containing the same number of beads of each shape and colour. Do not cut or bend the posts at this stage.

2 Begin to position the beads on the silver dome, working from left to right. Thread a beaded head pin through the perforated dome so the bead sits against the convex side. Cut the post with the side cutters, leaving approximately 7 mm (¼ in) of pin protruding at the back.

3 As you go, turn the dome over and loop the post of the head pin you have just

step four Repeat steps two and three until all beads are used.

step five Crimp the metal tabs to secure the earring back.

inserted (see Basic techniques, page 21) using the round-nose pliers. (See the photograph above for details.) Make sure the pin holds the bead securely to the frame. You may want to secure it in place with the snipe-nose pliers. Make sure the loops at the back of the dome aren't too big, or it will be difficult to secure to the earring back.

4 Attach the remaining beads by repeating steps two and three until all the beads are used. Randomly position the different shaped and coloured beads across the dome, noting the arrangement so that you can repeat it for the second earring.

5 When both domes are completely beaded and secure, attach the earring backs. Fit the back to the dome. If you have difficulty positioning the components closely together, clamp the edges of both pieces with the flat- or snipe-nose pliers. Secure the pieces by pushing the metal tabs flat over the edge of the dome one at a time, with the snipe-nose pliers.

Drop cluster earrings

These little grapelike clusters frame the face and provide movement and sparkle. Silver findings and opaque white beads as in the pictured example result in a simple, delicate look. Smoky crystals and blackened findings would give a more sultry effect, or combine beads in a variety of colours and finishes for a bolder approach.

Materials
34 head pins, 4 mm (3/16 in) long
16 jump rings, 4 mm (3/16 in) diameter
1 pair earring hooks
34 opaque white oval beads, 7 x 6 mm
(1/4 x 5/16 in) diameter

Tools
Side cutters
Safety glasses
Round-nose pliers
Snipe-nose pliers

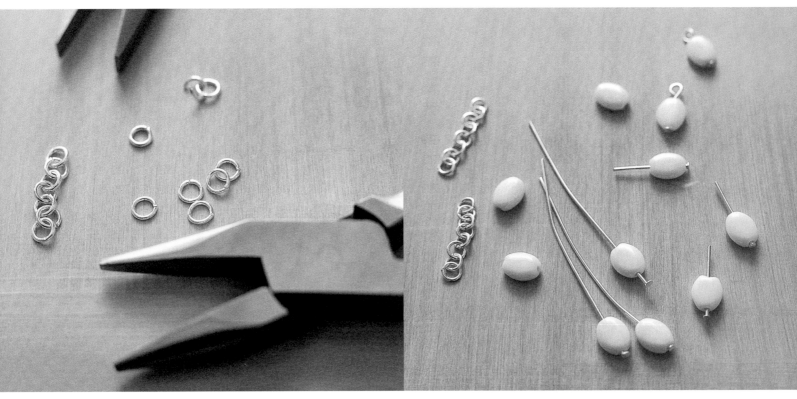

step one Using the snipe-nose pliers, connect the jump rings into two lengths of eight.

step two Thread each bead onto a head pin and cut the posts to the correct lengths.

1 Connect the jump rings together into two lengths of eight using the snipe-nose pliers (see Basic techniques, page 20).

2 Thread each bead onto a head pin and trim the excess wire with end cutters. Trim 32 of the pins to leave 7 mm (⁵⁄₁₆ in) excess and 2 pins to leave 15 mm (⁵⁄₈ in) excess.

3 Attach the earring hook to the jump rings with the snipe-nose pliers.

4 Connect the beaded head pins to the jump rings using the snipe-nose pliers (see Basic techniques, page 23). Swing open and attach the longest head pin to the last free

jump ring, and then connect a shorter beaded pin either side. Continue attaching the remaining beaded pins either side of the jump rings until you reach the top.

5 Repeat this process to make a pair.

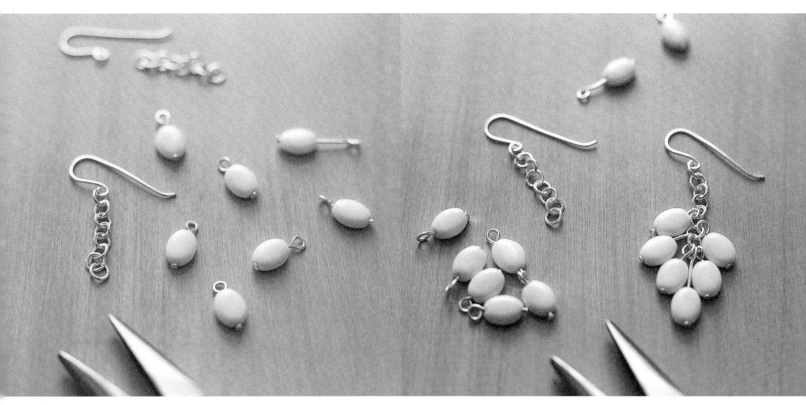

step three Attach the earring hook to the top of the jump rings.

step four Connect the beaded head pins to the jump rings.

Variations

By altering the size of the components used, you can create multiple styles using the same technique. To either reduce or extend the length of the earrings, simply add or deduct jump rings, but always hang three beads off the last jump ring to complete the earring.

If you use larger beads, also use larger jump rings so that the proportions of the earring remain the same and the beads have enough room to hang elegantly.

You can also use this technique to make a matching bracelet or necklace. Use a belcher chain instead of jump rings and make all of the beaded end posts the same length. Fasten with a parrot clasp.

Brooch

In this design, a large kilt pin supports multiple strands of chain dressed with beads, charms and other trinkets.

This is a rather heavy item, so is best worn with thick or heavy-weight winter garments. Use it to decorate a jacket or coat lapel, or to fasten a woollen shawl over your shoulders.

Materials
Large safety pin (kilt pin)
Blackened chain, 25 cm (10 in) each of
   five types
Artist's wire, 0.6 mm (22 gauge)
11 blackened head pins, 40 mm (1½ in) long
6 blackened eye pins
Assorted grey, purple and blackened silver
   beads (approximately 23 beads in total)

Tools
Round-nose pliers
Snipe-nose pliers
Side cutters
Safety glasses

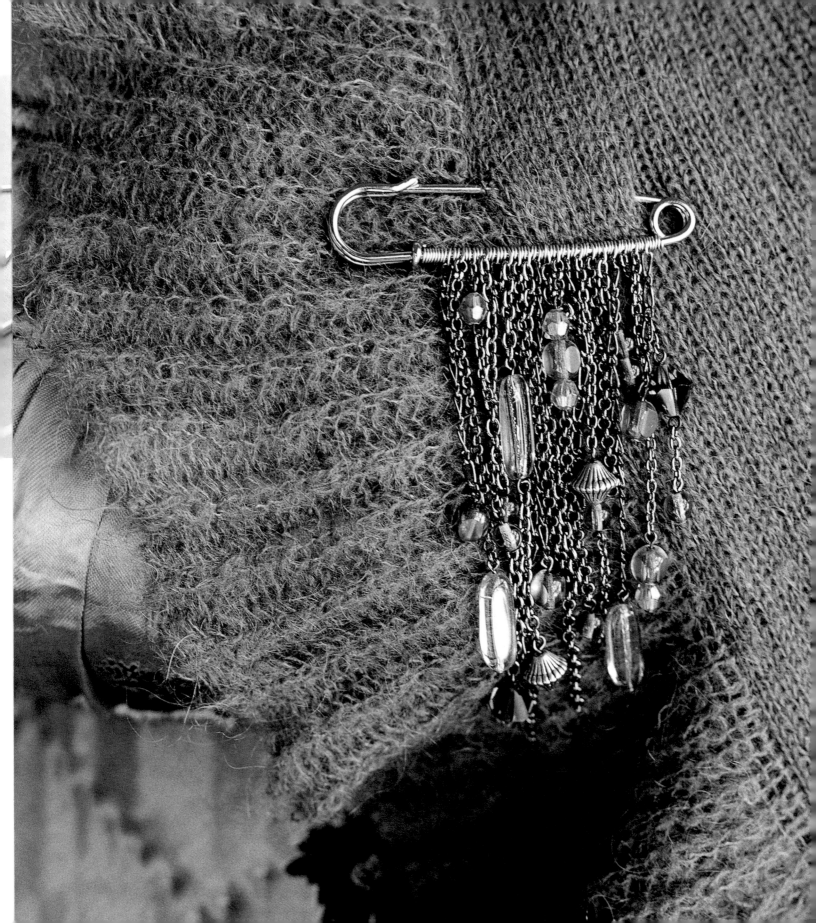

Cuff

This exuberantly embellished cuff bracelet

features rows of sparkling seed beads and

a cluster of pearls and gems in its centre.

Materials
Memory wire in small bangle shape

4 separator bars, 7-hole (approximately
3.5 cm or 1⅜ in long)

12 cm (4⅝ in) belcher chain, medium size;
alternatively, you can link sixty 4 mm (³⁄₁₆ in)
jump rings

28 silver head pins, 30 mm (1¼ in) long

2 cream pearls, 15 mm (⅝ in) diameter

8 cream pearls, 12 mm (½ in) diameter

6 cream pearls, 7 mm (¼ in) diameter

2 Czech crystals, clear AB 11 mm
(⁷⁄₁₆ in) diameter

2 Czech crystals, clear AB 10 mm
(⅜ in) diameter

7 pink AB beads, 7 mm (¼ in) diameter

364 pink seed beads, 4 mm (³⁄₁₆ in) diameter

Tools
Side cutters

Safety glasses

Round-nose pliers

Snipe-nose pliers

step one Thread beads onto head pins then make loops in the ends of the posts.

step four Construct the first row of the cuff.

1 Thread beads (except for the seed beads) onto head pins. Cut the posts with side cutters, leaving 10 mm (⅜ in) of post, and create an eyelet using the round-nose pliers (see Basic techniques, page 21). Divide the beads into three similar groups.

2 Cut the belcher chain into three 85 mm (3⅜ in) lengths or link three lengths of 18 x 4 mm (³⁄₁₆ in) jump rings.

3 Cut the memory wire with side cutters into seven 22 cm (8½ in) lengths. Create a loop in one end of each length by bending the wire around the round-nose pliers (see Basic techniques, page 17).

4 Begin constructing the seven rows of the cuff. For row one, thread the memory wire through a spacer bar, then thread on the components in the following order: 20 seed beads, a second spacer bar, 12 seed beads, a third spacer bar, 20 seed beads, and a fourth spacer bar. Finish the row by making a loop in the end of the wire close to the bar, so that the beads sit tightly together.

5 Repeat this process for rows 3, 5 and 7.

6 For row two, thread a spacer bar then the other components in the following order: 20 seed beads, a second spacer bar, one seed bead then one length of chain

step six Add the lengths of belcher chain to the even numbered rows.

step eight Attach the groups of beads to the chains.

(through the first link). Continue to thread
10 seed beads, and then thread on the last
link of chain, so the links sit across the top
of the seed beads. Continue threading
components in this order: one seed bead,
the third spacer bar, 20 seed beads, and the
fourth spacer bar. Finish by making a loop
in the end of the memory wire (as above).

7 Repeat this process for rows 4 and 6.

8 Link the beaded head pins (see Basic
techniques, page 23) onto the chains one
at a time, using the smaller beads on the
outsides and a large one in the middle.
Repeat this process for each section of chain.

Hints

For this design, belcher chain is
preferable to jump rings, which
may open over time.

To turn this design into a
choker, use 38 cm (15 in) of
necklace memory wire and add
two extra spacer bar sections
around each side for support.

embroidery

About embroidery

Embroidery is the art of embellishing or decorating textiles with a needle and thread. Although textiles, by their very nature, rarely survive the vicissitudes of time and climate, the existence of crude needles dating from the Stone Age tends to suggest that embroidery is certainly almost as old as humankind itself. As form followed function – and human nature being what it is – it can hardly have been a giant leap from sewing skins together in a simply functional way to adding stitching that was purely decorative.

We certainly have archaeological evidence that in the centuries well before the birth of Christ, civilizations around the world practised sophisticated and various forms of embroidery, much of it instantly recognizable in the stitches we still use today. It seems that this very human desire to embellish and beautify arose spontaneously and coincidentally in almost every early culture, developing in different ways from place to place. Of course, as trading routes opened up and communication became more sophisticated, techniques and patterns were shared and embroidery styles evolved over the centuries in response to different influences. Thus we have the white-on-white funerary cloth of ancient Egypt, the amazingly intricate Chinese two-sided silk embroidery, the bold colours and patterns of traditional Mayan motifs, the extraordinary opulence and diversity of Mughal embroidery, the delicate beauty of Norwegian hardanger, the elegant simplicity of Japanese sashiko and the magnificent ecclesiastical embroideries (opus anglicanum) of medieval England – to name but a few of the more famous examples.

By the time of the Middle Ages in Europe, richly embroidered textiles had become much prized as symbols of wealth, status and power, both sought after and ostentatiously displayed by the wealthy, worn as a symbol of majesty and the glory of God by kings and popes respectively, and frequently offered as expensive gifts in international diplomacy.

It is important to remember, however, that awe-inspiring as much of this museum-quality embroidery most certainly is, a greater part of the history of embroidery involves the countless generations of anonymous embroiderers that have carried on the time-honoured traditions of their forebears. This is the embroidery that was worked on domestic items, to decorate a trousseau or a shroud, to hold padded layers together for warmth, to welcome the safe arrival of a baby, to mark a rite of passage, to make an ordinary life a little less ordinary. This is the history that we tap into today, no longer embroidering because we have to, but because we can. And in an age where everything is mechanised and mass-produced, the sheer pleasure of producing something beautiful slowly by hand is not to be underestimated.

Cross stitch

Of the many types of embroidery, cross stitch is the most popular, and is practised by hobby embroiderers worldwide. It is also a very old craft; the earliest known piece of embroidered cloth includes cross stitching, and has been dated to between 200 and 500 AD.

There are examples of cross stitch from the T'ang dynasty in China (618–906 AD), and cross stitches were an element in Spanish Blackwork, a style of needlework that is believed to have been taken to England by Catherine of Aragon, the Spanish first wife of King Henry VIII. Due to her influence, it became very popular in her adopted home and also spread to other parts of Europe. During this time, folk art incorporating cross stitch was fashionable in Eastern Europe, and was used to decorate all types of household objects with floral and geometric designs. Different regions and countries each had their own styles of cross-stitch embroidery.

Samplers were the beginning of cross stitch as we know it today; the earliest dated sampler known was made in England in 1598. Samplers were so named because they contained samples of a variety of stitches; they were originally made to act as a reference for the stitcher rather than for any decorative purpose. Gradually, samplers developed from their original form into decorative and predominantly cross-stitch versions that told a story, even recorded history, and taught girls how to perform needlework. As letters and numbers usually featured in such samplers, they also helped teach children basic literacy.

The popularity of embroidered designs in Europe spread with the invention of printing in the sixteenth century. The earliest recorded patterns are from a book produced in Germany in 1525. Then, in 1804, the printed form of cross stitch, in which a design is printed onto cloth to be stitched over, took over from the counted form for at least a century. Since the late 1950s and early 1960s, cross stitch has again become popular as a leisure activity. Many designs are now commercially available; as well as modern designs, there are also charts and patterns depicting traditional motifs and samplers.

The aim of traditional cross stitch is to create a design or pattern on the background fabric. The background fabric may be totally covered with stitching, or more sparsely covered, depending on the design (unlike tapestry, for example, in which every thread of the canvas is covered). The designs are usually referred to as 'counted' cross stitch; that is, the design is worked from a chart by counting the stitches and rows. Cross stitch may also be done on fabric that has been commercially printed with a pattern to be stitched over, following a chart that indicates the colours required to complete the design; this is known as stamped cross stitch. Another type of cross stitch is applied to a background fabric over a type of canvas known as waste canvas. Once the design is finished, each thread of the waste canvas is withdrawn, leaving the cross-stitched design on the background. This technique is useful for doing cross stitch on non-evenweave or otherwise unsuitable fabrics, such as velvet.

Materials and tools

Fabrics

Almost any type of fabric, both woven and non-woven, can be used for surface embroidery, even those you might not initially think of as suitable, such as textured or printed fabrics, or even stretch knits. However, you do need to think about what the embroidered item is ultimately to be used for – does it need to be laundered, for instance? It is also important to consider the relation between thread and fabric: the fabric needs to be able to support the weight of the stitching. Thus, heavier fabrics are usually more suitable for thicker and heavier threads while, conversely, delicate fabrics are best suited to embroidery with very fine threads. But rules are made to be broken – don't be afraid to experiment with the wonderful variety of fabrics and threads that are now available.

Linen is one of the oldest and most widely-used fabrics for embroidery, from evenweave linen (used for counted thread work, such as cross stitch; see page 119) to firmly woven linen, ranging from heavy twill – the traditional choice for crewel embroidery – to the finest handkerchief linen. It is beautiful to work with and is very hard wearing, but it is more expensive than other closely woven fabrics.

Cotton is used to make a bewildering array of fabrics, almost all of which are suitable for surface embroidery. Calico is an inexpensive, firmly woven, unbleached cotton fabric that is very easy to work on. Other cotton fabrics range from very fine voile, lawn and batiste to heavier poplins, twills, waffle weaves and furnishing fabrics. Denim and velvet – both used for embroidery – are also made from cotton.

Silk is a luxury fabric that comes in a variety of weights and styles, from delicate chiffon and organza to lustrous silk dupion and beautifully draping silk velvet. They are expensive, but offer exquisite results, especially when they are embroidered with silk threads.

Wool, like linen, is a traditional and popular choice for many types of embroidery and comes in a broad range of weights – from a very fine fabric, suitable for layettes, to thick, soft blanketing.

Felt is a non-woven, non-fraying fabric that suits a variety of styles of embroidery. Although felt is often produced from synthetic fibres, pure wool felt (or one with a high proportion of wool) is a vastly superior product and is worth seeking out.

Knit fabrics can present a problem to the embroiderer because they all stretch to some degree. However, the stretch can be stabilized by pressing interfacing to the back of the knit before embroidering.

Evenweave fabrics

Evenweave fabrics suitable for traditional and contemporary cross stitch are characterized by a weave that has the same number of warp (vertical) and weft (horizontal) threads over a measured square, thus forming a very even grid over which to stitch. Evenweave fabrics are available in many weights, and are categorized by 'thread count'; this relates to the number of threads per inch (2.5 cm). Weaves range from the finest, almost transparent weave of a 55-count linen through to a rustic-looking cloth produced by a 12-count cotton or hessian.

When working traditional cross stitch, it is important to have a smooth, regular surface on which to work; this is the advantage of using evenweave linen, which has been produced specifically for this type of stitching. Contemporary cross stitch, however, can be worked just as easily on a rough or uneven surface as on smooth, even fabrics. Fabrics for contemporary cross stitch can be made of natural fibres or a blend of natural and synthetic fibres, according to the project you are undertaking and its uses. Consider what you are going to make, whether it needs to be laundered, and also the types of thread you will choose to decorate the surface. These threads need to complement the fabric and its uses (and, if the item is to be laundered, they must have the same laundering qualities).

If using fine or gauzy fabrics, as in contemporary or free cross-stitch designs such as the Lavender sachets on page 228, you will probably need to back the fabric with another fabric before stitching, to increase the strength and reduce the show-through of threads from the back of the work.

evenweave linen A higher number in the thread count indicates a finer fabric.

other evenweaves As well as linen, cotton and synthetic fabric can be used.

pre-finished Bands of varying widths, and cloths and towels with evenweave panels, are available.

Although fabrics are traditionally categorized by threads per inch, there are metric equivalents. The metric names of linen relate to the number of threads per centimetre; thus linen 10 has ten threads per centimetre. The following list gives the metric name and its imperial conversion.

linen 8   20 threads per inch

linen 10   25 or 26 threads per inch

linen 11   20 threads per inch

linen 12   30 threads per inch

linen 13   32 threads per inch

linen 14   35 threads per inch

linen 16   40 threads per inch

Other embroidery fabrics

Aida cloth is a cotton or cotton-blend evenweave fabric with a very distinct grid of warp and weft threads. It is available in a wide range of thread counts and colours.

Hessian is similar to old-fashioned sacking. Generally woven from jute fibres, it gives a coarse, rustic appearance to the work. Colours tend to be neutral.

Prairie cloth is an evenweave fabric with an open grid of thick fibres. It is generally 28-count, and is available in a range of colours.

Zweigart Anne (used for the Tablecloth, page 196) is an 18-count evenweave fabric woven with a grid of 12.5 cm (5 in) squares defined by slightly thicker lines in the weave. The grid provides a simple way of defining areas for cross-stitch designs in larger projects such as throw rugs and tablecloths.

Nearly all evenweave fabrics — for example Aida, evenweave linen, prairie cloth and hessian — are available in the form of pre-finished bands. These bands are designed to allow borders of cross stitching to be applied to non-evenweave fabrics.

Organza is a crisp, sheer fabric usually of silk or rayon but sometimes of other synthetic fibres. It gives a touch of opulence to contemporary cross-stitch designs.

Cotton muslin is a light- to medium-weight fabric with a fine, even weave; however, it is not considered an evenweave fabric for cross stitch purposes as the threads are too fine to be counted easily. It is inexpensive and therefore good to use as a lining or stabilizing fabric in embroidery projects.

Metallic threads come in a wide range of colours and thicknesses, from very fine stitching thread to thicker cords and braids that need to be couched in place. Metallic embroidery threads can be a little tricky to manage as the metallic finish makes them slippery and liable to tangle, and the thread has a tendency to wear badly in the needle. Use short lengths to prevent this.

Crewel wool is the finest of the embroidery wools and, as its name suggests, is used traditionally for crewel embroidery. The name can be slightly confusing, because these days, crewel wool is produced in several thicknesses, from very fine Broder Médicis to the thicker, divisible Persian yarn.

Tapestry wool is a thicker, twisted 4-ply yarn, used of course, for tapestry, but also for other types of wool embroidery.

Machine thread, although not traditionally thought of as a yarn for hand embroidery, can still be used to great effect. Using several lengths of different but similar-toned colours in the needle allows for interesting variegated results.

Visit a needlework shop to discover a wealth of interesting yarns – beautiful hand-dyed threads from boutique manufacturers, variegated and over-dyed yarns that change colour as you stitch, sparkling threads that catch the light, softly hued linen thread. Ask for help and don't be afraid to give different yarns a try.

Other than these traditional types of threads, it is possible to use silk ribbons and a large variety of other wools and cottons that are available from specialty embroidery and craft stores.

Colours and threads may be mixed or blended to create a larger variety of effects and colour schemes for your designs. For example, if using stranded threads, you can use two strands of one shade and one strand of another shade to give a variegated effect (as in the Christmas tree picture, page 166).

Remember that a stitch can be made with almost anything you can thread through a needle. This gives you great freedom for experimentation and innovation, especially when creating contemporary designs.

Threads should always be tested on a sample piece of the fabric before starting the actual project; if the result is unsatisfactory, try another type or thickness of thread. Testing the thread is especially advisable if you intend changing the threads and/or fabrics from those suggested in the design. In your eagerness to start your new project it is tempting to skip this step, but it is essential to get these matters right before commencing. A little experimentation at this stage may save a lot of time, money, effort and disappointment in the long run.

General sewing supplies

As well as the materials and tools specified in the individual projects, you will need general sewing supplies, such as:

- Dressmaker's scissors
- Paper scissors (paper tends to blunt scissors, so do not use the same pair for cutting both paper and fabric)
- Small, sharp embroidery scissors
- Dressmaker's pins
- Needles and machine sewing thread
- Tailor's chalk or water-soluble fabric marker (see page 129)
- Tracing paper
- Safety pins
- Transparent template plastic
- Tape measure
- Iron, ironing board and pressing cloth
- Sewing machine (optional)
- Embroidery hoop or frame

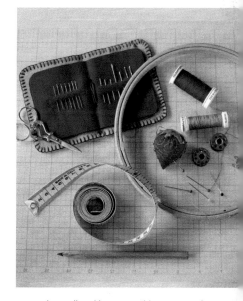

general supplies Keep everything you need close at hand in a basket or workbox.

needles Choose the appropriate needle for the type of embroidery and fabric that you are using.

Needles

It is important to choose a needle that suits both the type of fabric you are stitching on and the thread that you are stitching with. A rule of thumb says your needle should never be any thicker than the thread you are using. The thread must be easily passed through the eye of the needle, causing no drag or tension on the thread, and the needle should also move easily between the fibres of the fabric, without having to be forced and without leaving a hole.

Needles used for embroidery generally have longer eyes than those used for plain sewing, with the exception of straw, or milliner's, needles. Needle size is designated by number – the higher the number, the finer the needle.

Do not leave needles or pins stuck in your fabric, as they will eventually rust and leave a stain that is almost impossible to remove.

Crewel (or embroidery) needles are medium-length, sharp needles with a large, long eye, that come in a size range from 1 to 10. They are the most commonly used and versatile needles for embroidery, with the finer sizes (9 and 10) suited to one or two strands of thread, and the thicker needles used with 3-6 strands of stranded cotton or with cotton à broder and perlé cotton.

Chenille needles are longer and thicker than crewel needles, with larger eyes. They are suitable for thicker threads, such as tapestry wool, crewel wool and thick perlé cotton.

Straw (or milliner's) needles have a very small eye at the end of a long, fine shaft, which makes them useful for beading, or working very neat knot stitches, such as French knots and bullions.

Tapestry needles are like chenille needles, but they have blunt tips that push between the fibres of a fabric, rather than splitting them. Mostly used for counted thread embroidery, a tapestry needle is useful when whipping or braiding an embroidery stitch, when you don't want to pierce the fabric.

Getting started

Transferring a design

There are a number of different ways to transfer an embroidery design onto your embroidery fabric. The method you choose will depend on the type of fabric you are using and whether the sort of embroidery you are planning will completely cover the transfer marks or leave some that will need to be removed. Fabric markers include 2B lead pencils, chalk pencils, water-soluble pens, fade-out pens, heat transfer pencils and permanent pens.

Direct tracing can be used when the background fabric is smooth and light in colour. If you cannot see through your chosen fabric, you will need to use a light box or a window as a light source. When placing the fabric over the design, take care that the design is centred. To do this accurately, fold the fabric into quarters, finger press the folds and open out again. Place the design under the background fabric and line up the centring lines on the design sheet with the folded lines on your fabric. Pin or tape the design in place to help prevent slipping whilst tracing. Trace the design using a sharp 2B lead pencil or other fabric marker. Trace lightly, as you will need to cover your lines with embroidery.

Dressmaker's carbon comes in several colours, including a white version that can be used to mark dark fabrics. The fabric should be smooth for best results and, as the carbon marks could be permanent, the carbon colour should blend with that of the embroidery thread. Tape the fabric to your work surface, place dressmaker's carbon on top (ink side down) and then the design on top of this, right side up. Using a stylus or a sharp pencil, draw over the design, pressing firmly. Take care not to make any unnecessary marks, as these will be transferred as well.

Transfer pencils are heat-sensitive pencils that leave permanent lines on fabric, much like commercial iron-on transfers, so the design must be completely covered with embroidery. They are useful when the background fabric is too thick to see through. Trace a mirror image of your design onto tracing paper using a sharp transfer pencil. (The easiest way to do this is to place your design face down on a light box and trace it from the back.) Place the tracing, ink side down, on your fabric, cover with a sheet of baking parchment to prevent scorching, and iron the design onto the fabric.

Basting around a design takes more time than using a fabric marker, but it leaves no permanent mark and is a very useful method for wool blanketing and other textured surfaces where use of a marker is difficult. Trace the design onto thin tracing paper with a fine sharp pencil or felt-tip pen. Pin the design onto the background fabric and baste along the design lines with running stitch, working through both paper and fabric. Carefully tear away the paper, leaving the basted design on your fabric.

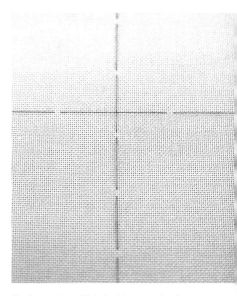

finding centre of fabric Use a contrasting thread and large running stitches to mark the centre.

transferring a design Choose the most appropriate method for your fabric and style of embroidery.

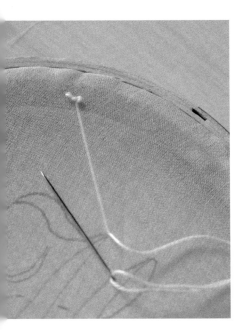

Using an embroidery hoop

Although not absolutely essential, for most embroidery techniques, you will achieve a better and more consistent result if you use an embroidery hoop or frame to hold the fabric taut, so that it is not distorted during stitching. It is also easier to stitch fabric that is held in a hoop or frame rather than loosely in the hand.

Various types and sizes of hoops and frames are available. The traditional round hoops, as shown in the photograph at right, consist of two wooden rings. The fabric to be embroidered is placed over the inner ring (which should be covered with protective bias binding or bias-cut fabric). The outer ring is then placed over the whole thing and tightened by means of a screw attachment. Choose a hoop that is big enough to hold the entire design area to avoid flattening the finished sections of your embroidery.

The simplest embroidery frames to use are usually made of plastic tubing and are square or rectangular. The fabric is placed over the tubes that form the framework, and half-round pieces are then snapped in place over the top, holding and tightening the fabric. Hoops with table-top stands or floor stands are also available.

When placing fabric into an embroidery hoop or frame, adjust it so that the weave is straight, not distorted. When tightening the fabric in the hoop, never pull on the bias as this will cause the fabric to stretch and distort. Do not pull the fabric drum tight; it should be firm, but still have a little give in it. When stitching, use a stabbing action from the back to the front of the fabric, and vice versa. Stitch all the parts of the design that fall within the framed area, then undo the frame or hoop and reposition it over the next area to be stitched. Do not leave the fabric in a hoop or frame for an extended length of time, as this will mark it; remove the fabric from the hoop once your sewing session is over.

wrapping an embroidery hoop Use pressed bias binding to wrap a hoop, securing the ends with a few stitches.

Making a waste knot

For a neat finish and to avoid unsightly knots, embroiderers often use a 'waste knot' when starting work. Knot the end of the thread and put the needle into the right side of the fabric, about 5 cm (2 in) away from your starting point, leaving the knot on the right side of the fabric. When the embroidery is finished, snip off the knot, thread the end into a needle, take the needle to the wrong side and weave the tail under completed stitches on the wrong side of the work.

waste knot A waste knot will ensure a neat, smooth finish with no bumps.

Finishing

Removing transfer marks

Fade-out pens will do what their name implies – slowly disappear within 2–14 days. If you need a design to last longer than that, choose a different form of marker instead. Water-soluble pen marks can be removed by dabbing them with cold water on a cotton bud. Chalk pencil marks can be brushed away or dabbed with a damp cloth.

If your embroidery has pencil marks on it, wash it in pure soap in warm water, as described below.

For fabric markers of all kinds, do not leave your work in the sun nor iron it before all traces of the marker have been removed. Heat can permanently set a marker, even those that are supposed to fade out.

Washing and pressing

Sometimes, despite the best intentions, embroidery can show signs of being a little grubby after having been repeatedly handled. If your embroidery needs to be washed, do this before making up the project. Wash it in warm water and pure soap, moving it gently in the water. Never rub nor pull at the fabric or stitching. This is particularly important for wool fabrics and threads, as the fibres will felt if they are over-agitated. Rinse gently and thoroughly, but do not wring – roll the work in a soft, clean, light-coloured towel and gently squeeze out the excess water.

Place a folded towel on the ironing board, place a piece of fabric on top – a clean white tea towel works well – then place the wet embroidery face down and another piece of fabric over the back. Press dry with the iron. The fabric over the back helps to prevent scorching and the towel underneath will prevent your embroidery from being flattened.

If your embroidery does not require laundering before making up, simply place face down on a towel as above, and press.

Ending a line of stitching

Once a row of stitching or a section of one colour is finished, take the thread to the back of the work and make a clove hitch knot (below).

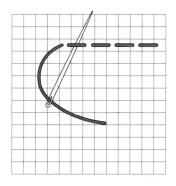

Bring the thread through to the back and through the last stitch.

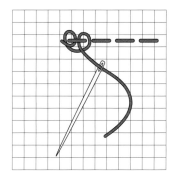

Work a clove hitch knot as shown to fasten off.

Then run the thread under the back of a few stitches to conceal and secure it (as pictured below), and cut off the excess.

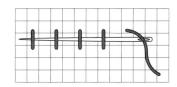

Run thread under the back of the stitching to avoid bulky knots.

How to mitre a corner

On each raw edge of the hem, turn under or overlock the allowance for the first hem, wrong sides together. Press well. At the corner, turn in the second hem if required. Press well. Unfold each corner, then fold up the edge of the fabric so that there is an exact diagonal at the point of the corner. Press, then trim the excess near the diagonal fold, as shown by the diagonal line in Diagram 1 below. Turn the diagonal over along the pressed line, then fold each side back up along its pressing lines to form a neat mitred corner (see Diagram 2). Neatly slipstitch the hem, then overstitch the mitred corners (see Diagram 3).

Diagram 1

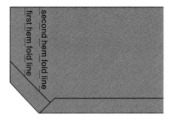

Diagram 2

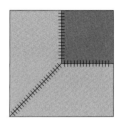

Diagram 3

Mounting embroidery

Before framing a piece, you will need to mount it. Cut a piece of heavy card the finished size of the piece, plus about 6 mm (1/4 in) added all round for the recess in the frame. Find the centre of the top and bottom, and mark lightly with pencil on the back.

To mount a small, lightweight piece, place the embroidery face down, then centre the cardboard on top of it, matching the pencil marks on the card with the centre line of the design. Fold each corner over and secure with masking tape (see Diagram 4). Fold in first one side, then the other, securing firmly with masking tape. Use the weave of the fabric as a guide so that the fabric is not distorted by being pulled unevenly. Neaten the mitred corners, pulling firmly and securing with more tape to give a smooth finish (see Diagram 5).

For a heavier or larger piece, fold in the corners as described above, then fold in opposite edges of the fabric and lace across the piece in both directions, using strong thread. Overstitch the mitred corners to secure them (see Diagram 6).

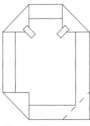

Diagram 4

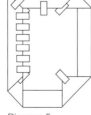

Diagram 5

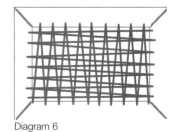

Diagram 6

Other techniques

Pulling threads

A thread can be pulled to give a guide for a straight cutting line or fold line. To pull a thread, use a needle to tease out the end of one thread of the fabric, near to the cut edge at the desired point. Then continue pulling it out, using the needle to extract the thread as you go.

When beginning a decorative effect such as hem stitching, two to four threads are commonly pulled (see also page 142).

Attaching seed beads

Seed beads are attached with a small half-cross stitch. You will need a beading needle (a very thin, long needle) or a fine, sharp needle. Work the first half of the cross stitch, then bring the needle up where the second half of the stitch begins. Pass the needle through the hole in the bead and down again through the fabric where the second half of the stitch ends. Continue cross stitching as normal until the next bead needs to be attached.

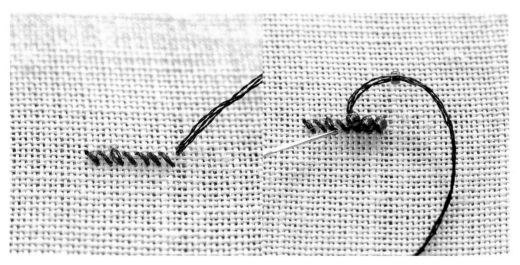

attaching seed beads Work the bottom diagonals of the cross stitches in the usual manner.

Thread beads onto the needle when working the top diagonal.

Resizing designs

The count of the fabric on which you work affects the finished size of the cross-stitch design. For this reason it is important to use the count of fabric specified, or your embroidered design may be bigger or smaller than you wish. However, it is possible to resize a design, as follows:

Count how many squares of the chart the design covers. Multiply the result by the number of threads of fabric covered by each stitch (usually, but not always, two). This is the number of threads of fabric that the finished design requires.

Now divide this number by the number of threads per centimetre or inch of the fabric you intend using. The result will be the finished size of the resized design.

For example, a design worked over two threads of fabric and 40 squares of the chart covers 80 threads. The following would be the size of such a design on a variety of counts of fabric:

28-count: 7.25 cm (27/8 in)

24-count: 9.2 cm (35/8 in)

20-count: 10 cm (4 in)

16-count: 12.5 cm (5 in)

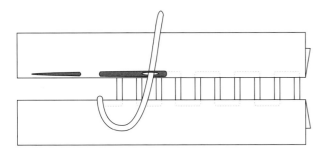

Ladder stitch

This stitch is used to make a strong and almost invisible join between two pressed edges, such as the opening in a seam.

Knot the thread and conceal the knot inside one end of the opening. Bring the needle out through the fold of the fabric, about 6 mm (1/4 in) from the raw edge. Insert the needle into the other side of the opening directly opposite where you brought it out. Take a small stitch along the inside of the fold, then bring the needle out on the same side. Take it back to the opposite side and take a small stitch along the inside of the fold. Repeat this process, working from side to side, until you've stitched the entire opening. Pull the thread taut to close the gap securely. Fasten off and trim thread.

Slip stitch

Slip stitch is used for an almost invisible finish on hems, or as an alternative to ladder stitch when closing an opening.

Slide the needle through one folded edge, pick up a thread or two of the opposite fabric, then push the needle directly back into the fold and take a stitch along the fold before picking up another two threads.

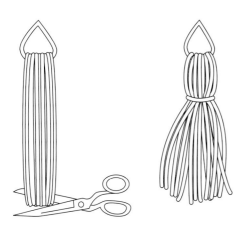

Making a simple tassel

Cut a rectangle of firm cardboard that is as wide as the desired length of your finished tassel. Wrap thread around the cardboard until you have the thickness of tassel that you desire. Thread a holding thread under the wraps at the top of the cardboard and tie securely. Cut the threads at the bottom, to release the tassel from the cardboard and form the skirt. To form the neck of the tassel, wrap a separate length of thread around the tassel a little way below the holding cord and tie off securely.

Making a twisted cord

Cut a minimum of four lengths of thread (stranded cotton, perlé cotton or embroidery wool, for example), at least four times the finished length required, and fold in half. Knot the ends and loop them over a hook (or jam the knot in a closed drawer) while you slip a pencil through the folded part at the other end. Twist the pencil in one direction, keeping the threads taut, until the cord is very tight and starts to kink back on itself. Place your finger at the halfway point and, relaxing the tautness just a little, allow the cord to twist back on itself from this point. Run your fingers firmly over the cord to smooth it.

twisted cord, step one Slip a pencil through the folded threads and twist tightly.

twisted cord, step two Place your finger at the halfway point, before letting the cord twist back on itself.

twisted cord, step three Remove the pencil and knot the ends together.

Stitch library

Back stitch

Bring the needle through the fabric from the wrong side to the right side at A. Insert the needle at B, and come out again at C. Insert the needle at A again and go an equal distance further on, past C. Repeat until you reach the end. Back stitch can be used to outline designs and to form a border. When working on non-evenweave fabrics, changing direction in back stitch is easy. If working on evenweave fabric, the curve will be staggered, as illustrated in the following diagrams.

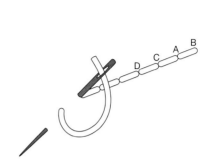

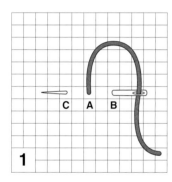

1

The first part of a back stitch is worked backwards.

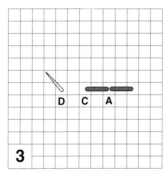

2

The stitches on top of the fabric go backwards; those on the back of the fabric go forwards.

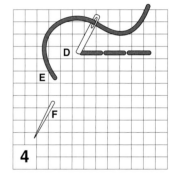

3

Work each stitch over the same number of threads (usually two).

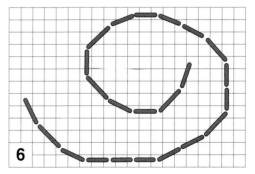

4

Back stitch may be worked in curved lines and around corners.

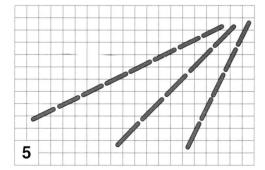

5

When working stitches at an angle, the steepness or shallowness of the line formed depends on how many threads across the needle is brought up at.

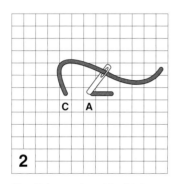

6

Curves can be created by combining horizontal and vertical stitches with those worked at an angle.

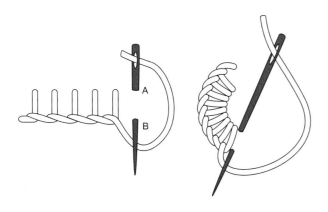

Blanket and buttonhole stitch

These stitches are worked in the same manner – buttonhole stitch is simply a close version of blanket stitch. Insert the needle from front to back at A, bringing it out again at B, keeping the thread under the needle point. Pull up the stitch to form a loop. Work the next stitch as close or as far apart from the first stitch as desired.

Buttonhole stitch is often often used to finish a piece of fabric, especially on blankets (hence the name) or in place or a machine-neatened edge such as zigzag or overlock. When buttonhole stitch is worked in a circle, it is known as a pinwheel flower.

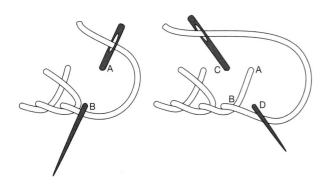

Buttonhole stitch, crossed

Insert the needle from front to back at A, bringing it out again obliquely at B, keeping the thread under the needle point. Insert it again at C, to the left of A, bringing it out again in the opposite oblique direction at D, keeping the thread under the needle point. Proceed in this manner, forming crosses as you stitch.

Chain stitch

Bring the needle through to the front at the desired starting point, A. Insert it again in the same place, then bring the point out again a short distance away at B, looping the thread under the needle before pulling it through. To make the next stitch, insert the needle again at B, and come out again a short distance away, looping the thread under the needle, as before. To finish, anchor the last loop with a tiny straight stitch.

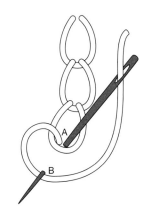

Chain stitch, back-stitched

This stitch is worked in 2 parts. First work a length of chain stitch. Then work a row of back stitch along the centre of the chain stitch loops, using the same coloured thread, or a contrast shade.

Chain stitch, braided

This stitch is worked in 3 steps. Work a length of chain stitch, then work a second row of chain stitch alongside the first. Using a contrast thread, and a blunt-nosed needle (such as a small tapestry needle), lace the adjacent chain stitch loops together, picking up the threads only, without piercing the fabric.

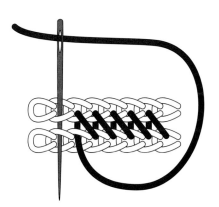

Chain stitch, Vandyke (Zigzag chain stitch)

Work this stitch in the same way as ordinary chain stitch, but work each chain loop at right angles to the previous one, thus creating a zigzag line. To make sure the stitches lie flat, pierce the end of each preceding loop with the point of the needle.

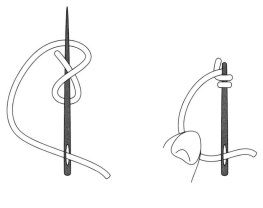

Colonial knot

Bring the needle to the front of the fabric. Wrap the thread over, under and around the tip of the needle in a figure-of-8. Insert the needle tip into the fabric a couple of fabric threads away from where it emerged. Pull the wraps firmly and push the needle through to the back. Pressing the knot and loop with your thumb, continue to pull the thread gently through.

Couching

Lay a thread along the line of the embroidery design and, using another thread in the same shade or a contrast colour, stitch the laid thread in place at regular intervals, taking a tiny stitch over the thread

Cross stitch

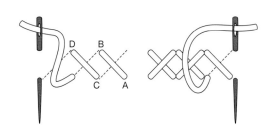

Cross stitch is used for the main body of the design and to fill in patterns.

Cross stitches should be always worked in the same direction, stitching a row of half crosses first, then turning back and completing the crosses. However you choose to work, it is essential that the top diagonals of all crosses lie in the same direction. Cross stitch is generally, but not always, worked over two threads of the fabric.

The following diagrams show cross stitch worked over evenweave fabric, as is common, but it can also be worked on other fabrics.

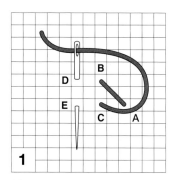

1

After completing each diagonal stitch, bring the needle through to the front.

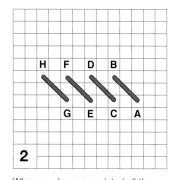

2

When you have completed all the stitches in a row, it is time to turn.

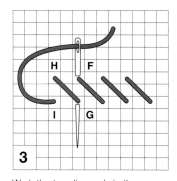

3

Work the top diagonals in the opposite direction to the bottom.

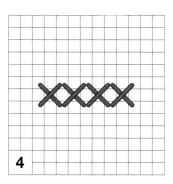

4

When the row is finished, move on to the next area.

Feather stitch

Bring the needle to the front at the top of the line to be covered (A). Holding the thread down with your left thumb, insert the needle a little to the right at B and take a slanting stitch back to the centre, bringing the needle out again at C (which becomes the starting point for the next stitch). To make the next stitch, holding the thread down with your left thumb, insert the needle a little to the left of centre, thus reversing the direction of B and C. Continue in this manner, alternating from side to side.

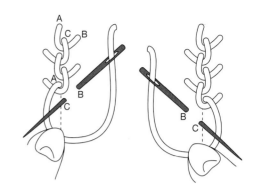

Fly stitch

Bring the needle to the front at A. Take a slanting stitch from B to C. Loop the thread under the needle tip and, holding the loop with your left thumb, pull the needle gently through. Anchor the loop by inserting the needle again at D, making a small stitch. Rows of fly stitch can be worked horizontally or vertically, and the length of CD can be varied as desired.

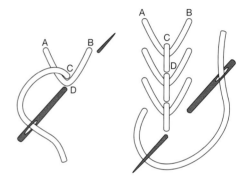

Four-sided stitch

This decorative stitch is always worked in horizontal rows, running with the grain of the fabric. Follow the numbered points illustrated and always pull each stitch tight. Tension is the most important part of this stitch, so don't put your work down in the middle of a row; instead, finish each row. When you come to the end of a row, turn the fabric upside down. Work the next row in the same manner as the first.

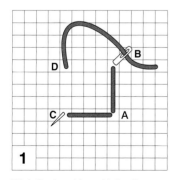

1

Work the top side and bring the needle out again at C.

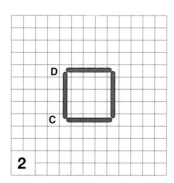

2

The fourth side of the square is also the first side of the next stitch.

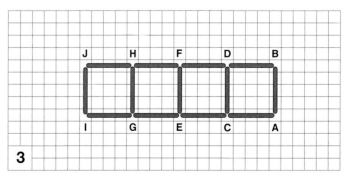

3

Continue along the whole row without stopping your work.

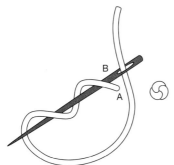

French knot

Bring the needle to the front at A and, holding the thread taut with one hand, wind the thread around the needle twice (or more, if the design specifies a number of wraps or you want a bigger knot). Keeping the thread taut, turn the needle and insert it again close to A, at B. Holding the knot in place with your thumb, pull the thread through to form a firm knot.

Hem stitching

This is a decorative method of stitching a hem or grouping several threads together. It is worked after the hem has been sewn in place.

Variations

The diagrams below show hem stitching worked over two threads, but it can be worked over more as you desire, so long as the number of threads over which it is worked is kept consistent throughout the piece.

Hem stitching can be worked along one or both sides of the pulled threads, either in mirror image (see Step 4, below) or in a V-effect (see Tissue sachet and makeup purse, page 288).

The threads pulled in hem stitching can be woven in along the 'furrows', from the intersections at the corners to the edges of the fabric, for a neater effect (see page 150).

Pull out the required number of threads along the stitching line (see page 26), then turn the hem up and sew it in place. Bring the needle through from back to front at A, through the hem. Take the thread to the right; then, pointing the needle towards the left, pass it under the required number of threads from B to C. Pull the thread through, then, with the needle at an angle, insert it at B and bring through to the front of the fabric at D, in line with the point at which the thread came up first.

Repeat to end of work, working around the same number of threads each time, and keeping a constant check on your stitch tension.

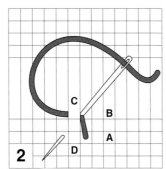

1 Bring the needle through the hem at A, then behind the desired number of threads from B to C.

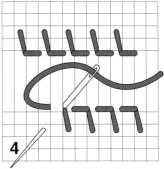

2 Wrap the needle around the threads, then insert it from back to front, bringing it out at D.

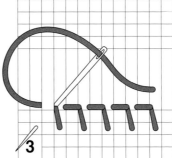

3 Continue along the hem until all stitches are worked.

4 For a double row of hem stitching, work the opposite side also.

Herringbone stitch

Bring the needle to the front at A. With the thread below the needle, insert it again at B and take a small stitch to the left, emerging at C. Pull the thread through. With the thread above the needle, insert it on the lower line at D and take a small stitch to the left, emerging at E. Pull the thread through. Continue in this manner, alternating between upper and lower lines.

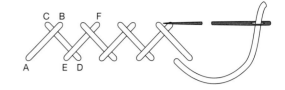

Herringbone stitch, closed

This is worked in the same way as ordinary herringbone stitch, but there is no space left between the stitches.

Lazy daisy stitch (Detached chain stitch)

Work in the same way as chain stitch, but anchor each loop with a small stitch. When worked singly, this stitch is mostly referred to as Detached chain stitch. When worked in a circular group to form a flower, it is called Lazy daisy stitch.

Pekinese stitch

This stitch is worked in 2 parts. Work a foundation row of back stitch. Using a blunt-end tapestry needle and the same shade or a contrast colour, lace through the back stitches from left to right, as shown, without picking up any of the background fabric. Slightly tighten each loop after it has been formed.

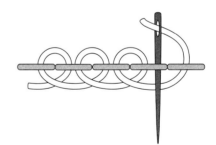

Pistil stitch

This is simply a straight stitch with a French knot at one end. Bring the needle to the front at A (base of stitch). Holding the thread taut with one hand, wind the thread around the needle twice, as for a French knot. Keeping the thread taut, insert the needle again at B, the desired distance from A. Holding the knot in place with your thumb, pull the thread through.

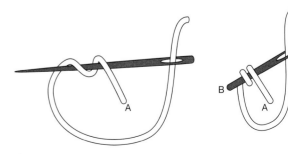

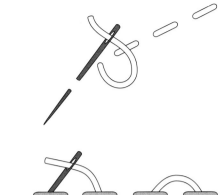

Running stitch

Thread the needle in and out of the fabric, keeping the stitches equal in length.

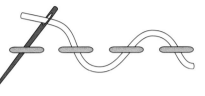

Running stitch, whipped

This stitch is worked in two parts. Work a foundation row of running stitch. Using a blunt-end tapestry needle and the same shade or a contrast colour, weave in and out of the stitches, as shown.

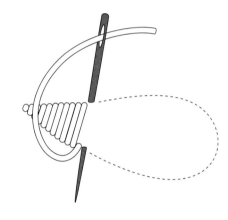

Satin stitch

Satin stitch should always be worked on fabric in a hoop to maintain an even tension in the stitching. Work a series of straight stitches close together across a shape to be filled. Do not make stitches too long.

Seed stitch (Kantha stitch)

This is used as a filling stitch or, on Indian Kantha embroidery, as a quilting stitch. Work small, straight stitches of fairly even length to fill a shape.

Shadow stitch (Double back stitch)

Bring the needle to the front at A, on one side of the design outline. Take a small back stitch to B and bring the needle to the front again at C, on the opposite side of the design outline, directly below A (Diagram 1). Take a small back stitch to D, then bring the needle to the front again at E, one stitch length away from A (Diagram 2). Take a small back stitch back to the same hole as A (F), then bring the needle to the front again at G, one stitch length away from C (Diagram 3). Proceed in this manner, making sure that when each back stitch is made, it goes into the same hole as the end of the previous stitch. The wrong side of the work will be a closed herringbone stitch, that will show through the transparent fabric as a shadow (Diagram 4). When working on a curved area of a design, the back stitches on the inside of the curve need to be shortened, while those on the outside need to be lengthened, so that you reach the end of the curved area simultaneously on both sides.

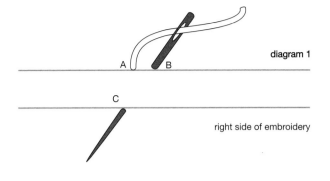

diagram 1

right side of embroidery

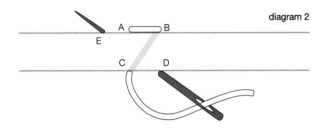

diagram 2

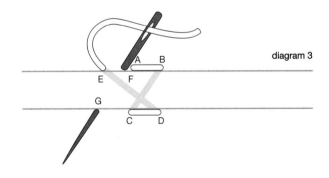

diagram 3

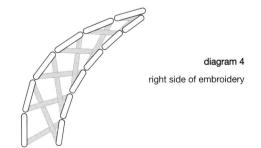

diagram 4

right side of embroidery

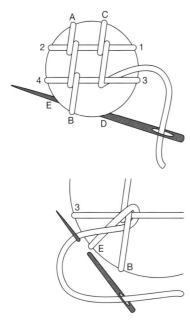

Shisha stitch

Holding the shisha mirror in place with your left hand, make two parallel horizontal stitches across the glass (1-2, 3-4). Bring the needle out at A, take it over, then under, then back over the first of the horizontal threads to form a holding stitch. Repeat this process on the remaining horizontal thread and insert the needle at B. Take the needle across the back of the work and bring it out at C. Work another 2 holding stitches across the parallel threads, as before, and insert the needle at D. Bring the needle to the front again in the lower left corner, close to the edge of the mirror, at E. Weave it over the holding threads, as shown, then take a small stitch close to the edge of the mirror, keeping the thread below the needle. Proceed in this manner clockwise around the mirror, taking the needle over the holding threads, then anchoring it each time at the edge of the mirror.

Spider's web

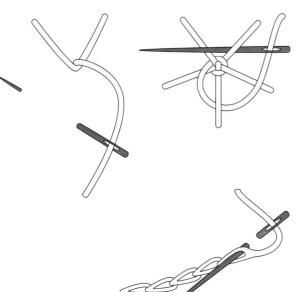

This stitch is worked in 2 parts. First work a foundation of spokes, using a fly stitch and a couple of straight stitches (you should always start with an uneven number of spokes). Using a blunt-end needle and the same shade or a contrast colour, weave over and under the spokes from the centre outwards, without piercing the background fabric.

Split stitch

This is worked in a similar manner to back stitch, except that the thread of the previous stitch is split by the needle as it emerges from the fabric to make the next stitch. The effect is like a narrow chain stitch.

Star stitch (Double cross stitch)

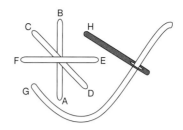

This is a series of straight stitches worked around the points of a compass to form a star shape. Bring the needle to the front at A, insert it at B, bring it out again at C, and insert it at D. Proceed in this manner around the circle, as shown. If desired, you can take a small anchoring stitch across the intersection of the spokes at the centre.

Stem stitch

Work along an outline from left to right, as shown, taking small, regular stitches. Always keep the working thread below the needle.

Straight stitch

This stitch can be worked singly, or in a group, as shown. Bring the needle to the front, then insert it again at the desired distance from the starting point. Groups of stitches can be all the same length or random lengths. It is important to keep an even tension.

Trellis couching

This stitch is worked in 2 parts. First lay a foundation trellis of threads, laid vertically and horizontally (A), or on the diagonal (B), across the area to be filled. Using a thread of the same shade or a contrast colour, take a small holding stitch across the threads at each intersection on the trellis. The holding stitch can be one small diagonal stitch or a cross, as desired.

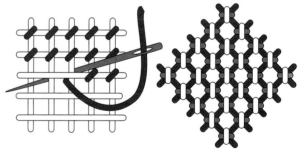

Diagram A   Diagram B

Table runner

From the refectory to the breakfast nook, a runner provides a unifying element to the table setting, whether the meal is a simple sandwich or a six-course banquet. Use a runner refectory style, down the centre of the table, as a mat for condiments, serving dishes and centrepieces; or make matching runners to use across the table instead of placemats.

This simple embroidered and hem-stitched runner can be made in any length to suit your table, and any colour to match your china. The elegant, geometric four-sided stitch will complement any mood, from formal to casual.

Materials
52 x 156 cm (21 x 61½ in) 28-count evenweave linen in ecru
4 skeins DMC stranded embroidery cotton, 3371 (black-brown)
4 skeins DMC stranded embroidery cotton, 840 (medium beige-brown)

Tools
Tapestry needle No 24
Embroidery scissors
General sewing supplies

Notes
The table runner shown is 36 cm (14 in) wide and 140 cm (55 in) long when finished. The dimensions may be changed to suit any size of table, or even reduced to a placemat size. The runner has a 4 cm (1½ in) double hem so that there is no shadow at the hemline. The corners are mitred and the hem is hem stitched with contrasting thread all round the runner. The hem stitching and the four-sided stitching are worked in four strands of DMC stranded embroidery cotton: two strands each of 3371 (black-brown) and 840 (medium beige-brown). This blending of shades gives a subtle variegated effect.

step two To prepare for hem stitching, draw threads along the line of the second hem. From the intersections, weave the thread back along the 'furrow' towards the edge.

ready to hem Showing the corners of the line of threads to be hem stitched, with the threads neatly woven back into the fabric.

Hint

When cutting fabric or folding hems, you might find it helpful to first withdraw a thread along the cutting or fold lines as a guide; this will enable you to fold or cut a very accurate line.

1 If changing the dimensions of the runner, decide on the finished size required and add 8 cm (3¼ in) to each edge. This is the actual size to which the fabric should be cut, including the allowance for a double 4 cm (1½ in) hem. Before cutting, withdraw a thread at the cutting position on all four sides to ensure that you get a perfectly straight line in the evenweave fabric.

2 To prepare for hemming and hem stitching, completely withdraw a thread along the line of the second hem on all four sides. Next, partially withdraw a thread alongside the first, to the point at which the previously withdrawn threads intersect.

Thread this thread into a tapestry needle and weave it back into the fabric along the 'furrow' left by the previously drawn thread, from the intersection to the edge of the fabric. Do this on all four sides.

3 On each side, withdraw one more complete thread, then partially withdraw and weave in one more thread as before.

4 Press the double hem on all four sides (see Hint at left). Following the instructions on page 132, mitre each corner. Slip stitch the hem into place. Once the hem is complete, you are ready to work the hem stitch (see page 142).

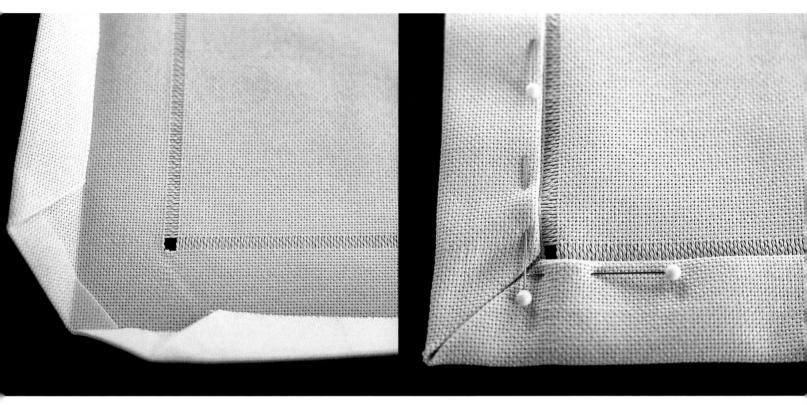

step four Press a 4 cm (1½ in) double hem, then mitre the corners.

step four continued Pin and neatly slip stitch the hem. Once the hem is finished, work the hem stitching.

5 Before beginning the hem stitching, work a small sample to check your tension. When you have a good even tension, start stitching at a corner, working over four threads with each stitch.

6 The four-sided stitch pattern along the sides is worked after the completion of the hem. Measure in 2 cm (¾ in) from the hem-stitched line at each corner to mark the starting point for the embroidery. From this point, work four-sided stitch over four threads for the desired length of the design, parallel to the hem (the length may vary with the size of your table runner). On the table runner shown here, work 21 stitches (about 8 cm/3¼ in) from the corner towards the middle of the short sides of the runner, at all four corners. Then, on the right-hand corner at each end, work 56 stitches (23 cm/9 in) along the long edge. On the left-hand corner, work approximately 100 stitches (42 cm/16½ in) along the long edge.

7 Measure in 2 cm (¾ in) from the outer edge of the first row of hem stitch in each corner to mark the starting point of the inner rows of embroidery. Work as before, stitching 11 stitches (4.5 cm/1¾ in) towards the middle on the short sides and, on the long sides, 26 stitches (11 cm/4¼ in) on the right and 40 stitches (29 cm/11½ in) on the left.

Hint

Try to complete a whole side of hem stitch or a complete row of four-sided stitch before taking a break, as your tension can change slightly if you put your work down for a while.

Cushion covers

These simple cushion covers are an effective way to create a casual, modern pairing, with the design of the first echoed but not exactly replicated in the other. In creamy linen with the sharp contrast of deep navy and cinnamon embroidery and a navy trim, the basic cross-stitched designs create a subtle repetition.

If your sewing skills do not extend to piping and zippers, you can work the embroidery, then send the materials to be professionally assembled at your local sewing supplier or by a dressmaker.

Materials (for each cushion)

50 cm (20 in) square of 28-count evenweave linen in ecru
1 skein cinnamon-coloured silk embroidery thread
1 skein DMC stranded embroidery cotton, 823 (dark navy blue)
40 cm (16 in) cushion insert
50 cm (20 in) square of dark navy cotton velvet for cushion backing: note that 1 m (39 in) of 120 cm (47 in) wide velvet is enough for the backing and piping for two cushions
180 cm (70 in) piping cord
30 cm (12 in) zipper

Tools

Tapestry needle No 24
Sewing machine with zipper foot
General sewing supplies

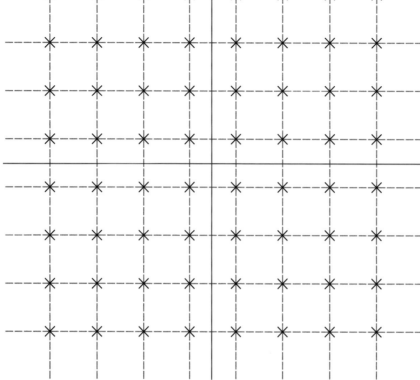

— back stitch worked over six
threads, using one thickness of
cinnamon silk embroidery thread

X cross stitch worked over
eight threads, using four strands
of DMC 823 (dark navy blue)

diagram 1 Stitching diagram for
Cushion 1. The centre lines are
marked in red.

1 To start the embroidery you need to mark the centre of your evenweave linen fabric. An easy way to do this is to fold the square of linen in half, then stitch a row of large running stitches between the two threads at the halfway point. Repeat this at a 90 degree angle: the stitches will cross at the centre of the fabric. Use a contrasting coloured sewing cotton for this stitching and leave the running stitches in place until the project is complete, when they can easily be pulled out.

2 The grids are back stitched in cinnamon silk embroidery thread, with each stitch worked over six threads of the linen. The smaller grid's squares are 30 threads (five back stitches) wide. To begin stitching, count 15 threads up and 15 threads across from the centre of the fabric. The total grid is nine squares in each direction. You may begin with a knot, or a short tail of thread on the wrong side of the work; be aware that, because of the dark colours used, any thread tail may be visible through the light-coloured linen. Work the entire grid in back stitch before working the cross stitches.

3 The cross stitches are worked over eight threads, with the middle of each cross centred over the junctions of the back-stitched grid, using four strands of the dark

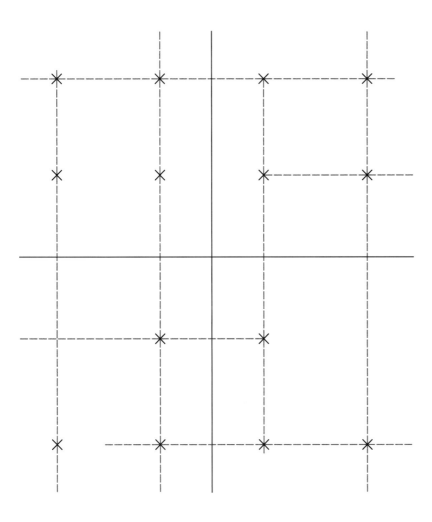

— back stitch worked over six
threads, using one thickness of
cinnamon silk embroidery thread

X cross stitch worked over
eight threads, using four strands
of DMC 823 (dark navy blue)

diagram 2 Stitching diagram for Cushion 2. The centre
lines are marked in red.

navy blue stranded embroidery cotton.
Each cross stitch should be started and
finished independently (using a clove hitch
knot; see page 131), so there is no shadow
of thread showing through to the right side
of the cushion.

4 The design for the second cushion is
not based on a regular grid. From the
marked centre, count 36 threads to the
left and commence with a line of back stitch
at this point, according to Diagram 2, then
count 48 threads down and work another
line of back stitch at this point. Work the
remaining lines of back stitch according
to the chart.

5 Note that the lines of the grid continue
beyond the main lines in some cases, for up
to 30 threads (five back stitches). Work
selected lines of the grid in the cinnamon
silk thread as before, in back stitch over six
threads. Work cross stitches in four strands
of dark navy blue embroidery cotton over
eight threads at the junctions of some of
the squares, as indicated in Diagram 2.
Remove the lines of running stitch when
you have finished all the embroidery.

6 Make up as instructed at right.

Making up the covers

Trim the edges of the linen so
that you have a precise 43 cm
(17 in) square, and neaten the
edges to prevent fraying. Cut a
square of navy velvet the same
size. Use the leftover velvet,
cut on the bias, to cover the
piping cord, and lay the piping
between the right sides of the
cushion front and back. Stitch
around three sides, adding a
zipper on the fourth side. If you
are not confident with this,
take your cushion materials to
a professional to be made up.

Crewel pincushions

Traditionally, this very old form of embroidery was worked on heavy twill linen using two-ply worsted wool yarn, known as 'crule' or 'croyl'. Dating from much earlier, but reaching the height of its popularity during the seventeenth century, crewelwork was used to decorate all kinds of furnishings – curtains, cushions, fire screens, bell-pulls, bed and wall hangings – as well as clothing. If an entire curtain seems a little ambitious, a small pincushion might be the perfect introduction to this lovely technique. The square pincushion is worked entirely in chain stitch, using stranded cotton. The hexagonal pincushion is worked in a variety of stitches, using the traditional fine crewel wool.

Materials
(For each pincushion)
30 cm (12 in) square linen, linen/cotton blend or Osnaberg fabric
25 cm (10 in) square wool or cotton print fabric, for backing
Polyester fibrefill
Matching machine thread

(For square pincushion)
One skein DMC Stranded Embroidery Cotton in each of the following colours: 728 (Medium Topaz), 3051 (Dark Green Grey) and 3052 (Medium Green Grey)
Two skeins DMC Stranded Embroidery Cotton in each of the following colours: 347 (Very Dark Salmon) and 899 (Medium Rose)

(For hexagonal pincushion)
One skein Cascade House Crewel Embroidery Wool in each of the following colours: 1520, 1780, 2380 and 3390
Two skeins Cascade House Crewel Embroidery Wool in each of the following colours: 1840 and 3990

Tools
Crewel needles, No 7 or 8
Small embroidery hoop
General sewing supplies
Template plastic, for hexagonal pincushion

Size
Square pincushion measures 13 cm (5 in) square
Hexagonal pincushion measures 15 cm (6 in) across widest point

Stitches
Back stitch (page 137)
Chain stitch (page 139)
Closed herringbone (page 143)
French knot (page 142)
Satin stitch (page 144)
Stem stitch (page 147)
Trellis couching (page 147)

step one A light box will make it easier to trace the design onto thicker fabric.

detail A tassel on each corner is an effective way to finish the square pincushion.

Hints

Don't have your thread too long, as wool wears when it is being pulled through the fabric.

Use a hoop for all filling stitches, such as herringbone or satin stitch, and try not to pull the stitches too tight, as it may pucker the fabric and ultimately distort the shape of your work.

1 The two designs are printed opposite. Enlarge as required and transfer your chosen design to the fabric using your preferred method (see page 129), taking care that it is centred on the fabric. Do not transfer the hexagon shape to the fabric at this stage.

2 Using the embroidery guides, opposite and on page 160, work your chosen design in the colours and stitches as given. The design for the square pincushion is worked entirely in chain stitch, using two strands of cotton. All the flowers and leaves are filled with chain stitch, starting on the outside and filling in towards the centre. On the

flowers, however, it is easier to stitch the centre first, then work outwards. The design for the hexagonal pincushion is worked with one strand of wool throughout, following the colours and stitches on the guide. When all embroidery is complete, press work on the wrong side on a well-padded surface.

3 To make up the square pincushion, trim embroidered fabric back to 14 cm (5½ in) square, keeping the design centred. Cut two pieces of backing fabric, each 7.5 x 14 cm (3 x 5½ in). With right sides together and allowing a 6 mm (¼ in) seam, join the backing rectangles to each other along one

embroidery guide
square pincushion
DMC Stranded Embroidery Cotton

■	347
■	899
■	728
■	3051
■	3052

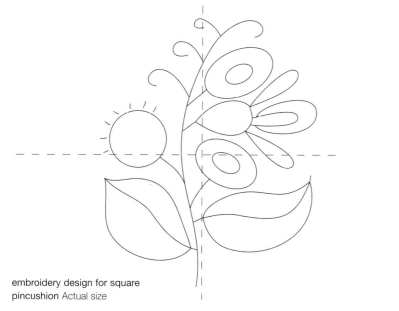

embroidery design for square
pincushion Actual size

embroidery design for hexagonal pincushion Enlarge by 200%

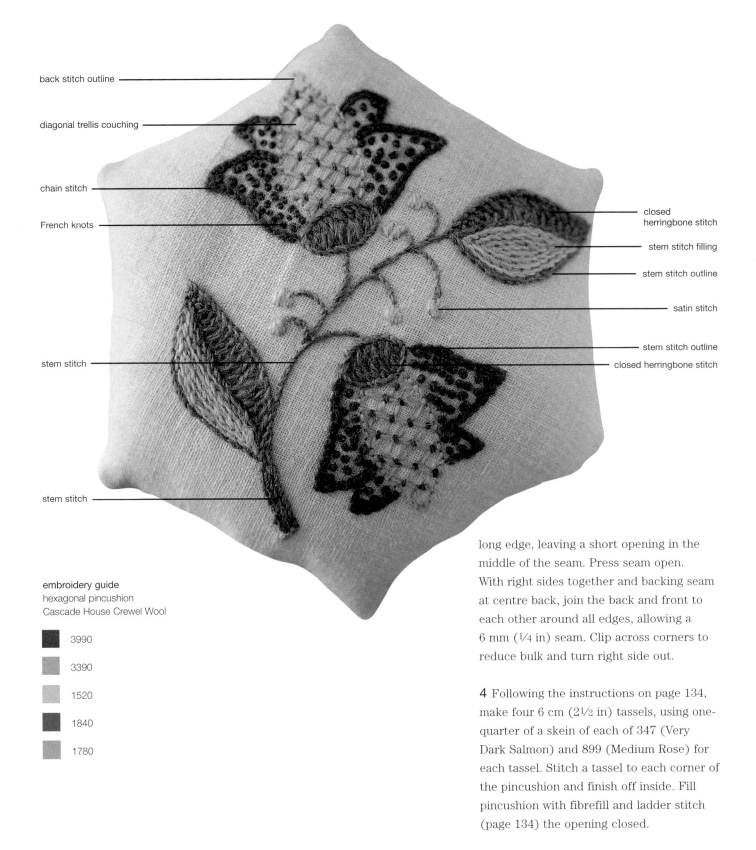

back stitch outline

diagonal trellis couching

chain stitch

French knots

stem stitch

stem stitch

closed herringbone stitch

stem stitch filling

stem stitch outline

satin stitch

stem stitch outline

closed herringbone stitch

embroidery guide
hexagonal pincushion
Cascade House Crewel Wool

3990

3390

1520

1840

1780

long edge, leaving a short opening in the middle of the seam. Press seam open. With right sides together and backing seam at centre back, join the back and front to each other around all edges, allowing a 6 mm (¼ in) seam. Clip across corners to reduce bulk and turn right side out.

4 Following the instructions on page 134, make four 6 cm (2½ in) tassels, using one-quarter of a skein of each of 347 (Very Dark Salmon) and 899 (Medium Rose) for each tassel. Stitch a tassel to each corner of the pincushion and finish off inside. Fill pincushion with fibrefill and ladder stitch (page 134) the opening closed.

step five When the pincushion is turned right side out, the opening should be in the middle of the centre back seam.

detail A twisted cord made from the same threads as used for the embroidery gives a professional finish to the edge.

5 To make up the hexagonal pincushion, make a plastic template of the hexagonal shape, on page 159. Place the template over the back of completed embroidery, keeping the design centred, and trace around the hexagon. The traced line will be the sewing line. Cut two pieces of backing fabric, 10 x 15 cm (4 x 6 in). With right sides together and allowing a 6 mm (¼ in) seam, join the backing rectangles together along one long edge, leaving a short opening in the middle of the seam. Press seam open. With right sides together and backing seam at centre back, join the back and front to each other around all edges of the hexagon, stitching on the traced line. Trim excess fabric on both back and front, leaving a 12 mm (½ in) seam allowance. Clip across corners and turn right side out.

6 Following the instructions on page 135, make a twisted cord using the extra skeins of 1840 and 3990. Hand-stitch the cord in place around the outer edge (it is much easier to do this before filling the pincushion), fill with fibrefill and ladder stitch (page 134) the opening closed.

Variation

If you prefer a scented sachet to a pincushion, fill the cushions with dried lavender or pot-pourri and place the sachet in your wardrobe where it will delicately scent your clothing as well as deter moths and silverfish.

Toile doorstop

The delicate tracery of the crewel-inspired

embroidery on this eye-catching doorstop is a

perfect foil to the toile de Jouy fabric used to

complete the project. Toile de Jouy originated in

France in the late eighteenth century and is easily

recognised by its white or off-white linen

background printed with complex pastoral

scenes in a single contrasting colour, usually

black, dark red or blue. Here, the black

embroidery on a cream background is also

a reminder of blackwork, another form of

traditional counted thread embroidery that was

immensely popular during Elizabethan times.

Materials
30 cm x 60 cm (12 x 24 in) cream linen
30 cm x 90 cm (12 x 35 in) black and white
    toile (or other black and white print) – allow
    extra for matching or centring toile pattern
One skein DMC Stranded Embroidery Cotton,
    310 (Black)
8 cm (3 in) purchased or handmade black
    tassel (see page 134)
Approximately 2 kg (4½ lb) plastic filler beads
    or rice, for filling
Machine thread to match

Tools
Crewel needles, No 10
Small embroidery hoop
General sewing supplies
Template plastic

Size
20.5 cm across base x 24 cm high
    (8 in x 9½ in)

Stitches
Back stitch (page 137)
Buttonhole stitch (page 138)
Chain stitch (page 139)
Colonial knot (page 140)
Herringbone stitch (page 143)
Lazy daisy stitch (page 143)
Stem stitch (page 147)
Straight stitch (page 147)
Trellis couching (page 147)

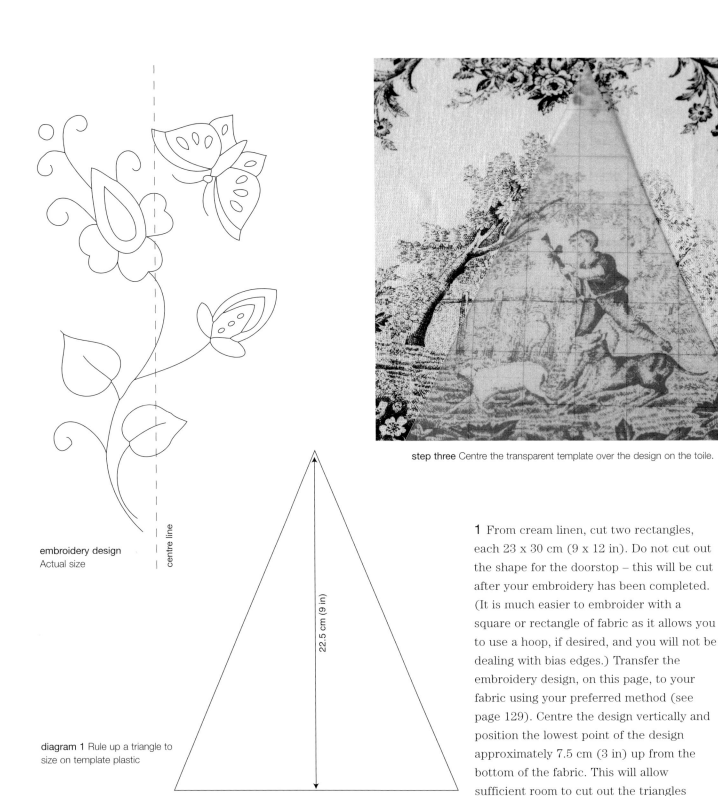

embroidery design
Actual size

centre line

diagram 1 Rule up a triangle to size on template plastic

22.5 cm (9 in)

19.5 cm (7¾ in)

step three Centre the transparent template over the design on the toile.

1 From cream linen, cut two rectangles, each 23 x 30 cm (9 x 12 in). Do not cut out the shape for the doorstop – this will be cut after your embroidery has been completed. (It is much easier to embroider with a square or rectangle of fabric as it allows you to use a hoop, if desired, and you will not be dealing with bias edges.) Transfer the embroidery design, on this page, to your fabric using your preferred method (see page 129). Centre the design vertically and position the lowest point of the design approximately 7.5 cm (3 in) up from the bottom of the fabric. This will allow sufficient room to cut out the triangles when embroidery has been completed.

2 Following the embroidery guide, at right, and using one strand of thread throughout, work the design on both pieces of fabric.

3 Following Diagram 1, opposite, rule up an isosceles triangle on template plastic. Cut the template out, place on the back of the completed embroidery and trace around the edge (this will be the stitching line). Doing this allows you to centre the template over your worked design. When cutting the fabric, remember to add 1 cm (⅜ in) seam allowance all round. Use the same method to cut two toile triangles. Move the template over the fabric until you find an appropriate part of the design that can be centred. You can also choose two matching motifs, if desired. Remember to add a seam allowance when cutting.

4 With right sides together, pin the embroidered triangles and toile triangles to each other, alternating linen and toile, until you have a square pyramid shape. Baste as pinned, then machine-stitch along your traced lines.

5 Measure the base edge of your pyramid, and cut a square of fabric to this measurement, plus 1 cm (⅜ in) seam allowance all round. Pin or baste the base square to the pyramid, right sides together, taking care to match the corners of the square with the seams of the pyramid – it may help to open out the seams. Stitch as basted, leaving an opening in the middle of one edge for filling. (It is easier to sew with the bulk of the pyramid on top). Clip across the corners and turn doorstop right side out through the opening.

embroidery guide

6 Stitch tassel in position through top of doorstop. Fill doorstop through opening in base. If using rice rather than filler beads, microwave 2–3 cups at a time on HIGH for 2–3 minutes, to dry it out and ensure there are no weevils. Ladder stitch (page 134) the opening closed, using tiny stitches.

Hint

You can make a simple funnel from paper to fill the doorstop or you could cut the bottom off a plastic drink bottle and use the top as a funnel.

Christmas tree picture

Celebrate the festive season with this sparkling

embroidery design, combining the rich colours

of traditional Christmas decor with the sheen of

metallic beads and buttons.

For a basic counted-thread cross-stitch pattern

such as this, be sure to start your stitching at the

centre of the chart and the centre of the fabric.

When the embroidery is complete, display your

work in a frame, as pictured, use it to cover

a book or box, or turn it into a wall-hanging.

Materials

45 x 40 cm (17¾ x 16 in) piece of 28-count
  evenweave linen in natural
1 skein DMC stranded embroidery cotton,
  ecru
1 skein DMC stranded embroidery cotton,
  3782 (beige)
1 skein DMC stranded embroidery cotton,
  500 (dark green)
1 skein DMC stranded embroidery cotton,
  3371 (dark brown)
1 skein DMC stranded embroidery cotton,
  3799 (dark grey)
Mill Hill seed beads in colours 03021 (cream),
  03039 (copper), 03037 (mixed metallics),
  02021 (pewter grey)
About 30 extra glass beads approximately
  7 mm (¼ in) diameter in warm natural
  colours
Machine sewing thread to match design
30 cm (12 in) of 6 mm (¼ in) silk ribbon
  to tie gifts

Tools

Tapestry needle No 24
Beading needle

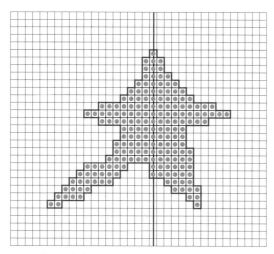

Cross stitch worked over two threads, using two strands of DMC 3782 (beige) and one strand of DMC ecru

Back stitch worked over two threads, using one strand of DMC 3371 (dark brown)

materials The tree design is worked in stranded cotton and embellished with metallic seed beads and larger glass beads in warm neutral tones.

stitching charts Stitch the star (above) on top of the tree (opposite), matching the centre lines of the grid (marked in red).

Cross stitch worked over two threads, using two strands of DMC 500 (dark green) and one strand of DMC 3371 (dark brown)

Cross stitch worked over two threads, using three strands of DMC 3371 (dark brown)

Cross stitch worked over two threads, using two strands of DMC 3371 (dark brown) and one strand of DMC 3799 (dark grey)

Tie silk ribbon around gifts at this point

1 The Christmas tree design is worked in cross stitch over two threads in three strands of the stranded cotton.

2 Mark the vertical centre of the fabric with a line of long running stitches in a contrasting thread, as described on page 129.

3 Start cross stitching the design at the star in the centre of the fabric, 8 cm (3¼ in) down from the top edge.

4 Work the star, tree and gifts according to the graphs and thread guides. Match the centre lines and the top and bottom of the two charts.

5 Next, scatter the small Mill Hill beads and the larger beads over the surface of the tree, arranging them in a pleasing design, and stitch into place with a single strand of light-coloured machine sewing thread and a beading needle.

6 Lastly, thread the silk ribbon onto the tapestry needle and tie it around the gifts below the tree.

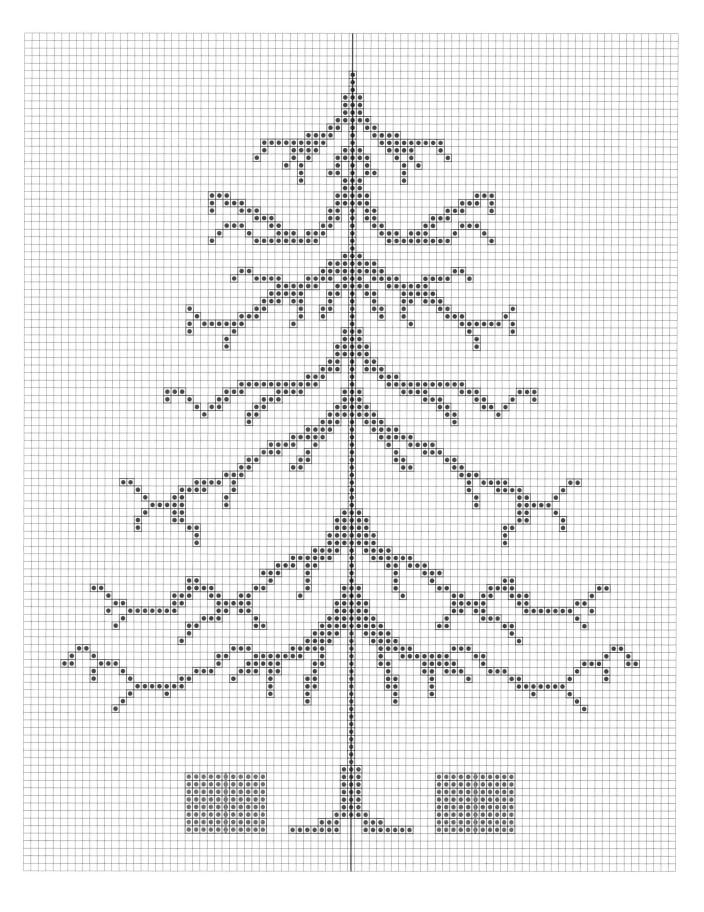

Paper cut-out cushion

Remember the childhood magic of cutting

shapes from folded paper, then opening it out

to reveal a lacy pattern? This is a lovely project

with which small children could be involved, and

they can watch their design grow into a beautiful

embroidered object. If you haven't a four-year-

old handy, release your inner child and have fun

cutting the paper shapes yourself.

Materials
Sheet of A4 paper
Spray adhesive (optional)
43 cm (17 in) square firmly woven cotton,
 for embroidery
Two 43 cm x 30 cm (17 in x 12 in) pieces
 fabric, for cushion back
One ball DMC Broder Spécial No 16, in the
 colour of your choice
40 cm (16 in) cushion insert
Matching sewing thread
Two or three large press-studs

Tools
Crewel needle, No 9
General sewing supplies
Embroidery hoop

Size
40 cm (16 in) square

Stitch
Star stitch (page 147)

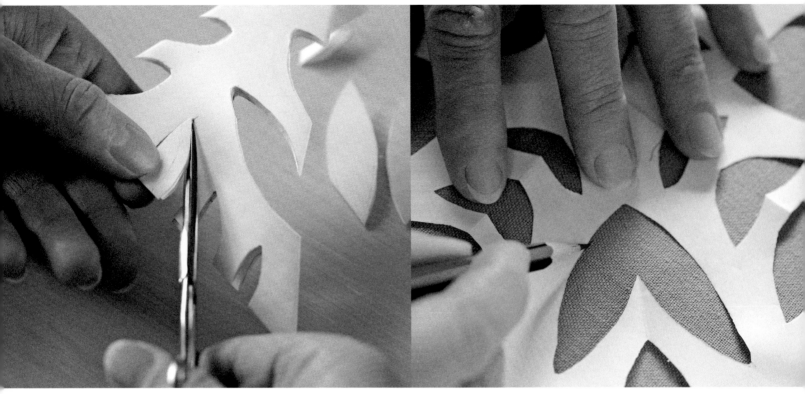

step one Cut a pattern of shapes from a folded sheet of paper.

step two Pin the cut-out paper to cushion fabric and trace the pattern.

Hint

If your young helper is not competent with scissors, ask him or her to draw the design on the folded paper and then help to cut it out. The unfolding part is always magical and fun.

1 Fold a sheet of paper in any way you like – concertina, quarters or sixths (if you want a snowflake design). Cut shapes into the paper – they can be as complex or as simple as you like. The pictured cushion is based on a simple quartered design.

2 Open out the template and centre it on the fabric for the cushion front, pinning it down securely. (If you have trouble getting it to lie flat, give the wrong side of the paper a light spray with adhesive. This will make it tacky for a short while and make it much easier to trace accurately.) Trace the outlines onto the fabric using a 2B pencil or your preferred marker (see page 129).

3 Decide whether to embroider a positive or negative of the cut-out pattern (or do both – delightful matching pairs of cushions can be made in this way). You can begin stitching by leaving a tail of thread to be secured later (see page 130), or simply tie a knot. Working within the traced outlines, work star stitch (double cross stitch), making sure the space is well covered. It is easier to maintain an even tension if you work with a hoop. The stitches will need to be of different sizes to accommodate the curves on the traced shapes.

4 When all areas have been embroidered, press the work on the wrong side, on a

step three Staying within the traced outlines, work star stitches of various size.

well-padded surface, using a steam iron, taking care not to flatten the embroidery.

5 To make up the cushion cover, machine-stitch a narrow double hem on one 43 cm (17 in) edge of both backing pieces. Overlap the backing pieces until they measure 43 cm (17 in) square and baste at the sides to hold. With right sides together, stitch embroidered front to cushion back around all edges, allowing 1.5 cm (⅝ in) seams. Trim corners and turn cover right side out through back opening. Sew press-studs in place to secure the opening. Place cushion insert into cover.

Hint

Make a flat sachet, about 40 cm (16 in) square. Fill this lightly with scented foliage such as dried pine-needles, dried leaves from *Eucalyptus citriodora*, or with dried lemon verbena or lavender. Place the sachet in front of, or behind, the cushion insert. This will add a fabulous scent to your room whenever the cushion is gently plumped or when someone sits against it.

Table runner

Real leaves have been used as the models for

this unusual project – collect and trace your own

interesting specimens or use the templates

provided. A sheer fabric is placed over the top of

the darker fabric leaf shapes to create a shadow

effect, then each leaf is outlined and highlighted

with surface embroidery that can be as simple or

elaborate as you like. The effect is charming.

Materials
Fresh leaves to photocopy (or trace from
the templates on page 176)
Double-sided appliqué webbing (Vliesofix)
25 cm x 115 cm (10 in x 45 in) cotton or fine
linen fabric in a shade to harmonise with the
embroidery threads
Purchased table runner
25 cm x 115 cm (10 in x 45 in) silk organza
or similar transparent fabric
Stranded embroidery cottons in a range of
green tones (or choose reds and oranges
for an autumnal sampler)

Tools
Crewel needle, No 9
General sewing supplies

Size
Technique can be varied to suit any size runner

Stitches
Back stitch (page 137)
Blanket stitch (page 138)
Buttonhole stitch (page 138)
Chain stitch (page 139)
Cross stitch (page 140)
Fly stitch (page 141)
Running stitch (page 144)
Running stitch, whipped (page 144)
Satin stitch (page 144)
Stem stitch (page 147)
Straight stitch (page 147)
Trellis couching (page 147)

leaf outlines Enlarge by 200%

1 If using fresh leaves, photocopy them, enlarging or reducing as desired. Otherwise, enlarge the outlines above by 200%.

2 Trace each leaf outline onto the paper side of Vliesofix and cut out, leaving 6 mm (¼ in) all round. Using a hot, dry iron, press the leaf shapes onto the wrong side of cotton or fine linen fabric, then cut out accurately on the traced lines.

3 Remove backing paper, position leaf shapes along the centre of the table runner and press in place. Cut a strip of organza to cover the leaves, allowing a border all round. Press under a narrow single hem on all edges and lay organza over the top of the leaves. Pin and baste in place.

4 When stitching the leaves, remember that because the leaf shape will show through the organza, it is not essential to define it exactly – this is up to the individual embroiderer. Experiment with different shades of threads and any of the stitches found in the stitch library. You can use quite simple stitches based on running, stem and chain stitches. The embroidery is worked through all three layers of fabric. Areas of the organza can be cut away with small, sharp scissors to reveal more intense colour from the fabric leaf shape underneath.

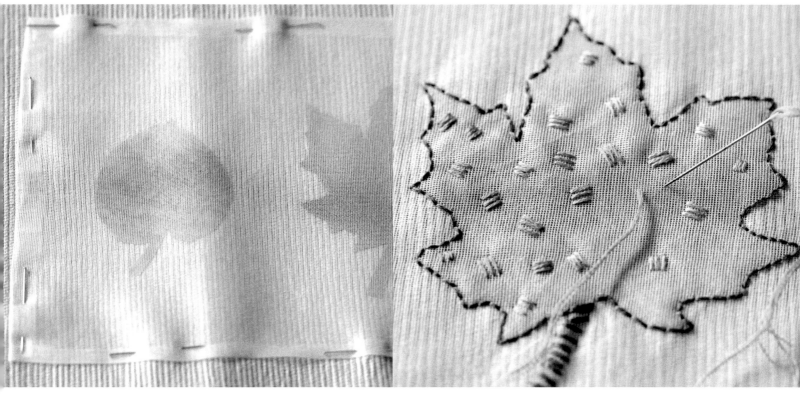

step three Pin and baste organza strip over the top of the fused fabric leaves.

step four Embroider over the leaf shape that is beneath the organza, using embroidery stitches of your choice.

Finish the cut edges of the organza with buttonhole or satin stitch, if you like.

5 Finish the basted edges of the organza with simple running stitch around the edge, then remove the basting.

Variation

This technique could also be used to make a delightful quilt-as-you-go quilt. Cut 15 cm (6 in) square pieces from fabrics of similar weight and baste under seam allowance on edges. Trace leaf shapes onto double-sided appliqué webbing and cut leaves from different-coloured fabrics. Press a leaf on a fabric square, then lay organza over the top and stitch as for the table runner, folding and basting seam allowances as you go. Embroider the leaves, as desired. To make up the quilt, you will need an equal number of plain squares the same size as the embroidered ones, with the seam allowance basted under. Cut quilt wadding into squares about 1 cm (⅜ in) smaller than the fabric squares, then sandwich a wadding square between two fabric layers. Outline quilt around the leaf shape first and then around the basted edges of the block. Quilt each block in this way, and then join one to another using decorative stitching, such as fly stitch or cross stitch.

Hint

Double-sided appliqué webbing (often sold in craft and fabric stores as Vliesofix) is a boon for projects such as this. Not only does it allow you to trace and cut very accurately, it also prevents fraying and holds the pieces firmly in place, without basting or pins, while you stitch.

Alphabet

This simple cross-stitch alphabet can be added to many items, incuding towels, cards, bags, bell pulls, samplers or bookmarks.

The sample shown is worked on 28-count ecru linen with DMC stranded embroidery cotton, but the design can be adapted for other evenweave fabrics and types of thread.

Materials
Evenweave fabric
Stranded embroidery cotton

Tools
Tapestry needles
Embroidery scissors
General sewing supplies

Appliqué cushions

These elegant cushion covers are a very effective way of tying a colour scheme together to complement your existing décor. Each cushion features a very simple pattern of appliquéd circles in soft tones and subtly contrasting textures to the background fabric. The embroidery is easy to work and the restrained use of beads and sequins adds just a hint of sparkle.

Materials
(For each cushion)
Two 45 cm (18 in) squares olive green suedette
Extra matching or contrast fabric, for flat piping
Double-sided appliqué webbing (Vliesofix)
Matching machine thread
30 cm (12 in) zip
40 cm (16 in) cushion insert

(For Cushions A and B)
Small amount silk dupion in each of the following colours: Taupe, Sea Blue and Ecru
One skein DMC Stranded Embroidery Cotton, 501 (Dark Blue Green)
One skein 100% cotton Floche in each of the following colours: Ecru and Antique Ecru or DMC Broder Spécial No 16: Ecru and 3032
Mill Hill Glass Seed Beads: 02047 (Soft Willow), 00557 (Old Gold) and 00123 (Cream)
Mill Hill Antique Glass Beads: 03028 (Juniper Green), 03037 (Abalone) and 03039 (Antique Champagne)
Thread to match beads

(For Cushion C)
25 cm (10 in) square real or artificial olive green suede
One skein DMC Stranded Metallic Thread, 5282 (Old Gold)
Metallic gold sewing thread
Metallic gold cup sequins
Mill Hill Glass Seed Beads: 00557 (Old Gold)
Thread to match beads

Tools
Crewel needles, No 9
Pair of compasses
Firm card or template plastic
General sewing supplies

Size
40 cm (16 in) square

Stitches
Blanket stitch (page 138)
Chain stitch (page 139)
French knot (page 142)
Running stitch (page 144)

materials Keeping beads, threads and fabrics restricted to a limited colour palette adds a subtle elegance.

step one Use a circular shape to trace multiple circles onto the paper side of Vliesofix.

1 Using compasses (or tracing around a circular object of appropriate diameter) draw a 5.5 cm (2¼ in) and a 7.5 cm (3 in) circle on cardboard or template plastic and cut out. For Cushion A, trace 12 small circles onto the paper side of Vliesofix; for Cushion B, trace 9 large circles; and for Cushion C, trace 3 small and 6 large circles. Cut out circles, leaving a narrow border all round. For Cushion A, using a hot, dry iron and pressing cloth, press 4 circles onto each of the three shades of silk. For Cushion B, press 3 circles onto each of the three shades of silk. For Cushion C, press all 9 circles onto suede. Cut out all circles accurately around the traced line.

2 **Cushion A** (see page 186) Position 12 small circles on background square in 3 vertical rows of 4 circles – one row of each colour. Remove backing paper and press circles into place. Work stitching across each row of three, working on each colour.

Row 1 Spiral of French knots: Floche (Antique Ecru) on Taupe; DMC Stranded Cotton 501 (3 strands) on Sea Blue; and Floche (Ecru) on Ecru.

Row 2 Spiral of running stitch: Floche (Antique Ecru) on Taupe; DMC Stranded Cotton 501 (3 strands) on Sea Blue; and Floche (Ecru) on Ecru.

step two Remove backing paper from each fabric circle before pressing onto background fabric.

cushion B, row 2 Stitch a seed bead to the end of every second blanket stitch.

Row 3 Spiral of detached chain stitches: Floche (Antique Ecru) on Taupe; DMC Stranded Cotton 501 (3 strands) on Sea Blue; and Floche (Ecru) on Ecru.

Row 4 Spiral of Mill Hill Seed Beads: 03037 on Taupe; 03028 on Sea Blue; and 00123 on Ecru.

3 Cushion B (see page 186) Position 9 large circles on background square in 3 vertical rows of 3 circles – one row of each colour. Remove backing paper and press circles into place, one at a time. Work stitching across each row of three, working on each colour.

Row 1 On one circle of each colour across the row, work a 15 mm (⅝ in) grid with 3 strands DMC Stranded Cotton 501. At the intersection of each grid on the Sea Blue silk, stitch two seed beads in 00557. At the intersection of each grid on the Taupe and Ecru silks, stitch a single seed bead in 03039. Scatter a few seed beads randomly onto one half of each of these 2 circles and stitch into place.

Row 2 On one circle of each colour across the row, work a row of blanket stitch around the edge, using three strands of DMC Stranded Cotton 501. On the end of every 2nd blanket stitch, stitch a seed bead:

Hint

The charm of this project lies in the perfect simplicity of the embroidered circles. You do not have to choose very difficult embroidery stitches, but you
do need to cut the circles accurately and embellish them as neatly as possible.

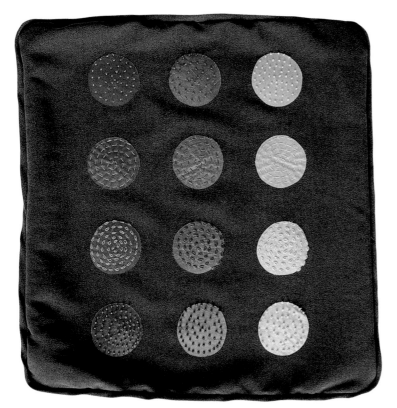

cushion A

cushion B

03039 on Taupe; 00557 on Sea Blue; and 02047 on Ecru.

Row 3 On Taupe circle, stitch a row of seed beads (03039) around the edge, 5 mm (³⁄₁₆ in) apart. On the Sea Blue circle, stitch a row of seed beads (00557) around the edge, 5 mm (³⁄₁₆ in) apart, and then a row of French knots (3 strands DMC 501) inside this row. On the Ecru circle, stitch a row of seed beads (03039) around the edge, 5 mm (³⁄₁₆ in) apart; inside this, work a row of French knots (3 strands DMC 501), then inside this, add a second row of seed beads (02047), off-setting them against the position of the French knots.

4 Cushion C (see page 187) On the background, position 2 rows of 3 large circles with a row of 3 small circles in the centre. Remove backing paper and, using a pressing cloth, press circles into place, one at a time. Work a 15 mm grid (⁵⁄₈ in) over each large circle and a 12 mm (¹⁄₂ in) grid over each small circle, using one strand DMC Metallic Thread 5282. At the intersection of each grid, stitch a gold cup sequin and a seed bead (00557), using metallic gold sewing thread.

5 When all embroidery is complete, trim embroidered square and backing square to 43 cm (17 in). For flat piping, cut

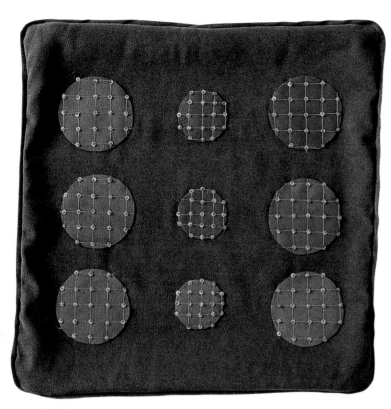

cushion C

4 cm-wide (1½ in) fabric strips on the bias, and join with diagonal seams to make a complete length of about 180 cm (70 in). Press strip in half lengthwise, wrong sides together. With right sides together and raw edges even, stitch flat piping strip to cushion front, easing around corners, allowing a 1.5 cm (⅝ in) seam and starting and finishing with a neat overlap in the centre of one side (bottom edge).

6 With right sides together, stitch the cushion front and back to each other along the top seam (opposite the side where the piping begins and ends), allowing a 1.5 cm (⅝ in) seam and leaving an opening in the centre for the zip. On the wrong side, baste one side of the zip against the piping line on the front of the cushion and stitch in place. Open out the cushion seam and carefully pin the other side of the zip in position on the cushion back, ensuring that the fabric butts up to the piping without gaping. Stitching from the right side, stitch the zip in place by machine or by hand, stitching across the top and bottom of the opening as well. Open the zip. With the right sides together, stitch the cushion front and back to each other around the remaining edges. Trim the corners and turn right side out through the zip. Place the cushion insert into the cover.

Hint

If your sewing skills do not extend to piping and zippers, you can work the cushion fronts, then send the materials to be professionally assembled at your local craft shop or by a dressmaker.

Dragonfly tablecloth

A series of simple chain stitch dragonflies flits

around the border of this pretty tablecloth.

Worked in cream thread on sheer white fabric,

the cloth has an ethereal beauty, but it would

also look stunning if the dragonflies were worked

in white on an indigo linen background – a

traditional Japanese combination. We've created

a circular cloth, but to save time, you could also

embroider on a purchased tablecloth of any

shape – and perhaps add a single motif to a set

of matching napkins.

Materials
115 cm (45 in) square handkerchief linen,
  or a purchased tablecloth of desired size
One skein DMC Stranded Embroidery Cotton
  (677) or Anchor Marlitt Stranded Rayon
  Embroidery Thread (1078)

Tools
Crewel needles, No 9
Embroidery hoop
General sewing supplies

Size
Finished cloth measures 112 cm (44 in)
  diameter, but method can be adapted to
  suit any sized cloth

Stitch
Chain stitch (page 139)

embroidery design Actual size

cutting a circle Fold cloth in quarters; anchor string in one corner, tie a pencil to remaining end and sketch a quarter-circle arc on the cloth.

1 Cut out a 115 cm-diameter (45 in) circle. Press under and stitch a 1.5 cm (⅝ in) double hem on the raw edge, by hand or machine.

2 Fold and press cloth into equal wedge-shaped segments – either six or eight. The dragonfly motif is printed actual size, at left. Trace and position motifs evenly around the edges of the tablecloth, placing one in the centre of each segment. Transfer the design to the fabric using your preferred method (see page 129).

3 Following the embroidery guide, opposite, work each dragonfly in chain stitch, using two strands of thread. A hoop is essential to maintain an even tension. It is also a good idea

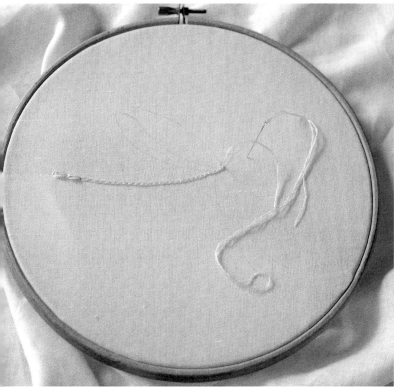

step three Placing your work in a hoop will ensure even tension.

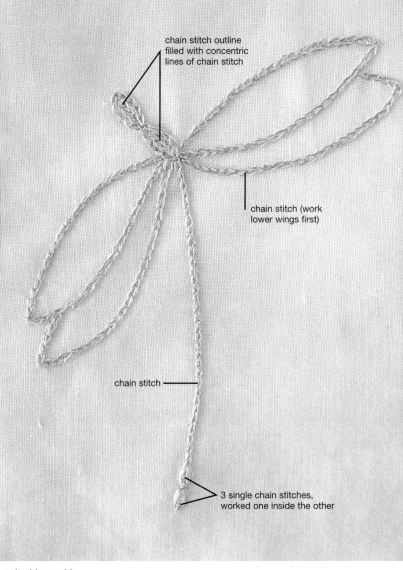

chain stitch outline
filled with concentric
lines of chain stitch

chain stitch (work
lower wings first)

chain stitch

3 single chain stitches,
worked one inside the other

embroidery guide

to finish a complete motif in one sitting so your stitch tension remains constant. Start by working the tail in a continuous row of chain stitch, then at the end of the tail, work 3 single chain stitches, one inside the other, to fill each tail piece.

4 Next, work the head and body by working a chain stitch outline, then filling the shapes with concentric rows of chain stitch inside the first row until the shape is filled. Lastly, stitch the wings with a continuous row of chain stitch to outline the shape.

Sheet banding

Crisp cotton bed linen needs little embellishment, but you can add homemade accents with hand-embroidered linen bands. Stitch a simple design in colours that complement your bedroom's decor and apply the finished band to the turn-down of your top sheet.

Choose colourfast threads for your embroidery to ensure that the sheets can be laundered as usual. You will need to press the band from the back of the sheet after washing, even if you don't wish to iron the entire sheet.

Materials

Bed sheet

Evenweave linen banding minimum of 8 cm (3¼ in) wide (such as Zweigart Faiden 100 per cent linen), the width of the bed sheet plus 5 cm (2 in) seam allowance

DMC pearl cotton No 8 in white

DMC stranded embroidery cotton, 613 (very light drab brown)

DMC stranded embroidery cotton, 844 (ultra dark brown-grey); note that the number of skeins of thread required will depend on the width of the sheet banding

Machine sewing thread to match banding

Tools

Tapestry needles Nos 24 (for pearl cotton) and 26 (for stranded cotton)

Embroidery scissors

General sewing supplies

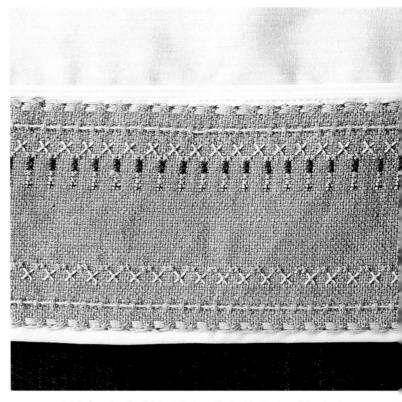

detail Showing the finished design attached to the top of the sheet.

1 To start, work running stitch in one thickness of white pearl cotton, about six threads in from one edge of the banding. Each running stitch goes over five threads and under two.

2 Leave a gap of four threads and work a row of large crosses in one thickness of white pearl cotton. These crosses are worked over four threads and with a four-thread gap between each one. A small upright cross is worked over two threads at the centre of the large cross in two strands of DMC 613 (very light drab brown).

3 Next, work two small crosses over two threads each, between the upper arms of the large crosses, using two strands of DMC 613.

4 Centred above these two crosses, work two crosses vertically over two threads using two strands of DMC 844 (ultra dark brown-grey), then another two using two strands of DMC 613. On top of this column, work one cross in one thickness of white pearl cotton, then superimpose a small upright cross in one strand of DMC 844.

5 Complete the banding with the large and small cross stitches and running stitch border at the top of the band, as indicated

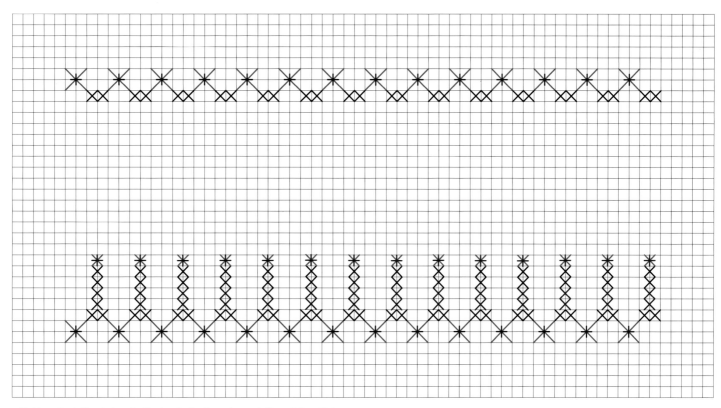

stitching chart See below for the key to the threads used. Repeat the stitch pattern along the whole length of the banding.

in the chart, repeating the design as necessary to embroider the entire band.

6 When the cross stitch is complete, the linen banding can be machine or hand stitched into position along the turn-down of the bed sheet.

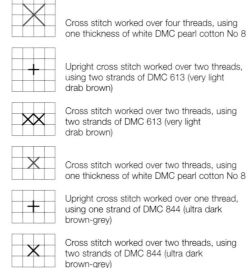

Cross stitch worked over four threads, using one thickness of white DMC pearl cotton No 8

Upright cross stitch worked over two threads, using two strands of DMC 613 (very light drab brown)

Cross stitch worked over two threads, using two strands of DMC 613 (very light drab brown)

Cross stitch worked over two threads, using one thickness of white DMC pearl cotton No 8

Upright cross stitch worked over one thread, using one strand of DMC 844 (ultra dark brown-grey)

Cross stitch worked over two threads, using two strands of DMC 844 (ultra dark brown-grey)

Tablecloth

Add extra pleasure to your dining with an elegant embroidered cloth such as this one. Worked on evenweave cloth woven with a self-colour grid, known as Anne cloth, the same design could easily be worked on any other 18- or 20-count evenweave fabric. The placement of motifs is made easier by the grid on the Anne fabric.

The thistle design on the pictured example is stitched in a subtle mix of dark navy blue and very light ash grey, but the colour scheme can easily be changed to suit your preference.

Materials

140 cm (55 in) square of 18-count Zweigart Anne evenweave fabric in oatmeal (if substituting a different fabric, buy a piece as long as it is wide, so that you end up with a square)

3 skeins DMC stranded embroidery cotton, 535 (very light ash grey)

4 skeins DMC stranded embroidery cotton, 823 (dark navy blue)

Machine sewing thread to match Anne cloth

Tools

Tapestry needle No 24

General sewing supplies

step three The thistle flowers and buds are worked in four strands of navy blue cotton, and the stems and thistle 'beards' in three strands of ash grey cotton.

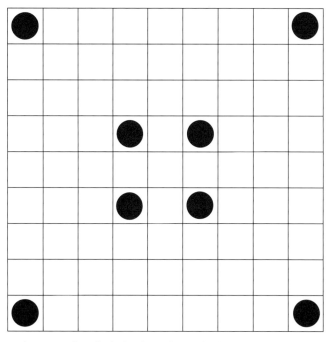

placement of motifs In the pictured example, the motifs are arranged symmetrically as shown, but they can be placed randomly if you prefer.

1 To begin the tablecloth, it is most important to draw a thread along each edge to find the straight grain. This needs to be at an equal distance from the grid that is woven into the fabric, along all four sides. Press and overlock or machine zigzag a single hem with mitred corners, to prevent fraying while working the cross-stitch.

2 Work cross-stitch motifs in the squares at each corner of the cloth and in four positions at the centre. The cross stitches in this design are worked over two threads of the evenweave fabric, using four strands of DMC 823 (dark navy blue).

3 The back stitches are worked over two threads of the fabric, using three strands of DMC 535 (very light ash grey), as shown in the chart. Be sure to start and finish securely, as this cloth will need to be laundered by hand after each use.

4 Upon completion and after laundering, press only on the wrong side of the embroidered cloth using a pressing cloth.

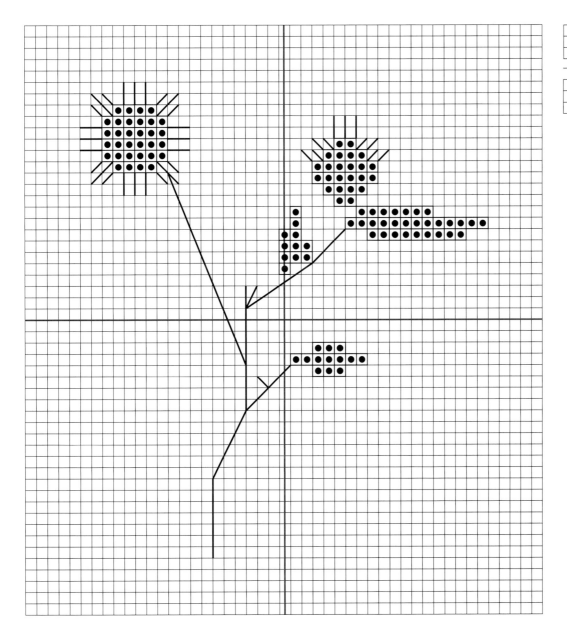

Cross stitch worked over two threads, using four strands of DMC 823 (dark navy blue)

Back stitch worked over two threads, using three strands of DMC 535 (very light ash grey)

Monogrammed sachet

Embroidered monograms are a delightful way to add a personalised touch to all sorts of small gift items, such as handkerchiefs and scented sachets. Suitable fabrics for the sachets are cotton voile, cotton batiste, handkerchief linen and cotton or silk organza. Organza is the most difficult to work on, so if you are a beginner, start with cotton voile and you will have great results.

Materials

14 cm x 48 cm (5½ in x 19 in) white cotton voile, batiste or handkerchief linen
One skein 100% cotton Floche (Ecru), or DMC Broder Spécial No 16 or No 20 (Ecru)
Extra thread for twisted cord, or 40 cm (16 in) silk ribbon
Matching machine thread
Dried lavender or pot-pourri, for filling

Tools

Crewel needles, No 9
Small embroidery hoop
General sewing supplies

Size

12 x 18 cm (4¾ x 7 in)

Stitch

Shadow stitch (page 145)

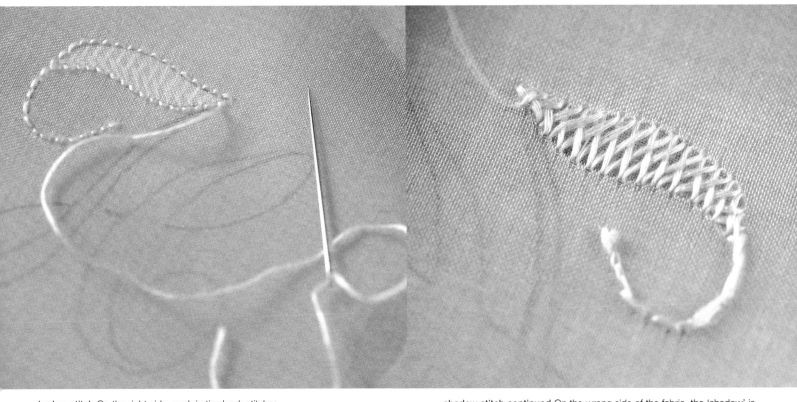

shadow stitch On the right side, work in tiny back stitches.

shadow stitch continued On the wrong side of the fabric, the 'shadow' is formed by a closed herringbone pattern.

Hint

If you have not done shadow stitch before, practise on a spare piece of fabric in a hoop until you get the hang of it. You might also want to work your first few letters in stem stitch or chain stitch, instead. They both look very effective and are a little easier for a beginner.

1 Press the voile strip in half crosswise to mark the bottom edge of the sachet. Enlarge the alphabet, opposite, by 200%. Transfer your chosen letter to the fabric using your preferred method (see page 129), centring it on the fabric and positioning the bottom of the letter about 3 cm (1¼ in) up from the pressed fold line.

2 Place fabric in an embroidery hoop – this is essential to maintain correct tension. Starting with a waste knot (see page 130), and using one strand of thread, work shadow stitch to fill in the letter. When finishing a thread, weave the end through the back of the work on the edge of the

shape (not through the centre), so that it is not visible from the front. Try to start and finish the monogram in one sitting – this is so you have the same tension from the beginning to the end of your work.

3 When all embroidery is complete, press under 5 mm (³/₁₆ in) along both short edges. With wrong sides together, fold fabric in half crosswise and stitch side seams, allowing 5 mm (³/₁₆ in) seams and leaving a 1 cm (³/₈ in) opening in one seam, starting 9 cm (3½ in) down from folded edge. (The opening in the seam is for a drawstring.) Carefully trim away half the seam allowance on both sides. Turn bag

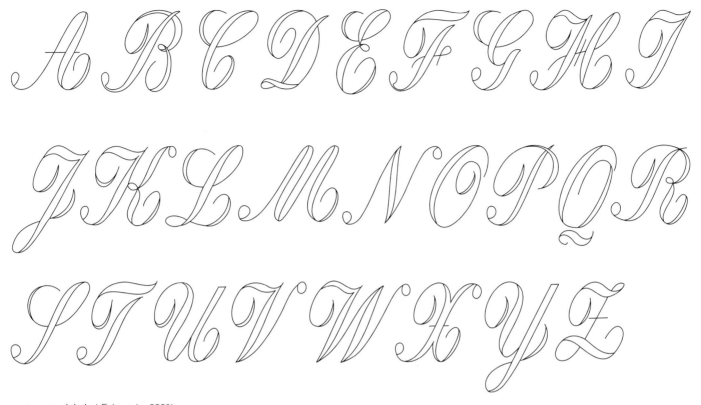

monogram alphabet Enlarge by 200%

inside out, bringing right sides together and, enclosing raw edges of seams, stitch each side seam again, this time allowing 6 mm (¼ in) seams and leaving the opening at the same place, as before. This double stitching forms a neat French seam.

4 Press down 5 cm (2 in) on upper edge, forming a hem, and stitch close to pressed edge. Make a parallel row of stitching, 1 cm (⅜ in) from the first, to form a casing. Turn right side out – the gap in the side seam should be in the centre of the casing. Press well, using a pressing cloth. Make a 40 cm (16 in) twisted cord (see page 135), and thread through casing. Alternatively, use a

length of silk ribbon. Fill the sachet with lavender or pot-pourri, pull up the cords and tie in a bow to secure.

Variation

Work a monogram on a set of purchased linen handkerchiefs for a beautiful and personalised gift. Experiment on different fabrics and try using coloured thread for a softly hued shadow effect.

Flower cushions

These beautiful, big stylised flowers are worked

on a patchworked background of neutral,

firmly woven furnishing fabrics. This adds a

subtle dimension to the finished cushion – and

is an ideal way to use up small scraps and

samples. If you prefer, you could work on a

single piece of background fabric instead.

Materials
(For 2 cushions)

Assorted firm, neutral fabrics for cushion fronts

0.4 m x 112 cm (½ yd x 44 in) of two different
    fabrics for cushion backs

0.2 m x 90 cm (¼ yd x 35 in) fabric, for
    covered buttons

Six 38 mm (1½ in) self-cover buttons

One skein DMC Perlé Cotton No 5 in each of
    the following colours: 920 (Medium Copper),
    921 (Copper), 936 (Very Dark Avocado
    Green), 937 (Medium Avocado Green), 783
    (Medium Topaz)

Size 20 (56 cm/22 in) cushion insert

Matching machine thread

Tools
Chenille embroidery needles, No 22

Embroidery hoop, optional

General sewing supplies

Size
37 x 53 cm (14½ x 21 in)

Stitches
Back stitch (page 137)

Chain stitch, back-stitched (page 139)

Chain stitch, braided (page 139)

Colonial knot (page 140)

Fly stitch (page 141)

Lazy daisy stitch (page 143)

Running stitch (page 144)

Stem stitch (page 147)

Trellis couching (page 147)

materials Choose a range of toning neutral fabrics for the cushion front and back.

step one Press patchwork seams open and topstitch on each side of each seam.

1 Using assorted neutral fabrics, cut and join large squares and rectangles as desired to make up a patchworked rectangle, 56 x 40 cm (22 x 15¾ in). Bear in mind that furnishing fabrics tend to fray, so allow 1.5 cm (⅝ in) seam allowances. Press seams open and topstitch 6 mm (¼ in) on each side of each seam, to flatten and hold in place. Press finished piece thoroughly.

2 Embroidery designs are printed opposite and on page 208. Enlarge design 400% on a photocopier and transfer to the prepared patchwork background or a single rectangle of natural coloured fabric, using your preferred method (see page 129).

3 Following the embroidery guides, opposite and on page 208, and using one strand of thread throughout, work embroidery designs as shown. After all embroidery has been completed, press well on a well-padded surface. Slightly round off the corners on the cushion front, using the edge of a cup or mug as a guide.

4 For the backing of each cushion, cut one rectangle of backing fabric, 45 x 39.5 cm (17¾ x 15½ in), and one rectangle from a second backing fabric, 31 x 39.5 cm (12 x 15½ in). Press under and stitch a double 4 cm (1½ in) hem on one 39.5 cm (15½ in) edge of each piece. Make three

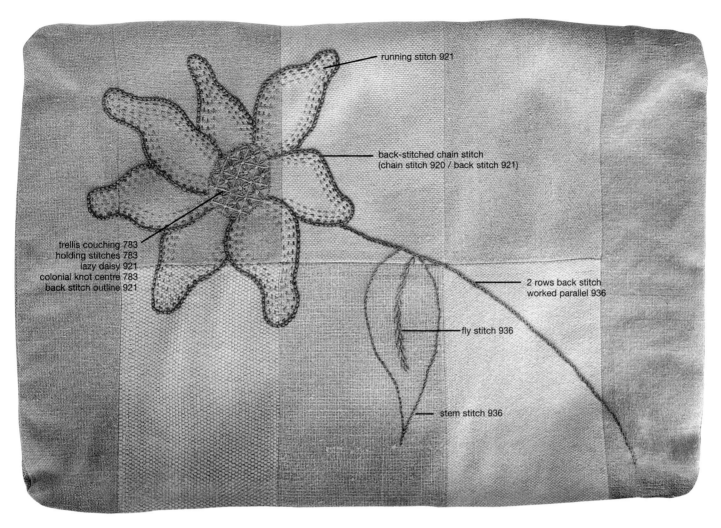

running stitch 921

back-stitched chain stitch
(chain stitch 920 / back stitch 921)

trellis couching 783
holding stitches 783
lazy daisy 921
colonial knot centre 783
back stitch outline 921

2 rows back stitch
worked parallel 936

fly stitch 936

stem stitch 936

design 1 embroidery guide

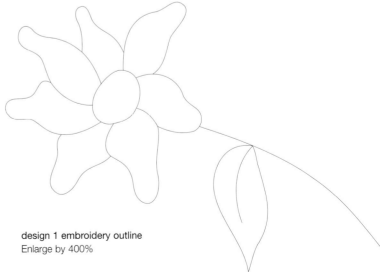

design 1 embroidery outline
Enlarge by 400%

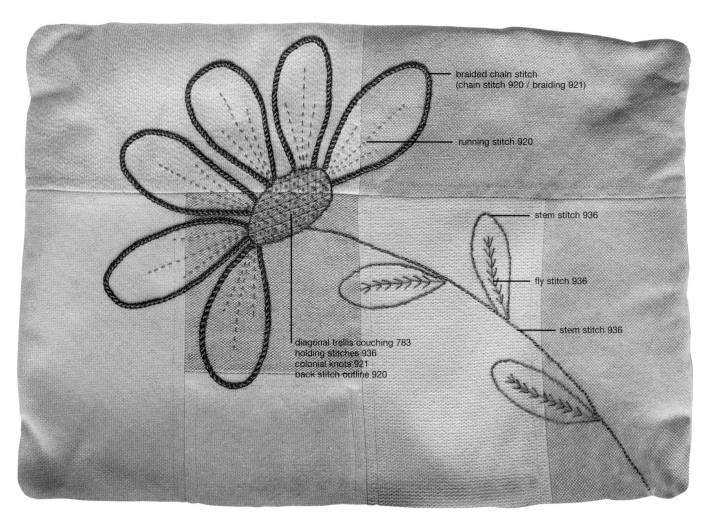

braided chain stitch
(chain stitch 920 / braiding 921)

running stitch 920

stem stitch 936

fly stitch 936

stem stitch 936

diagonal trellis couching 783
holding stitches 936
colonial knots 921
back stitch outline 920

design 2 embroidery guide

design 2 embroidery outline
Enlarge by 400%

detail In the flower centre of Design 2, colonial knots fill the trellis couching.

detail Using a small print fabric to cover buttons adds an interesting contrast to the back of the cushions.

evenly spaced buttonholes in the centre of the hem on the smaller backing piece. With right sides facing up, lap smaller backing piece over larger piece, lining up hems, and baste at sides to hold. (The complete back should measure 56 x 40 cm/22 x 15¾ in.) Round the corners as for the front. Place the cushion front and back with right sides together and pin or baste well. Allowing a 1.5cm (⅝ in) seam, stitch around edges as basted. Zigzag or overlock raw edges and turn right side out through back opening.

5 Cover buttons following manufacturer's instructions and sew to cushion backs to match buttonholes. Insert cushion filler.

Hint

The standard cushion insert is a square, but it can be squashed to fit into this rectangular cover. If you find it too big, simply remove a little of the stuffing.

Brooch cushion

Jewelled brooches never seem to go out of fashion. Whether you prefer a classic antique style or a funky art piece in modern materials, having a place to store and display your precious pins is essential.

This small and simple project is perfect to make as a gift for someone you love. The filling of sand and sawdust will help to keep the pins sharp and free of rust. Include some dried lavender flowers in the mix to add a delicate fragrance.

Materials
Two 10 cm (4 in) squares of 24-count
   evenweave linen in natural
1 skein DMC stranded embroidery cotton,
   816 (garnet)
1 skein DMC stranded embroidery cotton,
   838 (very dark beige-brown)
Two 10 cm (4 in) squares of cotton lawn
½ cup 50/50 mix of sand and sawdust
Machine sewing thread to match fabric

Tools
Tapestry needle No 24
General sewing supplies
Sewing machine (optional)

step two Work blocks of four cross stitches by four rows.

step six Whip stitch the chain-stitched borders together on three sides.

1 Cut two 10 cm (4 in) squares of evenweave fabric accurately by drawing a thread in both directions at opposite corners to ensure a straight cut.

2 The cross stitches in this design are worked with two strands of stranded embroidery cotton over two threads of the evenweave fabric. The checkerboard blocks consist of four stitches by four rows. The rows of blocks alternate colours; refer to the photograph on page 210 for the colours and the placement of the blocks.

3 Because this is such a small piece, it is not necessary to work the cushion front

design from the centre of the fabric, although this can be done if desired. Start the first block approximately 10 threads (at least 1 cm/⅜ in) from one corner, or locate the centre of the square and stitch the first block there. Work the five-block rows in DMC 816 (garnet) and the four-block alternate rows in 838 (very dark beige-brown), working the brown blocks between the corners of the red ones.

4 When you have completed the checkerboard pattern for the front of the cushion, take the remaining square of evenweave fabric and locate the centre. Work a four-stitch by four-row block in very

step seven Make the filling cushion from cotton lawn. Leave an opening at one side so that the square can be turned right side out.

detail The design on the back of the cushion.

dark beige-brown at the centre, followed by a single border of garnet cross stitches.

5 If necessary, trim the squares to 1 cm (⅜ in) larger than the centred checkerboard design. Now work a row of chain stitch around the edges of both front and back squares. Stitch two threads away from the front design and correspondingly for the back. Work chain stitches in three strands of DMC 838, over four threads of the fabric.

6 Finger press the seam allowance to the wrong side, away from the chain stitch. Hold the front and back squares with wrong sides together and the chain stitch rows aligned. Whip stitch the two rows of chain stitch together, using three strands of very dark beige-brown embroidery thread, until you have joined three sides of the squares.

7 Make the filling cushion of cotton lawn. With right sides together, stitch the squares of lawn together around the edges, leaving a small gap for turning. Clip the corners, then turn the square through to the right side. Fill with the sand and sawdust mix, then slip stitch to close the remaining seam. Insert into the cushion.

8 Whip stitch the remaining side of the brooch cushion, securing with a clove hitch.

Hint

These colours and the block sizes can be altered as desired: try an alternate design of five stitches by five rows in a checkerboard pattern using hand-dyed variegated cotton thread to create the colour change rather than two different solid-colour threads.

Tray cloth and napkin set

Breakfast in bed remains one of those

indulgences we permit ourselves too rarely.

Tempt someone who deserves a relaxing treat

by presenting their meal on a beautifully laid

tray, complete with embroidered table linen for

a touch of luxury.

Any evenweave fabric will do, although choosing

a finer linen cloth will mean the napkin is softer

to the touch and easier to fold when you create

the perfect tray setting.

Materials

32-count evenweave linen in ecru; note that
the amount required will depend on how
many placemats and napkins you wish
to make
Machine sewing thread to match linen
DMC stranded embroidery cotton, 500
(very dark blue green)
DMC stranded embroidery cotton, 3350
(ultra dark dusty rose)
DMC stranded embroidery cotton, 3363
(medium pine green)
DMC stranded embroidery cotton, 3685
(very dark mauve); note that the number of
skeins required for each shade will depend
on how many items you wish to make

Tools

Tapestry needle No 24
General sewing supplies

step two Fold and stitch the hems, firstly drawing a thread along the lines of the hem to provide a crisp and accurate fold line.

step three Scatter several strawberries over the placemat, making a mixture of right-facing and left-facing berries, as shown in the charts opposite.

1 Cut as many mats and napkins as you require to the sizes specified in the patterns opposite.

2 The placemats and napkins have double mitred hems on all sides. To provide a crisp fold line for the hems, draw a thread along the fold lines of each hem on all sides. Then mitre the corners of the placemats and napkins (see page 132). Once the hem is folded, slip stitch it into position. The hems must be completed prior to cross stitching your design.

3 Following the charts provided, stitch the berries as shown, one in one corner of the napkin and one in the lower right-hand corner of the placemat, as indicated on the patterns. Scatter three more berries on the placemat. The pictured example shows three berries stitched around the top right-hand corner. Change the placement of the berries as you wish, but be careful not to stitch them where you would place your dinner plate.

4 Once you have completed the cross stitch and outlines according to the chart, lastly stitch the French knots (see page 142) according to the positions on the chart.

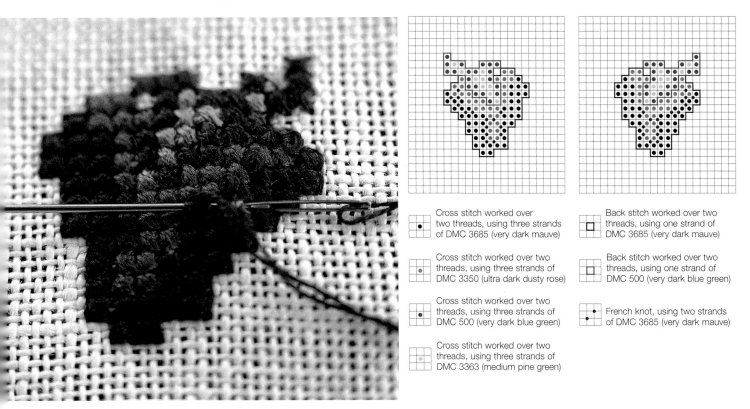

Cross stitch worked over two threads, using three strands of DMC 3685 (very dark mauve)

Cross stitch worked over two threads, using three strands of DMC 3350 (ultra dark dusty rose)

Cross stitch worked over two threads, using three strands of DMC 500 (very dark blue green)

Cross stitch worked over two threads, using three strands of DMC 3363 (medium pine green)

Back stitch worked over two threads, using one strand of DMC 3685 (very dark mauve)

Back stitch worked over two threads, using one strand of DMC 500 (very dark blue green)

French knot, using two strands of DMC 3685 (very dark mauve)

step four Add French knots for extra dimension to the strawberries.

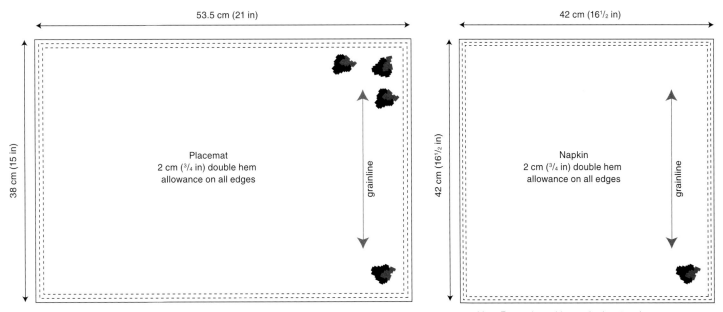

53.5 cm (21 in)

38 cm (15 in)

Placemat
2 cm (³/₄ in) double hem
allowance on all edges

grainline

42 cm (16¹/₂ in)

42 cm (16¹/₂ in)

Napkin
2 cm (³/₄ in) double hem
allowance on all edges

grainline

placemat For each placemat required, cut a piece of evenweave linen to the measurements shown.

napkins For each napkin required, cut a piece of evenweave linen to the measurements shown.

Paisley cushion

The comma-shaped motif that we know as 'paisley' derives from Mughal art in India, where it can be traced back some 2,000 years. Kashmiri shawls bearing the motif were much copied in Victorian Britain, most abundantly in the weaving town of Paisley – hence the name. This vibrantly coloured interpretation acts as a modern version of the traditional sampler, and offers you the chance to show off all your embroidery stitches on a cheerful cushion cover.

Materials

40 cm (16 in) square linen fabric, for embroidery
0.65 m x 115 cm (⅔ yd x 45 in) fabric, for cushion back and piping
1.5 m (1⅔ yds) piping cord
Three large buttons
Size 14 (35 cm/14 in) cushion insert
One skein DMC Stranded Embroidery Cotton in each of the following colours: 718 (Plum), 749 (Medium Yellow), 917 (Medium Plum), 991 (Dark Aquamarine), 992 (Light Aquamarine), 3607 (Light Plum), 3608 (Light Melon), 3834 (Dark Grape), 3835 (Medium Grape), 3836 (Light Grape)
Matching machine thread

Tools

Crewel needles, No 9 or 10
Small embroidery hoop
General sewing supplies

Size

Approximately 34 cm (13½ in) square

Stitches

Back stitch (page 137)
Chain stitch (page 139)
Chain stitch, back-stitched (page 139)
Buttonhole stitch (page 138)
Colonial knot (page 140)
Lazy daisy stitch (page 143)
Pekinese stitch (page 143)
Running stitch (page 144)
Running stitch, whipped (page 144)
Stem stitch (page 147)
Trellis couching (page 147)

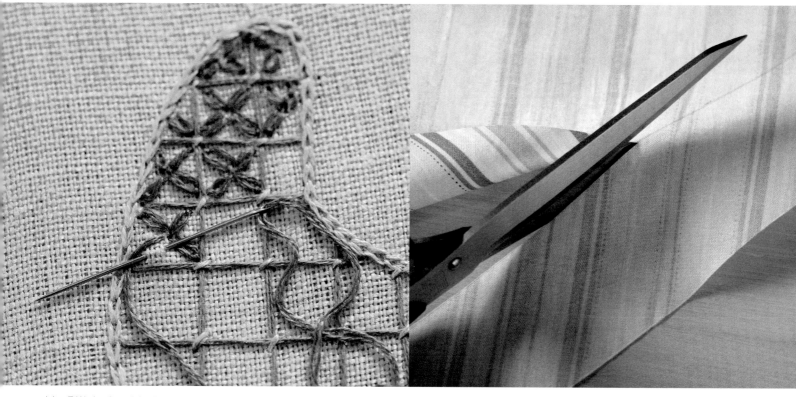

paisley E Work a lazy daisy in the centre of each square of trellis couching

step four Bias strips are cut at a 45° angle to the straight grain.

Hint

To find the correct bias of a piece of fabric, fold it diagonally so that the selvedges meet. The angle of the fold is at 45° to the straight grain of the fabric. Press the fold and use this line as a guide for cutting bias strips across the fabric, parallel to the pressed foldline.

1 Embroidery design is printed on page 223. Enlarge design by 200% on a photocopier and transfer to the linen using your preferred method (see page 129).

2 Following embroidery guide on page 223, work paisley motifs, using two strands of thread unless otherwise indicated.

3 After all embroidery has been completed, press on wrong side on a well-padded surface. Trim embroidery to 35.5 cm (14 in) square, making sure the embroidery is centred on the fabric before cutting. Round off the corners of your embroidery – a cup or mug works well for this.

4 For piping, cut 5-cm (2-in) wide bias strips to make up to approximately 150 cm (60 in) in length. Join as necessary on the diagonal and press seams open. Place piping cord in the centre of bias strip and, using a piping or zipper foot, stitch along the length of the bias strip, enclosing the cord. Trim back excess fabric so you have a 6mm (¼ in) seam allowance. With raw edges of cushion and piping even, stitch piping in place. To finish, neatly overlap the ends of the piping in the centre of the bottom of the cushion.

5 For the cushion back, cut two pieces of backing fabric, one 35.5 cm (14 in) square,

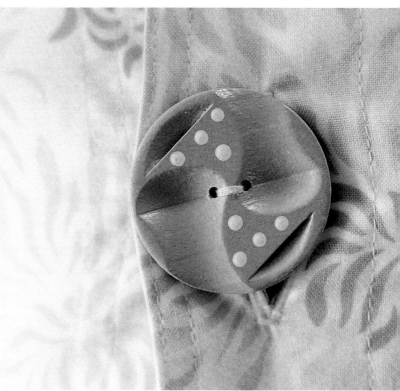

step four continued Join bias strips at right angles, to give a diagonal seam.

detail Choose large decorative buttons for the back of the cushion.

and the other 35.5 x 25 cm (14 x 10 in).
Press and stitch a double 5 cm (2 in) hem
on one side of the square. Make three
evenly spaced buttonholes in the centre of
the hem. Press and stitch a double 5 cm
(2 in) hem on one 35.5 cm (14 in) edge of
remaining backing piece. With right sides
facing up, lap larger backing piece over the
smaller, lining up hems, and baste at sides.
Complete back should measure 35.5 cm/
14 in square. Pin cushion front and back,
right sides together. Stitch around edges,
allowing a 6mm (¼ in) seam, again using a
piping or zipper foot. Turn right side out
through back opening, sew buttons in place
to match buttonholes, then insert cushion.

EMBROIDERY GUIDE

Paisley A

Paisley outline – chain stitch – 3608
Trellis couching diagonally – 718
Holding stitches – 3608
Colonial knots (3 strands) – 743

Paisley B

Paisley outline – chain stitch – 991
Pekinese stitch worked in rows approximately
    6mm (1/4 in) apart
All foundation rows – back stitch – 991
Row 1 (shortest) – 3835
Row 2 – 718
Row 3 – 3836
Row 4 – 743
Row 5 – 917
Row 6 – 3834
Row 7 – 992
Row 8 – 3608
Row 9 – 3607

Paisley C

Paisley outline – chain stitch – 718
Buttonhole stitch worked in linking rows from top
    to bottom
Row 1 – 3607
Row 2 – 991
Row 3 – 3834
Row 4 – 743
Row 5 – 3835
Row 6 – 3607
Row 7 – 991
Row 8 – 3834
Row 9 – 743

Paisley D

Paisley outline – Chain stitch – 743
Running stitch worked in concentric shapes from
    outside in
Row 1 – 718
Row 2 – 991
Row 3 – 3835
Row 4 – 743
Row 5 – 3607
Row 6 – 992

Paisley E

Paisley outline – Chain stitch – 992
Trellis couching on the straight, 6 mm (1/4 in)
    apart. Work a four-petal daisy in lazy daisy
    stitch in each section; some half sections will
    have half a daisy. Add a colonial knot to the
    centre of each full or half daisy.
Couching lines – 991
Holding stitches – 992
Daisies – 3835
Centre – 743

Paisley F

Paisley outline – chain stitch – 3835
Laced running stitch worked in rows
    approximately 6 mm (1/4 in) apart
All running stitch lines – 3834
Lacing stitches:
Row 1 – 718
Row 2 – 3836
Row 3 – 3607
Row 4 – 992
Row 5 – 3608
Row 6 – 3835
Row 7 – 991
Row 8 – 718
Row 9 – 743

Paisley G

Paisley outline – chain stitch – 3607
Chain stitch worked in concentric shapes from
    outside in
Row 1 – 992
Row 2 – 3607
Row 3 – 3608
Row 4 – 991
Row 5 – 3834

Paisley H

Paisley outline – chain stitch – 3834
Alternate rows of stem stitch and back-stitched
    chain stitch
All rows of stem stitch – 3607
All alternate rows of foundation chain stitch – 743
Back stitching:
Row 1 – 991
Row 2 – 3607
Row 3 – 3835
Row 4 – 3834
Row 5 – 991
Row 6 – 3607
Row 7 – 3835
Row 8 – 3834

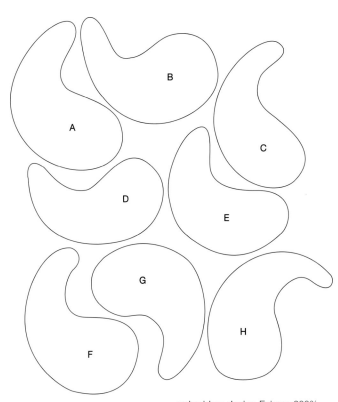

embroidery design Enlarge 200%.

Plum blossom tea towels

Once they are adorned with simple plum

blossom motifs, these domestic utility items

become decorative additions to the kitchen or

the picnic basket. If you are able to source plain

woven tea towels, stitch the designs directly onto

them. On the other hand, should you wish to

decorate items that have a variable woven

texture, you may find it easier to stitch the design

onto a smaller piece of cloth first, and then

appliqué the cloth to the object, using a

traditional Indian seed stitch known as Kantha.

This method allows you to work a small and very

portable project. It also has the advantage of

presenting a relatively tidy reverse to the item, so

that there are fewer threads to be snagged when

the cloth is in use.

Materials
Plain tea towels
Selection of machine sewing threads to blend
    together for interesting striped thread
    variations
Scraps of cotton or linen fabric, for appliqué
    (optional)

Tools
Crewel needle, No 9
General sewing supplies

Stitches
Back stitch (page 137)
Chain stitch (page 139)
French knot (page 142)
Pistil stitch (page 143)
Running stitch (page 144)
Satin stitch (page 144)
Seed stitch (page 144)
Split stitch (page 146)
Stem stitch (page 147)

step one To create the rough bark of the plum stems, cover a running stitch foundation with uneven satin stitch.

step two Work pistil stitch stamens in the centre of each simple flower.

To work the design directly onto the tea towel

1 Blend three or four threads in different browns and thread a needle. Create the outline of the plum stems using running stitch (at a slight angle across the tea towel), and then cover the outline with slightly uneven loose satin stitch to suggest a bark-like effect. Work another stem in the same manner, crossing the first at an acute angle. The stalks do not need to be perfectly straight.

2 Draw a simple five-petal flower with tailor's chalk or water-soluble fabric marker. Work around the outline in split stitch or a small chain stitch using a selection of pink threads. Strengthen the outline of the flower by working a line of rustic satin stitch around the inside of the petal outline. Work a series of pistil stitch stamens in the centre of the flower, with a few extra French knots for good measure.

3 To add leaves to your design, sketch leaf outlines in various sizes with tailor's chalk or water-soluble fabric marker. Using mixed green threads in your needle, work around the outline of the leaf in split stitch or stem stitch. Fill in the interior area using contour lines in back stitch or running stitch.

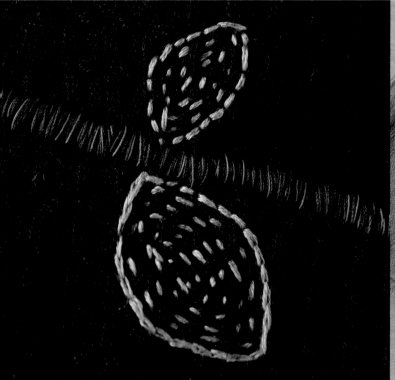

step three Add leaves of various sizes and fill in with contour lines of running stitch or back stitch.

variation Use the same method to add appliquéd designs to a set of purchased or homemade napkins, making each one slightly different.

Working a design to be appliquéd

1 Take a small rectangle or square of fabric, about 10 x 10 cm, or 10 x 12 cm (4 x 4 in, or 4 x 5 in), and turn under a narrow single hem, using a small running stitch in the same colour that you plan to use for the seed (Kantha) stitch when the fragment is appliquéd to the larger cloth.

2 Create a five-petal flower shape, using the colours and stitches of your choice, mixing and changing threads to make the work interesting. We've used simple combinations of satin stitch, running stitch and French knots. Using brown threads, add a suggestion of stems in the stitch of

your choice – we used split stitch on one sample, and loose satin stitch worked over running stitch in another.

3 Pin or baste the work to the napkin or tea towel and proceed to attach it using seed (Kantha) stitch. It is best to work with the needle at right angles to the cloth in a kind of back stitch, rather than attempting to make a number of stitches at once.

Lavender sachets

The fresh scent of lavender will permeate your wardrobe and your clothing when you use these aromatic sachets. As well as lavender, you can include herbs such as mint and rosemary to help repel moths and other destructive insects.

Silk organza has a lovely crisp finish and the translucency required for this design, while a muslin lining keeps the pot pourri from seeping out and staining your clothing. Hang the sachet over the hook of a coathanger, tie it around the clothes rail in your wardrobe, or place it in your lingerie drawer.

Alternatively, the sachet can be filled with dried culinary herbs and hung in the kitchen or pantry.

Materials (for each hanger)
40 cm (16 in) square silk organza
40 cm (16 in) square cotton muslin
DMC pearl cotton No 5 *or* DMC stranded
  embroidery cotton
Dried herbs, dried lavender, dried rose petals
  or pot pourri, for filling
1 m (1 yd) of 6 mm (¼ in) grosgrain ribbon
  or silk organza ribbon for ties

Tools
Pencil
Compass
Water-soluble fabric marker
Crewel embroidery needle
Embroidery hoop

step two Using a water-soluble marker pen, mark dots all over the inner circle on the organza fabric, to show the placement points for the groups of cross stitches.

step three Work groups of five cross stitches over the marked dots, stitching through both layers of fabric. Do not extend the stitching beyond the inner circle.

Hint

The finished silk organza circles need to be at least 30–35 cm (12–14 in) in diameter. If you wish to make smaller hangers than the size given at right, remember to keep the stitches at least 15–20 cm (6–8 in) from the edges of the fabric to allow for a 10 cm (4 in) ruffle when the organza is drawn up.

1 Using a pencil and compass (or dinner plates of the correct size), mark two concentric circles, 22 cm (8½ in) and 36 cm (14¼ in) in diameter, on the organza fabric. (If you wish to make smaller hangers, see the hint at left.) Do not cut out the circles until after all the cross stitching has been worked on the organza, so that the raw edges of the circle remain crisp.

2 Using a water-soluble fabric marker, mark placement points for groups of cross stitches (see chart) all over the centre of the organza fabric. Do not extend the placement points beyond the inner circle. Note that towards the outer edge of the

circle, you will need to mark partial groups of stitches (see the photograph above) to fit the design neatly into the circle.

3 Lay the organza over the muslin and place in an embroidery hoop. Work the cross stitches through both layers, using one thickness of pearl cotton or two strands of stranded embroidery cotton. After each group of stitches is completed, the thread should be fastened off to minimize shadows of threads behind the translucent fabrics.

4 When you have completed all the cross stitches, cut out both layers of fabric into a circle. If you have resized the hanger,

step five Pile pot pourri into the centre of the circle, then draw up the running stitch threads to form a neat ball.

step five continued Finish the hanger with a ribbon bow.

remember that the finished circle needs to be at least 10 cm (4 in) wider than the stitched area. In matching machine thread, work medium-length running stitches around the line of the inner circle. Do not fasten off.

5 Place the fabric circle face down and pile pot pourri in the centre. Draw up the edges of the fabric using the ends of the running stitch, ensuring the ball is well filled with pot pourri, then tie off and trim the threads. Decorate with a ribbon bow to finish.

chart 1 Repeat these groups of cross stitches all over the marked inner circle of the fabric.

Curtain

A lightweight curtain admits subtle light through a window. The shadowy shapes of simple stitched motifs on this curtain add a touch of embroidery magic to a plain fabric drop.

This design is made up of diagonal and upright crosses on top of each other, with loosely carried threads on the reverse adding depth to the shadow-work effect. This is a simple but effective way to dress up a purchased ready-hemmed curtain.

Materials

Ready-made cotton voile or muslin curtain
    in white or ecru
DMC stranded embroidery cotton,
    317 (pewter grey)
DMC stranded embroidery cotton,
    318 (light steel grey)
DMC stranded embroidery cotton,
    762 (very light pearl grey)

Tools

Embroidery hoop
Crewel embroidery needles
Water-soluble fabric marker
General sewing supplies

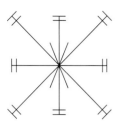

small star design (top row)

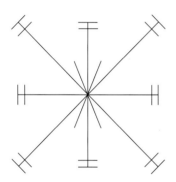

medium star design (middle row)

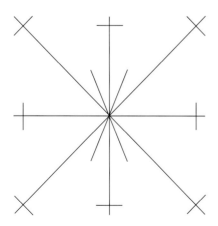

large star design (bottom row)

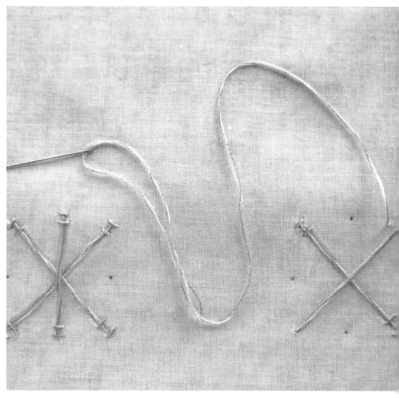

stitching in progress Work the stitches over the marker-pen dots.

1 Trace the stars at left onto the curtain using a water-soluble fabric marker. Following the curtain layout chart opposite, repeat the stars across the width of the curtain, working from the centre out. You can increase the spacing between rows as desired, and increase the number of rows in the design if you have a larger curtain.

2 Place the section of curtain to be stitched into an embroidery hoop. Be careful to start and finish each pattern securely with a clove hitch knot (see page 131). There will be some show-through of the threads at the back of the fabric; this is intentional and adds a soft, shadowy effect.

3 The bottom row of stars is stitched with one strand of DMC 317 (pewter grey) combined with two strands of DMC 762 (very light pearl grey).

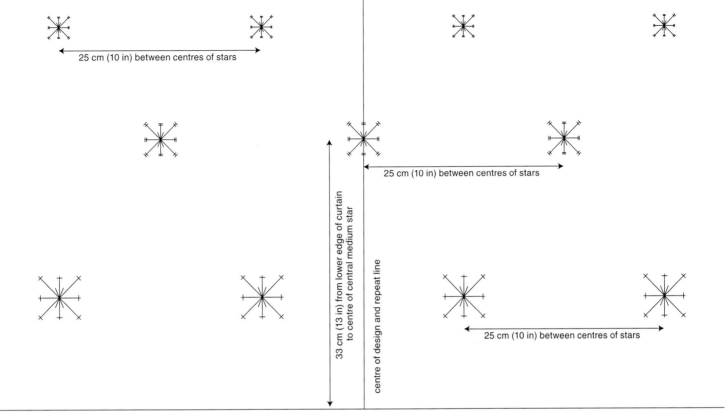

25 cm (10 in) between centres of stars

25 cm (10 in) between centres of stars

33 cm (13 in) from lower edge of curtain to centre of central medium star

centre of design and repeat line

25 cm (10 in) between centres of stars

curtain layout

lower edge of purchased ready-hemmed curtain

4 The middle row of stars is stitched with one strand of 762 (very light pearl grey) combined with two strands of 318 (light steel grey).

5 The top row of stars is stitched with one strand of 318 (light steel grey) combined with two strands of 762 (very light pearl grey).

6 When stitching the star motifs, first stitch the large upright cross and the bars at the end of each arm. Next, stitch the large diagonal cross and the bars at the end of each arm. Lastly, stitch the smaller diagonal cross at the centre.

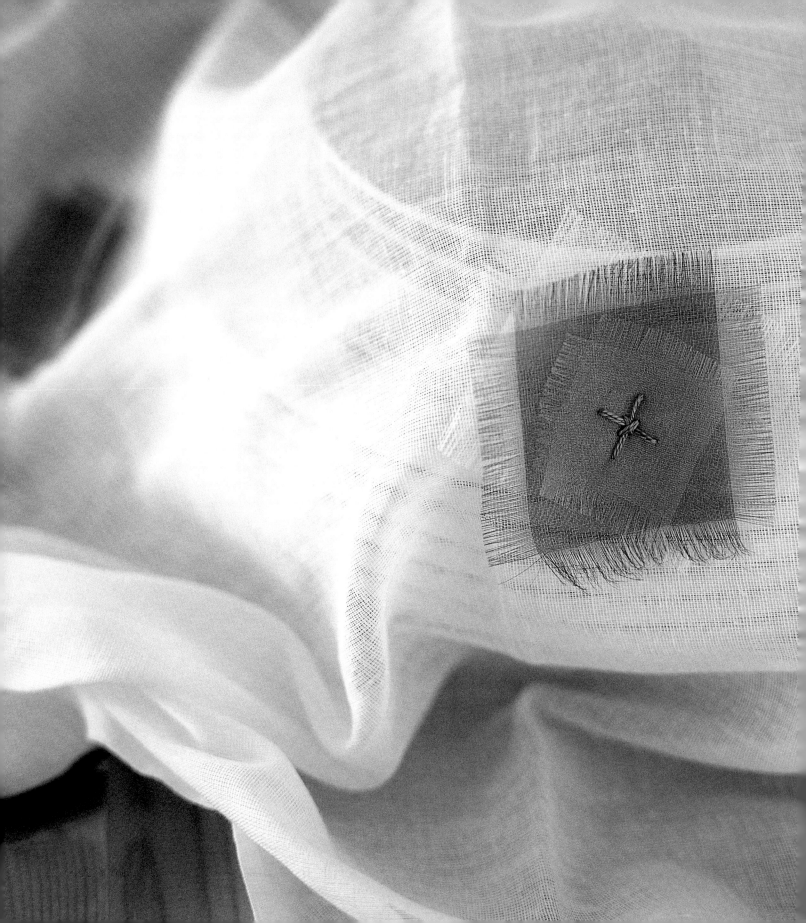

Table throw

A sheer covering of lightweight fabric will keep insects away from an outdoor table setting, allowing preparations to be completed well before the guests arrive.

Voile, organza or fine muslin fabrics are perfect for this project: contrasting patches with frayed edges are attached with large cross stitches to create a stunning effect, taking only a few minutes of your time.

Materials

A piece of cotton muslin or similar, as long as it is wide; for example 1.4 m (55 in) of fabric 140 cm (55 in) wide, or 1.5 m (59 in) of fabric 150 cm (59 in) wide

Small amounts of silk organza in two or three contrasting colours (in the pictured example, the organza patches are cream, coffee and steel blue)

DMC pearl cotton No 8, to attach the organza patches (in the pictured example, coffee-coloured thread 841 is used)

Tools

Straw hand-sewing needle

4 fabric weights (available from furnishing stores); or use coins

step one Draw a thread along all four sides of the piece of muslin to ensure you have a true square.

step one continued Cut along the drawn thread line.

Laundering

If you need to wash an embroidered piece, do so by hand using cold water and wool detergent or very diluted laundry detergent. Rinse well, then roll in a clean towel to get rid of excess water; never wring the fabric. Allow to dry completely, then press on the wrong side, using a pressing cloth.

Beaded embroidery can be dry-cleaned; or launder as above, then when dry, lay it face down on a thick towel

1 Draw a thread along all four edges of the muslin to ensure you have a true square, then cut along the drawn thread line.

2 Press a double 3 cm (1¼ in) hem along all four sides. Add a weight to each corner, pin the hem into place, then machine stitch the hem 2 mm (¹⁄₁₆ in) from the inner edge.

3 You are now ready to place the organza patches into position. To prepare the patches, cut about 15 pieces of organza in each colour, approximately 6 x 5 cm (2½ x 2 in). Cut them freehand, as they do not all have to be exactly the same size; some variation in size adds to the effect. Fray

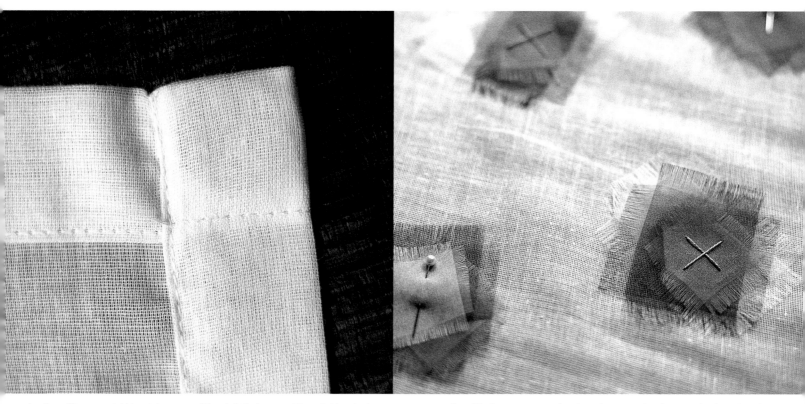

step two Place a weight in each corner of the cloth before machine stitching the hem.

step five Pin the organza patches into place, spacing them randomly and varying the order of the colours within the patches, then stitch down with a large cross stitch.

along all four sides of each piece for about 1 cm (⅜ in).

4 Make the patches into groups, giving some groups two layers and others three layers, and arranging the colours in different orders throughout the groups. Place each patch at an angle to the previous, to allow all the colours to show at the edge of the group.

5 Place the groups of patches onto the completed muslin throw. If you wish, lay the throw on a flat surface, such as the floor, so that you can rearrange the patches until you are pleased with the total effect. Pin them in place, then stitch them down using one or two thicknesses of pearl thread. On each patch, first work a single large uneven cross stitch; if the stitch size floats too much, secure the centre with a smaller upright cross stitch as pictured on page 236. Be sure to start and finish securely so that the stitching can withstand laundering.

Baby blanket and cot sheet

An interesting change from baby pastels, this charming cot set would make a beautiful and practical gift for a new arrival. The motifs are worked almost entirely in simple stem stitch on easy-to-launder 100% cotton – brushed fleece for the blanket and snowy white poplin for the sheet. You could also embroider the motifs directly onto a purchased throw, woollen cot blanket or packaged sheet set.

Materials

2.5 m x 115 cm (2¾ yds x 45 in) charcoal grey
   100% cotton brushed fleece
2 m x 112 cm (2¼ yds x 44 in) white
   cotton poplin
One skein DMC Perlé Cotton No 5 in each of
   the following colours: 321 (Christmas Red),
   550 (Very Dark Violet), 601 (Dark Cranberry),
   796 (Dark Royal Blue), 943 (Medium
   Aquamarine), 947 (Burnt Orange), 972 (Deep
   Canary) and 996 (Medium Electric Blue)
One skein DMC Perlé Cotton No 8, 310 (Black)
Matching machine thread

Tools

Mixed crewel needles
General sewing supplies

Size

Blanket: 104 x 120 cm (41 x 47 in)
Sheet: 108 x 148 cm (42 x 58 in)

Stitches

French knot (page 142)
Running stitch (page 144)
Satin stitch (page 144)
Stem stitch (page 147)
Straight stitch (page 147)

cot blanket Position the motifs evenly around the border as desired.

COT BLANKET

1 Cut two pieces of brushed fleece, each one 107 x 123 cm (42 x 48½ in). Press one piece in half crosswise and then lengthwise, and mark centre lines with basting stitches. The nursery motifs are printed on page 244 – enlarge 200% on a photocopier. Allowing for 1.5 cm (⅝ in) seam allowance, position motifs evenly around edges of fleece – three across the top, one on each side and three across bottom – about 7.5 cm (3 in) in from edges. Transfer designs to the fabric using your preferred method (see page 129). The Chicks are positioned at the centre bottom of the blanket; the Horse motif is used three times (centre top and on each side) and the Dog and Cat are each used twice, in the alternate corners.

2 Work all motifs in stem stitch, except where otherwise indicated, using one strand of thread and a different colour for each motif. Keeping the thread to the outside of the design at all times, work the motifs in the following order:

Dog Work the tail and patches. Stitch the body, chin, top of head and ears. Work the face details in black: mouth; nose (use double thread) in straight stitch; eyes in satin stitch.

Cat Work patches, tail, ears, body and face circle. Stitch face details in black: mouth; nose (use double thread) and whiskers in straight stitch; eyes in satin stitch.

Horse Stitch mane, tail, body, sides of face, ears and face. Stitch face details in black: mouth; eyes and nostrils in satin stitch.

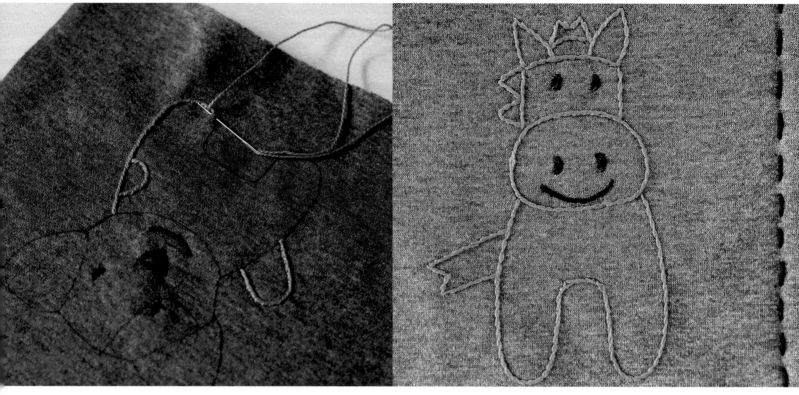

cot blanket step two Always keep the thread on the outside of the design when working stem stitch.

detail Horse motif on cot blanket.

Chicks Stitch bodies. Stitch remaining details in black: legs in straight stitch; eye (use double thread) in French knot; beak.

3 When all embroidery is complete, place front and back together, right sides facing, and stitch around all edges, allowing a 1.5 cm (⅝ in) seam and leaving a 20 cm (8 in) opening in one side. Trim corners, turn right side out and slip stitch (page 134) the opening closed. Press on the wrong side on a well-padded surface.

4 Using black perlé cotton, work a line of large, evenly spaced running stitch around the edge of the blanket, through both

layers, about 1.5 cm (⅝ in) from the edge. Lay the blanket on a flat work surface and lightly mark an inner rectangle, 20 cm (8 in) from the edges. Work over the marked line with running stitch, stitching through both layers.

Variations

For extra warmth and thickness, you could add a layer of cotton quilt wadding to the blanket before stitching the front and back together. Quilt through all the layers using large, even running stitches.

The motifs can also be worked on wool blanketing. You will only need one layer, so try to keep the back as neat as possible. Finish the edges with blanket stitch in a bright contrasting colour.

embroidery designs Enlarge 200% for blanket and 140% for sheet

COT SHEET

1 From white cotton, cut one rectangle, 134 x 112 cm (52½ x 44 in), and another strip, 36 x 112 cm (14 x 44 in), for the border. Press and stitch a 1 cm (⅜ in) double hem on two long sides and one short end of the sheet rectangle. Press border strip in half lengthwise to mark finished width; open out again.

2 Enlarge the nursery motifs, above, by 140% on a photocopier. Remembering that when the border is turned back, the motifs need to be right side up, and allowing for seam allowance, position motifs evenly along the border strip between the pressed foldline and one edge, using as many or as few as you wish. Transfer designs to fabric using your preferred method (see page 129). Embroider the designs, as for the cot blanket. Do not carry threads across the back, as these will show through.

3 To make up, use a pin to mark the centre of the unfinished edge of the sheet and the centre of the long edge on the non-embroidered half of the border. With right sides together and matching centres, pin edges together. The edges of the border will extend beyond the sheet on each side. Stitch as pinned, allowing a 1 cm (⅜ in) seam. Press under 1 cm (⅜ in) on

cot sheet step two Remember, when tracing the motifs, that the sheet border will be turned back, so trace the motifs upside down.

detail Cat motif on cot sheet.

remaining long raw edge of border. Fold border in half, right sides together and stitch sides. (The seam allowance should be about 2 cm (¾ in), but adjust this if necessary so that the width of the border matches the finished width of the sheet.) Trim seam allowance to 1 cm (⅜ in) and clip across corners. Turn border right side out and topstitch pressed edge in place over seam. The embroidered motifs should be upside down, on the wrong side of the sheet so that they will be the right way up on the right side when the sheet is turned down over a blanket.

Variations

Embroider a motif or two onto a matching purchased pillowcase.

You could also make a simple and charming patchwork quilt by working motifs onto squares of white fabric and alternating them with plain or print squares in colours that will match your embroidery thread.

Glasses case

Spectacles are delicate and easily damaged,

so a secure, protective case is essential.

There is no reason why such a mundane object

needs to look ordinary, though, and this project

will inspire you to look at other everyday objects

that can be personalized and embellished with

a little embroidery.

The given pattern fits a slim pair of spectacles;

if yours are wider, adjust the size accordingly.

Materials

32-count evenweave linen in ecru

Ecru cotton lining fabric

Ecru machine sewing thread

Small amount of DMC stranded embroidery
cotton, 3834 (dark grape)

Small amount of DMC stranded embroidery
cotton, 501 (dark blue green)

2 small bee charms

1 purse clip approximately 6 cm (2⅜ in) wide

30 cm (12 in) of braid approximately 1 cm
(⅜ in) wide

Tools

Tapestry needle No 24

General sewing supplies

detail The case is lined with cotton fabric and the upper edges of the lining are trimmed with braid.

variation If desired, the case can be worked in the alternative design given opposite, then made up as instructed.

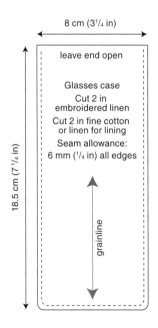

8 cm (3¼ in)

leave end open

Glasses case
Cut 2 in
embroidered linen
Cut 2 in fine cotton
or linen for lining
Seam allowance:
6 mm (¼ in) all edges

18.5 cm (7¼ in)

grainline

1 The cross-stitch design should be worked prior to cutting out the pattern shape, according to the chart provided and using two strands of stranded embroidery cotton.

2 Stitch the back stitch according to the chart, using a single strand of stranded embroidery cotton.

3 Attach the bee charms to the design with a small stitch across the body to hold them flat and in position.

4 Using the patterns provided, cut two shapes in linen fabric and two shapes in lining fabric.

5 Machine stitch the linen, with right sides together, leaving the end open as marked on the pattern. Turn the linen through to the right side and press carefully.

6 Repeat this using the lining fabric, but do not turn it to the right side. Insert the lining into the linen, with wrong sides together, then fold in the seam allowance along the top edges and press flat carefully. Whip stitch the purse clip into place along the open top edges of the case.

7 Hand sew a braid or ribbon trim to the inside upper edge of the purse to complete.

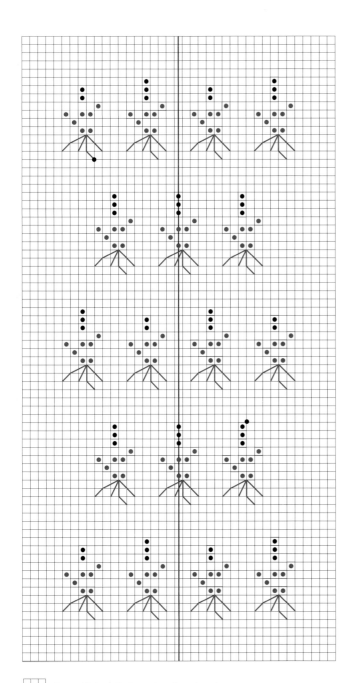

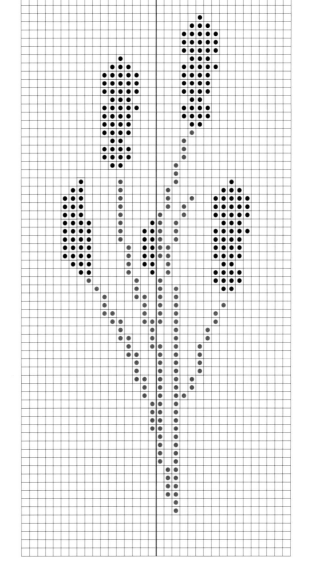

Cross stitch worked over two threads, using two strands of DMC 3834 (dark grape)

Cross stitch worked over two threads, using two strands of DMC 501 (dark blue green)

Back stitch worked over two threads, using one strand of DMC 501 (dark blue green)

Attachment point for bee charms

Cross stitch worked over two threads, using two strands of DMC 3837 (lavender)

Cross stitch worked over two threads, using two strands of DMC 503 (medium blue green)

Evening purse

This is the perfect project for using up odd pretty buttons, interesting fabric scraps and swatches gleaned at the haberdashers, fragments of old lace or favourite clothes, small beads, sequins and shisha mirrors. Even the small piece of multi-coloured cord stitched to this bag was twined from the thread ends of other projects. We give instructions for the construction of the basic bag, but the final embellishment will be up to you. The beauty of such a method is that no two bags are ever exactly alike.

Materials

Two 36 cm (14 in) squares cotton or linen fabric (use a contrasting fabric for the lining, if preferred)
36 cm (14 in) square firm interfacing
Small scraps of fabric, such as silk, satin, and so on
Shisha mirrors
Mother-of-pearl buttons
Assorted seed beads
Assorted threads
Press-stud fastener
Matching machine thread

Tools

Crewel needle, No 9
General sewing supplies

Size

The bag shown in the photograph (finished size approximately 13 x 16.5 cm, or 5 x 6½ in) was made from two squares of fabric 36 x 36 cm (14 x 14 in). The size can be varied as follows: 21 x 21 cm (8¼ x 8¼ in) makes a 10-cm (4-in) wide wallet. 50 x 50 cm (19½ x 19½ in) makes a bag 23 cm (9 in) wide.

Stitches

Back stitch (page 137)
Couching (page 140)
Star stitch (page 147)
Feather stitch (page 141)
Fly stitch (page 141)
French knot (page 142)
Running stitch (page 144)
Seed stitch (page 144)
Shisha stitch (page 146)
Straight stitch (page 147)

step one Pin an assortment of fabric scraps to one corner of fabric square.

step six Stitching only through two layers, secure side flaps together with decorative stitching. Stitch the bottom rows through all layers.

1 Baste or press interfacing to the back of one fabric square. Turn right side up and, keeping in mind a seam allowance of 1.5 cm (⅝ in), layer some small scraps of fabric across one corner of the work. Pin in place, and baste down (basting prevents pins from getting entangled in the stitching thread).

2 Use a selection of stitches to secure the scraps, such as French knots, running stitch, seed stitch, straight stitch and vertical fly stitch. Wrinkle some of your fabric during stitching, to create interesting texture. Add extra stitches, such as double cross stitch on various angles. Fray the edges of the fabrics if desired.

3 Add shisha mirrors to the surface, as desired, using shisha stitch. Attach mother-of-pearl buttons, stitching them on with boldly contrasting thread. Fill a few areas with seed beads, stitching them on using a back stitch through each bead.

4 To make an interesting decorative version of a twisted cord, follow the directions on page 135, using various thread trimmings. To make a longer cord, simply add handfuls of offcuts, overlapping them with the main body of thread slightly before twisting, or adding them in as you twist. Stitch the bundle onto the work using back stitch, or couching it down if desired.

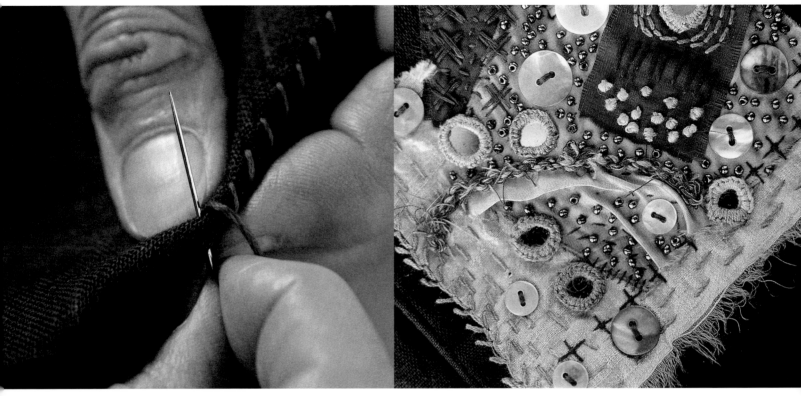

step seven Oversew the sides of the bag together using a contrast thread.

detail Fabrics and embellishments can be varied according to what you have on hand, making each bag unique.

5 Take the second square of fabric (lining) and place on top of the embroidered square, right sides together. With 1.5 cm (⅝ in) seams, stitch together around edges, leaving an opening in one side (not directly next to the embroidered corner). Clip the corners, turn work right side out, press and slip stitch the opening closed.

6 Place the square on a flat surface, lining uppermost, and turn it on its point so that the embroidered corner is at the top. Fold in the side corners, one overlapping the other, until the work measures 16.5 cm (6½ in) across. Secure the fold with pins, then hand-stitch together through the two top layers only, in a square and/or circular pattern of stitching that secures both corners, so that the work forms a kind of flat tube. Now stitch across the bottom of the tube, through all layers, decoratively by hand, or with a line of machine-stitching, so that a pocket is formed.

7 Fold lower part of the bag upwards, pin securely, and oversew the sides of the bag together using a contrasting colour. This creates a second pocket in front of the first.

8 Fold the embroidered flap over, and mark the position for the press-stud fastener. Attach with sturdy thread.

Variation

Add a handle in the form of a chain or cord, if desired. Experiment with different folds to make varying bag shapes with different pockets. Try making an all-white or all-grey version for a truly elegant bejewelled talisman.

Bag with pocket

This sturdy, lined bag is robust enough to carry
a load of shopping, but pretty enough to do duty
as a roomy carry-all or even, perhaps, as a
knitting or handwork bag. The outer pocket is
embroidered with a charming design of cottage
garden flowers in a variety of simple stitches,
using fine crewel wool. The bag itself is fully lined
with a fine cotton print and reinforced with thin
quilt wadding to make it extra soft and strong.

Materials

1.2 m x 115 cm (1¼ yards x 45 in) plain
cotton fabric for embroidered pocket, outer
bag and handles
1.2 m x 115 cm (1¼ yards x 45 in) lining
fabric
Thin quilt wadding
One skein Cascade House Crewel Embroidery
Wool in each of the following colours: 1780,
1840, 2130, 2180, 2350, 2660, 3135, 4280,
4470, 4570, 4650, 5290, 8300 and 8320
Small amount DMC Stranded Embroidery
Cotton 743 (Medium Yellow), for bee stripes
Matching machine thread
Button

Tools

Crewel needles, No 8
Small embroidery hoop
General sewing supplies

Size

Finished bag measures 39 cm wide x 38 cm
high (15¾ x 15 in), excluding handles

Stitches

Back stitch (page 137)
Buttonhole stitch (page 138)
Buttonhole stitch, crossed (page 138)
Chain stitch (page 139)
Colonial knot (page 140)
Fly stitch (page 141)
Lazy daisy stitch (page 143)
Pistil stitch (page 143)
Running stitch, whipped (page 144)
Spider's web (page 146)
Stem stitch (page 147)
Straight stitch (page 147)
Trellis couching (page 147)

EMBROIDERY GUIDE

Windflower

Stem Back stitch – 1840

Leaves Back stitch leaf outline – 1840;
straight stitch vein – 1840

Petals Back stitch petal outline – 8320

Stamens Pistil stitch – 8300 (work centre stitch first,
then one on either side)

Centre Fill with colonial knots (double thickness) – 2130

Cyclamen

Stem Stem stitch – 1780

Petals Three straight stitches worked in and out of the
same holes, surrounded by a lazy daisy. Work centre
stitch first, then one stitch on either side – 4280

Centre Three colonial knots – 2350

Forget-me-nots

Stem: Back stitch – 1780

Flowers: Colonial knots – 8320

Campanula

Stem Stem stitch – 1840

Leaves Lazy daisy stitch – 1840

Flower Back stitch outline, add a straight stitch towards
centre at each point – 5290

Centre: Lazy daisy stitches from centre – 2130

Coneflower

Stem Stem stitch – 1840

Leaves Three straight stitches in and out of the same
holes – 1840

Flower Chain stitch petal outline – 5290

Stamens One straight stitch on each petal – 2130

Centre Fill centre with colonial knots – 2130

Daisies

FULL DAISY

Stem Back stitch – 1780

Leaves Tiny lazy daisy stitches – 1780

Petals Work a lazy daisy stitch at 9, 12, 3 and 6 o'clock
then fill in between with more petals. The more
petals you have, the better your daisy will look.

Make stitches different lengths; don't worry if you have more stitches in one quarter than another – 2130

Centre Fill centre with colonial knots – about five – 2350

HALF DAISY

Stem and leaves As for Full Daisy

Petals Work petals at 9, 3 and 6 o'clock and fill in between as for Full Daisy – 2130

Centre Fill centre with colonial knots – approximately five – 2350

Cosmos

Stem Laced running stitch: running stitch in 1840, laced with 1780

Petals Crossed buttonhole stitch – 4280

Centre Back stitch outline – 2130, trellis couching diagonally – 2130

Bluebell

Stem Stem stitch – 1840

Leaves Lazy daisy stitch – 1840

Flower Buttonhole stitch – 8320

Centre 5–7 colonial knots – 2130

Hollyhock

Stem Stem stitch – 1840. It is better to work the stem after the flowers have been embroidered as then you will be able to use the back of your work to take the thread to the next section of the stem

Leaves Fly stitch vein, stem stitch leaf outline – 1840

Small leaves Lazy daisy stitch – 1840

Flowers Buttonhole stitch – 4570, 4470, 4650. Start buttonhole stitch on the outside then work in an anti-clockwise direction. Flowers graduate from larger at the base to smaller at the top. Colour graduates also from darkest shade at the base to lightest at the top. Where flowers overlap, stitch into the previous flower. Buds at the top are colonial knots in lightest shade

Snail

Shell Spider's web – 3135

Body Stem stitch – 3135

Eye French knot – 3135

Antennae Pistil stitches – 3135

Bee

Body Work 5–7 straight stitches in and out of the same holes – 2660

Head Colonial knot – 2660

Antennae Straight stitches – 2660

Wings Loose lazy daisy stiches – 2660

Stripes Straight stitches worked across the body – one strand DMC 743

Ground line

Back stitch – 1890

embroidery design Enlarge 200%

1 For pocket, cut a piece of fabric, 45 x 30 cm (18 x 12 in). Enlarge embroidery outline, above, to 200% on a photocopier. Transfer design to centre of fabric using your preferred method (see page 129).

2 Following embroidery guide on page 256, work embroidery using one strand of crewel wool (except for bee stripes). Trim embroidery to 40.5 x 21.5 cm (16 x 8½ in).

3 Cut remaining bag pieces as follows: **Front/Back** (43 x 40.5 cm / 17 x 16 in): 2 outer, 2 lining and 2 wadding; **Handles** (5 x 56 cm / 2 x 22 in): 2 outer, 2 lining and 2 wadding; **Flap** (9 cm / 3½ in square):

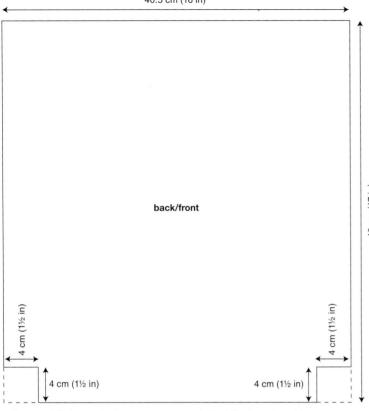

diagram 1 Cut away the lower corner on each Front/Back section of bag

40.5 cm (16 in)

43 cm (17 in)

back/front

4 cm (1½ in)

4 cm (1½ in)

4 cm (1½ in)

4 cm (1½ in)

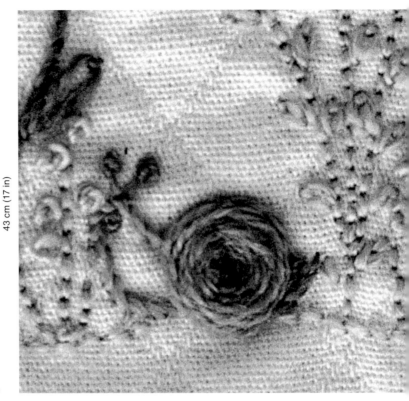

detail The snail shell is worked in spider's web, using a variegated thread.

1 outer, 1 lining and 1 wadding; **Pocket Lining** (40.5 x 21.5 cm / 16 x 8½ in): 1 lining and 1 wadding; **Pocket Binding** (21.5 x 6.5 cm / 8½ x 2½ in): 2 lining. All measurements include a 6 mm (¼ in) seam allowance, unless otherwise indicated.

4 Cut away a 4 cm (1½ in) square from each lower corner on all Front/Back pieces (Diagram 1). Use a glass to trace and cut a curved edge on one end of all Flap pieces.

5 Sandwich wadding between wrong sides of embroidered Pocket and lining. Baste all layers together. Press binding strips in half, wrong sides together. With raw edges

matching and allowing a 1 cm (⅜ in) seam, stitch a binding strip to the top and bottom edges of the pocket. Fold pressed edge of binding to the back and slip stitch in place over seam line.

6 Baste pocket on right side of bag Front, 9 cm (3½ in) up from bottom edge. Top-stitch lower edge of pocket to Front, stitching along the binding seam line. Baste wadding Front/Backs to wrong side of bag Front and Back around all edges.

7 Place Handle pieces right sides together with wadding on top. Stitch sides and one short end. Trim corners, turn right side out

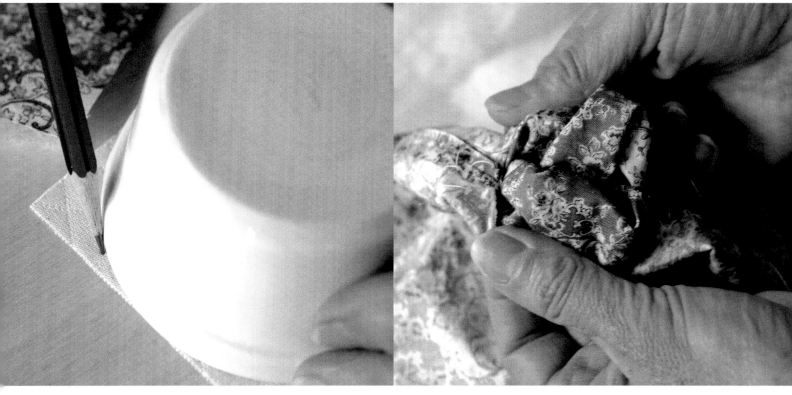

step four Use a glass or small bowl to round one edge of all Flap sections.

step eleven Turn completed bag right side out through opening left in the bottom seam of the lining.

and press. Top-stitch on both long sides, approximately 6 mm (¼ in) from edge. Repeat for remaining handle.

8 Place Flap pieces right sides together, with wadding on top. Stitch around edge, leaving straight end open. Clip curves and corners and turn right side out. Make a buttonhole approximately 1.5 cm (⅝ in) in from curved end of flap.

9 With right sides together and raw edges even, pin handles to bag Front and Back, 10 cm (4 in) in from each edge. Centre the flap on the bag Back, between the handles. Baste handles and flap in place.

10 With right sides together, stitch bag Front to Back at sides, and across bottom edge, catching edges of pocket in side seams. Matching side and bottom seams, stitch across the corners to form the boxed corners. Turn right side out.

11 Stitch lining pieces together as for outer bag, leaving an opening for turning in the centre of the bottom seam. With right sides together, stitch lining and bag together around upper edge. Turn right side out through opening in lining. Press well around top of bag, slip stitch (page 134) opening closed and push lining into bag. Sew a button to bag front to correspond to flap.

Hint

If you plan to use your bag for shopping, or even if you just like a carry bag with inner pockets for your keys or mobile phone, top-stitch a lined pocket square to the lining of the bag before joining it to the outer bag.

Apron

The simple embroidery on this apron sets

a tone for finding pleasure in homemaking tasks.

Make the apron in a fine evenweave fabric,

or simply insert a panel of evenweave for the

stitching. Alternatively, work the embroidery

on an evenweave band and attach it to a

homemade or purchased apron. Variegated

embroidery thread adds visual interest to the

cross-stitched border design without the need

to stop and change colours.

Materials
80 x 115 cm (31½ x 45 in) 22-count
   evenweave linen or cotton fabric in natural
2 skeins DMC pearl cotton No 5, 115
   (variegated garnet)
2 m (2 yd) cotton or rayon ribbon 25 mm
   (1 in) wide
Machine sewing thread to match fabric

Tools
Tapestry needle No 22
General sewing supplies

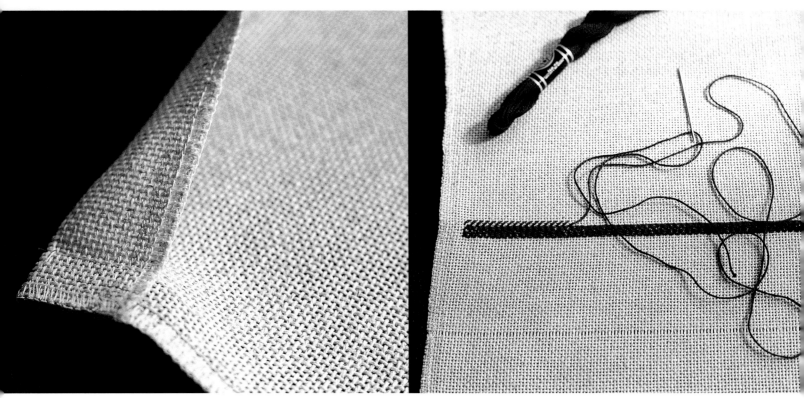

step two Overlock or zigzag the raw edges to prevent fraying, then press the hem up.

step five Work the cross-stitch design according to the chart.

1 Cut the apron from evenweave linen or cotton according to the pattern opposite, making sure the hem of the apron is cut on the true straight grain. (Check this by pulling a thread along the fabric before cutting.) The size can be adjusted by increasing or decreasing the length of the ties. Note that you will need to increase the amount of ribbon required if you do this.

2 After cutting out the apron, it is necessary to neaten the raw edges around the apron to prevent fraying while you work the cross stitch. This can be done by a machine zigzag stitch, with an overlocker, or in blanket stitch by hand.

3 The apron has a 1.5 cm (⅝ in) seam allowance around all side and top edges and an 8 cm (3¼ in) seam allowance at the bottom. At the hemline, press up the hem to give you a starting position for the cross stitch, which is worked above the hemline.

4 Next, mark the centre of the apron: this will match up with the centre of the chart (see page 264). Start your cross stitching at this point, according to the chart.

5 The cross stitches are worked over two threads, using one thickness of DMC pearl cotton No 5 in variegated garnet.

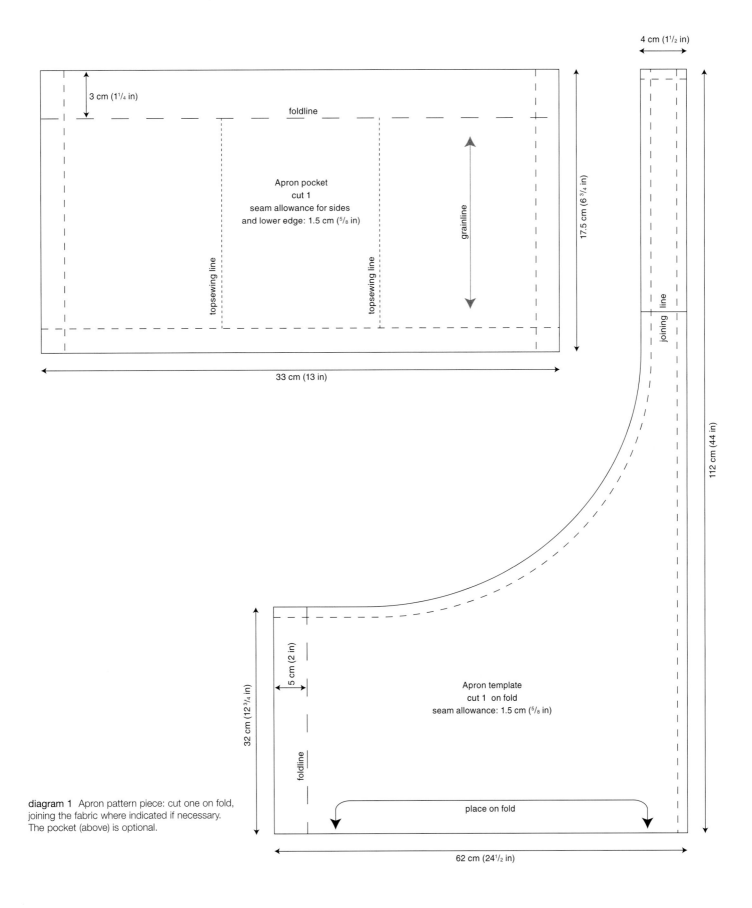

4 cm (1½ in)

3 cm (1¼ in)

foldline

Apron pocket
cut 1
seam allowance for sides
and lower edge: 1.5 cm (⅝ in)

grainline

17.5 cm (6¾ in)

topsewing line

topsewing line

33 cm (13 in)

joining line

112 cm (44 in)

5 cm (2 in)

32 cm (12¾ in)

Apron template
cut 1 on fold
seam allowance: 1.5 cm (⅝ in)

foldline

place on fold

diagram 1 Apron pattern piece: cut one on fold,
joining the fabric where indicated if necessary.
The pocket (above) is optional.

62 cm (24½ in)

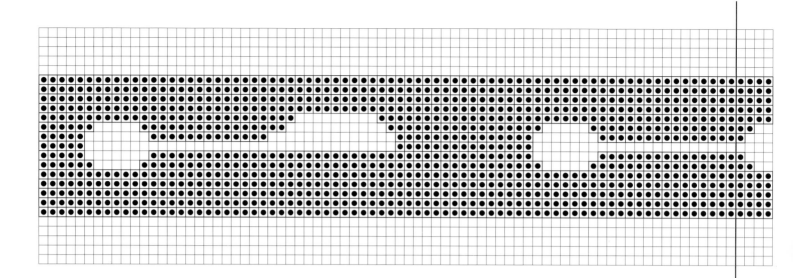

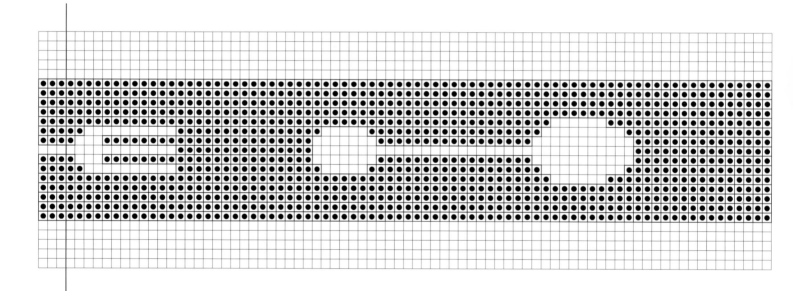

stitching chart The red line marks the centre of the design, and indicates where the two charts overlap.

Cross stitch worked over two threads, using one thickness of DMC pearl cotton No 5 in variegated garnet.

step six Make sure the top diagonals of the cross stitches all go in the same direction.

step nine Add a pocket to the apron. As a variation, the apron can be made in a plain fabric with or without a separate embroidered band.

6 Finish the cross stitches 1.5 cm (⅝ in) from the side edges. This makes it easier to turn over the side hem allowance. Be sure to work all your stitches with the diagonals going in the one direction.

7 After completing the cross stitch, press in the hem allowance around all edges of the apron. Slip stitch or machine stitch in place.

8 Lay the cotton or rayon ribbon across the top edge of the apron on the wrong side, covering the hem allowance. Turn under a small hem at each end of the ribbon and ties, and slip stitch the ribbon to the apron to reinforce the waistline.

9 If you wish to add a pocket to the apron, cut the pattern piece from the remaining fabric. Neaten the raw edges, then press under 1.5 cm (⅝ in) seam allowances on all sides. Centre the pocket on the front of the apron, about 12.5 cm (5 in) from the top edge. Top stitch around the side and bottom edges, about 6 mm (¼ in) from the edge, then stitch along the lines marked on the pattern to divide the pocket into sections.

Tote bag

This simple tote bag has a multitude of uses –

fold it and slip it into a basket to use as an extra

bag when shopping, take your swimming gear to

the beach, or use it for library books. With an

extra inner pocket for a coin purse or mobile

phone, the fully-lined bag is actually reversible (if

you omit the inner pocket), so if you're feeling

industrious, you could work the embroidered

motifs on the lining as well.

Materials
0.5 m x 115 cm (⅔ yd x 45 in) linen/cotton
   blend for outer bag
0.5 m x 115 cm (⅔ yd x 45 in) contrast
   linen/cotton blend for lining
One ball DMC Perlé Cotton No 8: Ecru
Matching machine thread

Tools
Crewel needle, No 8
Small embroidery hoop
General sewing supplies

Size
33 cm wide x 48 cm high (13 x 19 in) to the
   top of the handle

Stitches
Back stitch (page 137)
Buttonhole stitch (page 138)
Colonial knot (page 140)
Fly stitch (page 141)
Lazy daisy stitch (page 143)
Running stitch, whipped (page 144)
Stem stitch (page 147)
Trellis couching (page 147)
Vandyke chain stitch (page 139)

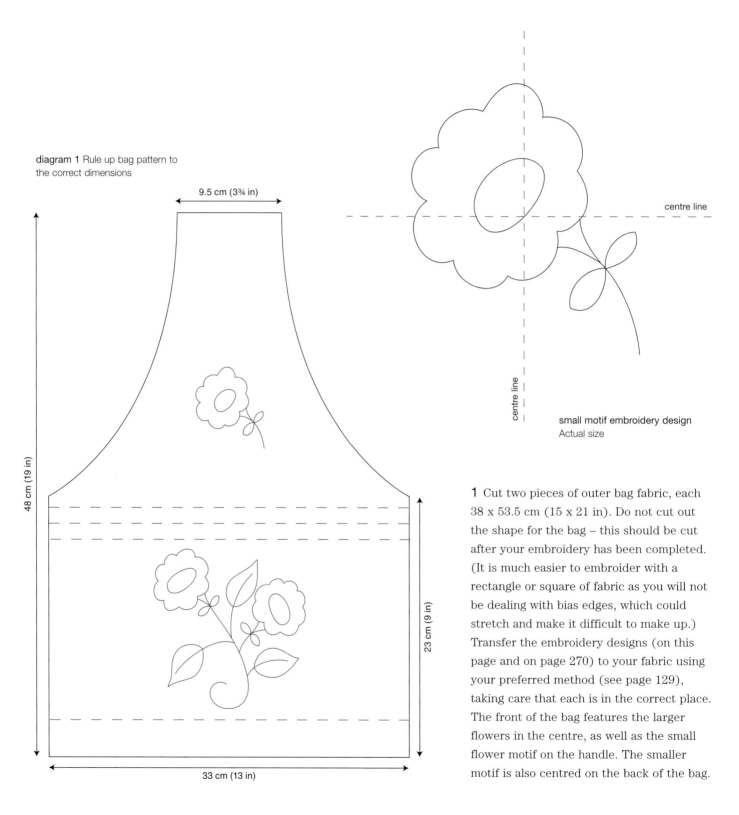

diagram 1 Rule up bag pattern to the correct dimensions

9.5 cm (3¾ in)

48 cm (19 in)

23 cm (9 in)

33 cm (13 in)

centre line

centre line

small motif embroidery design
Actual size

1 Cut two pieces of outer bag fabric, each 38 x 53.5 cm (15 x 21 in). Do not cut out the shape for the bag – this should be cut after your embroidery has been completed. (It is much easier to embroider with a rectangle or square of fabric as you will not be dealing with bias edges, which could stretch and make it difficult to make up.) Transfer the embroidery designs (on this page and on page 270) to your fabric using your preferred method (see page 129), taking care that each is in the correct place. The front of the bag features the larger flowers in the centre, as well as the small flower motif on the handle. The smaller motif is also centred on the back of the bag.

small motif embroidery guide

step three Work three rows of decorative stitching across pocket rectangle.

2 Using the embroidery guides (on this page and on page 271), work the designs in the stitches as given. Use one strand of Perlé No 8 thread throughout. Finish the embroidery by working evenly spaced, decorative rows of laced running stitch and Vandyke chain stitch on the bag Front as shown on the pattern diagram.

3 For the inner pocket, cut a 16 x 19 cm (6¼ x 7½ in) rectangle from both outer fabric and lining. Work a row of Vandyke chain stitch flanked by two rows of laced running stitch across the outer fabric rectangle. Begin the first row 4 cm (1½ in) down from the top edge and space the rows

about 1.5 cm (⅝ in) apart. After all embroidery has been completed, press on the wrong side on a well-padded surface.

4 Rule up a full-size pattern for the bag (Diagram 1). When you are sketching in the curved line of the handle, first sketch one side, then fold your pattern exactly in half lengthwise and cut along your sketched line – this way, both curves will be symmetrical. A seam allowance of 6 mm (¼ in) is included on all sides. Use the pattern to cut two Bags from the embroidered outer fabric, and two Bags from lining, keeping the pattern centred over the embroidery on both the outer Bags.

Variation

Reverse the colour scheme and work with red thread on an ecru background for a completely different effect, or do this for the lining only.

If you want a larger bag, scale up the bag measurements from Diagram 1, remembering also to scale up the corresponding embroidery designs.

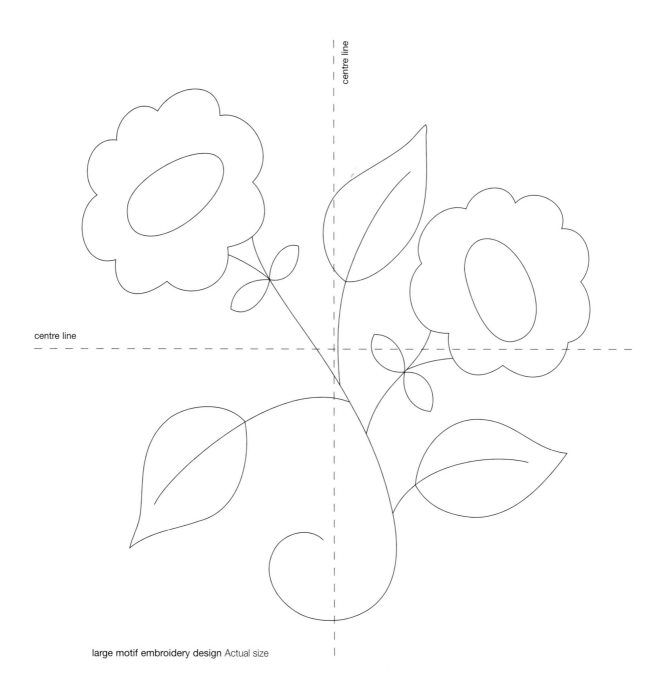

centre line

centre line

large motif embroidery design Actual size

large motif embroidery guide

detail Showing the line of even running stitch worked around curved opening edges.

5 With right sides together, stitch inner pocket rectangles to each other around the edges, allowing a 6 mm (1/4 in) seam and leaving a small opening in one side. Trim corners, turn right side out, press and slip stitch (page 134) the opening closed. Stitch pocket in place on the right side of one lining bag Front/Back, reinforcing upper corners with a double row of stitching.

6 With right sides together, stitch Bag Back and Front to each other along the sides and bottom and across the top edge of the handle. Press handle seam open. Repeat for the lining, but leave an opening in the handle seam. Press handle seam open.

7 With right sides together, stitch bag and lining to each other around curved edges. Clip around curves, taking care not to clip into stitching. Turn bag right side out through opening left in the handle of the lining – this step is a little fiddly and time consuming but it will work. Slip stitch (page 134) the opening closed.

8 Press well around curved edges. Using Perlé No 8 thread, work a line of evenly spaced running stitch around the curved opening edges, working approximately 6 mm (1/4 in) in from the edge.

Hint

If you are going to make your bag completely reversible, you should omit the inner pocket, since you don't want it on the outside of the bag where the embroidery should be. Alternatively, you could omit the smaller motif on the back of the bag and replace it with an embroidered pocket.

Persian shawl

Traditionally, an heirloom shawl like this would have been embroidered while stretched right side down, on a frame. The embroidery was worked from the back and the stretching ensured that the work would be perfectly smooth and unpuckered when it was finished. However, a frame of the size required would need a separate studio space, and creating chain stitches in reverse is rather tricky for the amateur. So this shawl is worked un-stretched, although care must be taken not to pull stitches too tightly. Embroidered in silk/cotton thread on luxurious 100% pure hand-dyed silk velvet, the design is not given as a printed pattern, but should simply grow as you work – beautiful, sinuous tendrils, covered with stylised embroidered leaves and flowers as the fancy takes you.

Materials
2.4 m x 115 cm (2¾ yds x 45 in) pure silk velvet
One hank silk/cotton embroidery thread (available in 'natural' but very easy to dye if desired)
Matching machine thread (preferably silk), for stitching completed shawl
Contrast colour thread, for basting

Tools
Crewel needle, No 9
General sewing supplies

Size
Approximately 240 x 115 cm (93½ x 45 in)

Stitches
Chain stitch (page 139)
Couching (page 140)
Running stitch (page 144)
Split stitch (page 146)
Other stitches of your choice

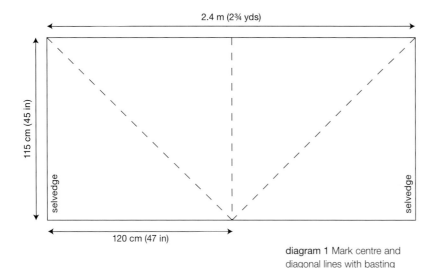

diagram 1 Mark centre and diagonal lines with basting

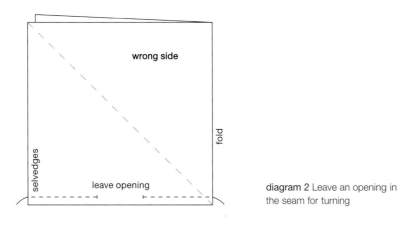

diagram 2 Leave an opening in the seam for turning

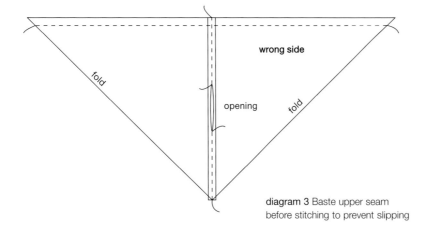

diagram 3 Baste upper seam before stitching to prevent slipping

1 Find the centre point of the velvet, that is, 120 cm (47 in) from each selvedge. Mark this line by basting with contrasting colour thread. Mark and baste the diagonal lines as well (Diagram 1).

2 While the shawl may look complex, the design is built 'freehand' on a very simple foundation – a sinuous curve stitched in chain stitch. Use the photograph as a guide to sketch in the basic curves of the design, then fill in details as you wish. Begin stitching the design in the middle triangle area of the cloth, as basted in Diagram 1. Using the diagonal and vertical markings as a guide, stitch wandering lines to left and right – these will form the 'stems' of the Persian garden shawl. Add small stems at various points on the curves.

3 Begin to add flowers and leaves using a combination of split stitch, chain stitch, couching, trellis couching, running stitch and any of the other stitches described in the stitch library.

4 Continue to add to your design, creating leaves of varying sizes and fanciful flowers based on tulips, carnations, peonies and the like. When all embroidery is finished, press the work flat from the wrong side, using a steam iron and a thick towel laid under the work so as not to squash the embroidery nor the pile of the velvet.

5 To create the lining, fold the velvet in half crosswise, right sides together, so that it forms a square. Allowing a 1.5 cm (⅝ in) seam, stitch the sides nearest the apex of the embroidered area together, leaving a 25 cm (10 in) opening in the middle of the

detail Add stylised flowers to the chain stitch stems, using stitches of your choice.

detail The design should grow organically from the apex of the triangle.

seam (Diagram 2). Now fold the work so that it forms a large triangle, with the seam you have just stitched running up the centre, from the apex. Pin and baste the top edges together, then stitch along the entire length (Diagram 3).

6 Turn right side out through centre opening and slip stitch opening closed using invisible (or very small) stitches.

Shoe bag

Whether you are travelling to a distant destination or just to the office, it's sometimes necessary to carry a change of footwear with you. A practical shoe bag such as this protects the shoes from being scratched and scuffed, and also prevents them from dirtying or damaging other items.

The bag is decorated with a richly beaded motif of an old-fashioned shoe, and embellished with a twisted cord. Make two matching shoe bags as a set for your wardrobe, make a bag to complement your luggage or simply use it as a protective cover for your favourite shoes. Alternatively, the bag, minus the embroidery, could be adapted as a book bag or as storage for craft or other items.

Materials
Evenweave fabric, or other durable, washable fabric, for bag
Lightweight fabric, for lining
Machine sewing thread to match
1 skein DMC stranded embroidery cotton, 939 (very dark navy blue)
1 skein DMC stranded embroidery cotton, 838 (very dark beige-brown)
1 skein DMC stranded embroidery cotton, 3799 (very dark pewter grey)
1 skein DMC stranded embroidery cotton, 5282 (metallic gold)
Gutermann seed beads, 603864 (metallic blue)
Silk thread for drawstring cord

Tools
Crewel embroidery needle
Machine sewing thread
General sewing supplies

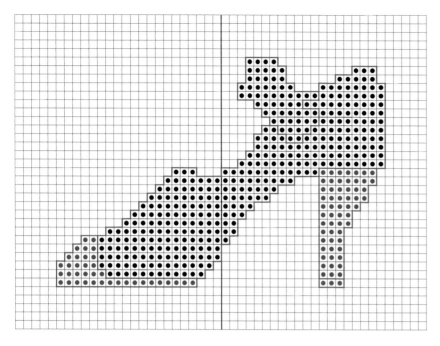

chart 1 Cross stitch and back stitch in stranded embroidery cotton

Cross stitch worked over two threads, using three strands of DMC 838 (very dark beige-brown)

Cross stitch worked over two threads, using three strands of DMC 939 (very dark navy blue)

Cross stitch worked over two threads, using three strands of DMC 3799 (very dark pewter grey)

Back stitch worked over two threads, using two strands of DMC 3799 (very dark pewter grey)

1 Cut the outer fabric and lining fabric according to the patterns and cutting instructions.

2 On one piece of outer fabric, mark the centre vertically with long running stitches in a contrasting machine sewing thread. Work the cross stitch and back stitch in stranded embroidery cotton using the colours and stitches indicated in Chart 1. Begin the cross stitching along the sole of the shoe, about 9 cm (3½ in) up from the lower edge of the fabric, centring it vertically according to the line on the chart.

3 When all the stitching from Chart 1 is completed, begin stitching from Chart 2. Work the long straight stitches in DMC 5283 (metallic gold) first, and lastly attach the seed beads where indicated.

4 With the right sides of the outer fabric together, machine around two sides (leaving small openings where indicated on Diagram 1 to allow the cord to be threaded through), and across the base. If desired, double-stitch the base for added strength.

5 Fold a hem along the top edge of the outer fabric and press to the wrong side. Turn right side out.

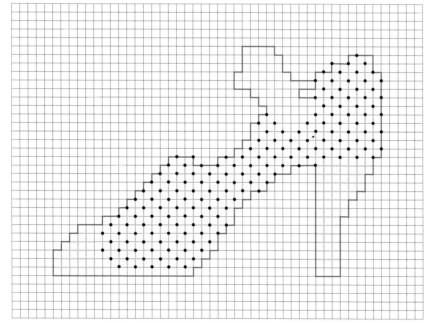

chart 2 Back stitch in gold stranded thread, and beading

Outline of shoe as worked in Chart 1

Long straight stitches worked over two threads, using one strand of DMC 5283 (metallic gold)

Placement points for seed beads, secured with 1 strand of DMC 939 (very dark navy blue)

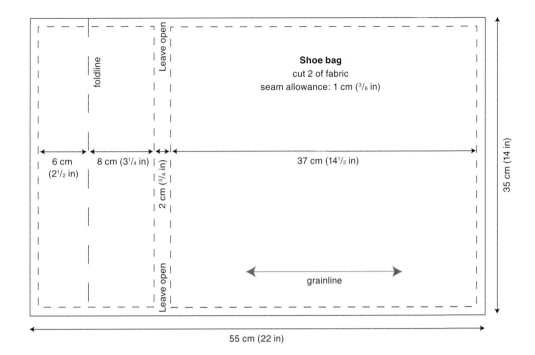

diagram 1 Cut evenweave fabric to the measurements specified

Shoe bag
cut 2 of fabric
seam allowance: 1 cm ($^3/_8$ in)

foldline

Leave open

Leave open

6 cm ($2^1/_2$ in)

8 cm ($3^1/_4$ in)

2 cm ($^3/_4$ in)

37 cm ($14^1/_2$ in)

35 cm (14 in)

grainline

55 cm (22 in)

diagram 2 Cut lining fabric to the measurements specified

6 Machine sew the lining together in the same way, remembering to leave small openings where indicated on Diagram 1 to allow the cord to be threaded through. Fold and press the hem allowance to the wrong side of the lining, then place the lining inside the shoe bag, with wrong sides together, and pin the two pieces together. Slip stitch the folded top edge of the lining to the facing of the outer fabric.

7 At the hemline, machine sew two parallel rows of stitching to thread the cord through, ensuring that they run on either side of the opening left in the side seams. Thread the cord through this casing and out through the openings in the side seams.

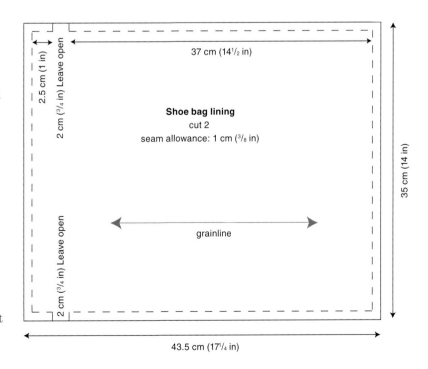

2.5 cm (1 in)

2 cm ($^3/_4$ in) Leave open

37 cm ($14^1/_2$ in)

Shoe bag lining
cut 2
seam allowance: 1 cm ($^3/_8$ in)

35 cm (14 in)

2 cm ($^3/_4$ in) Leave open

2 cm ($^3/_4$ in) Leave open

grainline

43.5 cm ($17^1/_4$ in)

Linen scarf

Stylised flowers in vibrant colours add a designer element to this striking linen scarf with a pure silk lining. It is important to use natural fibres for the outer fabric as well as the lining, so that when you need to have the scarf laundered, each fabric will react in the same way to the cleaning processes, rather than shrinking unevenly.

Materials

0.4 m x 180 cm (½ yd x 70 in) ecru embroidery linen
Matching silk fabric, for lining
Two skeins DMC Stranded Embroidery Cotton in each of the following colours: 550 (Very Dark Violet), 601 (Dark Cranberry), 907 (Light Parrot Green), 947 (Burnt Orange), 996 (Medium Electric Blue) and 3837 (Ultra Dark Lavender)
Matching machine thread

Tools

Crewel needles, No 9
General sewing supplies

Size

The scarf measures approximately 166 x 31 cm (65 x 12 in), including embroidered band, which is about 20 cm (8 in) in length.

Stitches

Chain stitch (page 139)
Colonial knot (page 140)
Feather stitch (page 140)
Straight stitch (page 147)

embroidery design
Enlarge by 200%

step two Work a single straight stitch in the centre of each chain stitch.

1 Cut a piece of linen, 35 x 25 cm (14 x 10 in). Enlarge embroidery design, at left, by 200% on a photocopier and transfer to linen using your preferred method (see page 129).

2 Following the embroidery guide, opposite, work embroidery using 3 strands of thread. For each flower, work a row of single chain stitches, working from the centre out, radiating stitches at the ends. When filling the centre with colonial knots, thread a separate needle with each of the 5 colours and work them one or two knots at a time to get a good balance of colour.

3 When embroidery is complete, press on the wrong side only, on a well-padded surface. Trim to 33 x 20 cm (13 x 8 in). Cut a rectangle of linen, 33 x 150 cm (13 x 58½ in). For flat piping, cut two linen strips, each 4 x 33 cm (1½ x 13 in). Press each strip in half lengthwise, wrong sides together. With right sides together and raw edges even, stitch a piping strip to each long edge of embroidered linen, allowing for 1 cm (⅜ in) seams. With right sides together, stitch the scarf rectangle to one piped edge of the embroidered linen. Press and topstitch by machine close to seam.

single chain
stitches 947,
filled with straight
stitch 907

single chain
stitches 3837,
filled with straight
stitch 907

colonial knots
550, 601, 907,
947, 996

single chain
stitches 601,
filled with straight
stitch 907

single chain
stitches 601,
filled with straight
stitch 907

single chain
stitches 947,
filled with straight
stitch 907

single chain
stitches 996,
filled with straight
stitch 907

feather stitch:
foundation row 3837;
second row (on top) 601

4 Cut a piece of silk lining to match scarf front (approximately 33 x 168 cm / 13 x 65¾ in). With right sides together and allowing a 1 cm (³⁄₈ in) seam, join scarf to lining around all edges, leaving an opening in one side for turning. Clip across corners, turn right side out and slip stitch (page 134) opening closed. Using a pressing cloth, press around all the edges so that seams will sit as flat as possible after turning.

Beaded cuff

This fabulous beaded cuff works as an unusual bracelet, but it could also be made in pairs to provide elegant matching cuffs for a sheer evening blouse. The secret to achieving a truly stylish look is to choose materials within a specified colour field for a sumptuous, yet subtle effect. Various shades of red look beautifully rich, but you could also choose black with very deep blue or green accents, or the soft beauty of mother-of-pearl on a cream background.

Materials
30 cm x 20 cm (12 in x 8 in) background cloth, such as cotton velveteen or corduroy (lighter fabrics will need to be reinforced with interfacing)
13–15 assorted buttons
Small glass beads in assorted sizes
Sequins
Range of threads: stranded cottons, machine sewing thread, lurex embroidery thread
Matching machine thread
Two large press-studs

Tools
Crewel needle, No 9
General sewing supplies

Size
Approximately 6 cm x 23 cm (2½ cm x 9 in), but can be varied to fit any sized wrist

Stitches
Blanket stitch (page 138)
Fly stitch (page 141)
Lazy daisy stitch (page 143)
Seed stitch (page 144)

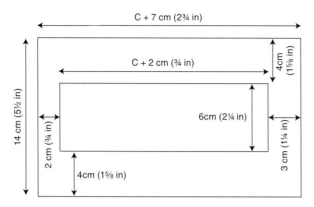

diagram 1 Dimensions for cuff and beaded area

step one Trace the outline for the beading area onto the wrong side of the cuff and baste over the traced lines.

1 Measure the circumference of wrist (C). Rule up a paper pattern, the length of which is [C + 7 cm (2¾ in)] x 14 cm (5½ in) wide. Measurements allow for 1 cm (⅜ in) seams. Rule up another rectangle, [C + 2 cm (¾ in)] x 6 cm (2¼ in) wide – the actual width and length of the beaded area. Cut out the two pattern pieces. Pin the larger rectangle to the fabric and cut out. Pin the smaller template on the larger fabric rectangle as shown in Diagram 1. Trace around the outline, then baste along the tracing line with a contrast thread to mark the working area. (If you are using interfacing, this is the area where it needs to be applied on the wrong side.)

2 Stitch buttons randomly in the working area, allowing the threads to travel across the buttons if desired, since they are decorative, not functional.

3 Working in lazy daisy stitch, create small random daisies in stranded cotton, or multiple strands of machine sewing thread. Stitch small pinwheel flowers (blanket stitch worked in a circle).

4 Stitch largest beads at random between buttons and daisies. Staying within the basted lines, keep adding beads and sequins as desired. Embellish the pinwheel flowers and daisies with smaller beads.

step three Once all the buttons are in place, add flowers randomly between them.

step six With the back seam in the centre, stitch across the short ends of the cuff.

5 Using a range of threads, including lurex, stitch small beads on top of buttons and add sequins and beads as desired. Choosing threads at random, fill any empty spaces with seed stitch or fly stitch until the surface is richly textured. When you have finished, remove the basting.

6 Bring the two long sides of the piece together with the right side of the work inside. Allowing 1 cm (3/8 in) seams, stitch along the long edge by hand or machine, leaving a 5 cm (2 in) opening in centre of seam. Finger press the seam open and position seam so that it will lie at the centre back of the tube, then stitch across both

short ends. (If stitching by machine, use a zipper foot with the needle positioned to one side to avoid crushing the beads.) You should have 2 cm (3/4 in) of unembellished fabric remaining on one end and 1 cm (3/8 in) on the other. Clip corners and turn right side out through centre back opening. Ladder stitch (page 134) the opening closed.

7 Stitch through all layers using random seed stitch (hiding the thread ends in the middle layer of the work). This will finish the unembellished ends nicely and give extra structure to the piece.

8 Sew on the press-studs to secure.

Variation

Make a collection of these pretty cuffs to use as napkin holders for special occasions.

Tissue sachet and makeup purse

This prettily embroidered toilette set has a

subdued elegance. The choice of colours for

the evenweave fabric, embroidery, ribbon and

even the lining will change the whole character

of the pieces: the lining shows through where

the threads are withdrawn for the hem stitching,

and you can also change the look by using

a matching or contrasting embroidery thread

and ribbon insertion.

Materials

32 cm (12½ in) square of 28-count evenweave
   linen in ecru (shown opposite) or mid-brown
   evenweave prairie cloth (shown on the
   following pages)

32 cm (12½ in) square of silk lining fabric
   to match the linen or prairie cloth

Stranded embroidery cotton to match
   or contrast with fabric

4 mm (³⁄₁₆ in) silk ribbon for insertion

7 mm (¼ in) clear plastic press stud

Machine sewing thread to match fabric

Tools

Tweezers

Embroidery scissors

Tapestry needle

Straw needle

General sewing supplies

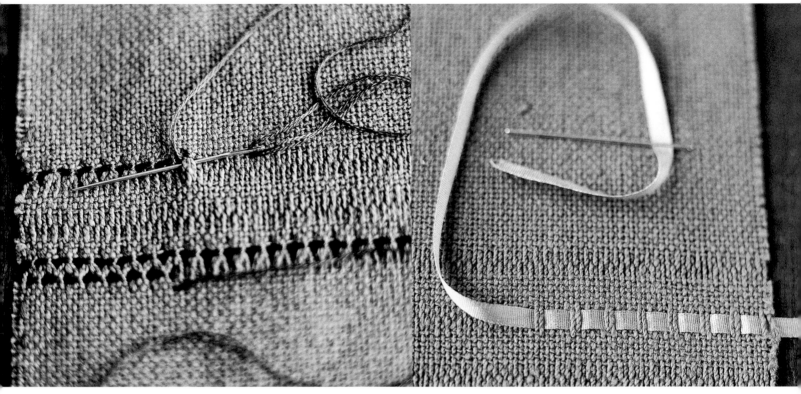

step three Work hem stitch on both sides of the withdrawn threads to form a V pattern.

step four Weave the silk ribbon through the space left by the withdrawn threads.

1 Using the patterns provided, cut one piece of evenweave fabric and one of lining fabric each for the purse and tissue sachet. Mark the fold lines and seam allowances.

2 Withdraw threads using a pair of tweezers, in the following order. For the front flap of the makeup purse, count 10 threads from the hemline of the flap and withdraw six threads; count six threads, then withdraw five threads; count another six threads, then withdraw six threads. For the tissue sachet, count eight threads from the hemline at the top and bottom and withdraw threads in the same arrangement as for the makeup purse flap.

3 Work hem stitch along both edges of the outer rows where threads have been withdrawn. Use two strands of embroidery cotton for this stitching. The hem stitch is worked by grouping four threads together across one side, then on the opposite side grouping two threads from each adjacent group to create the V-shaped effect.

4 Thread the straw needle with silk ribbon and weave the ribbon through the centre section of withdrawn threads, going under two threads, then over four threads. Ensure the ribbon lies flat as you draw it through.

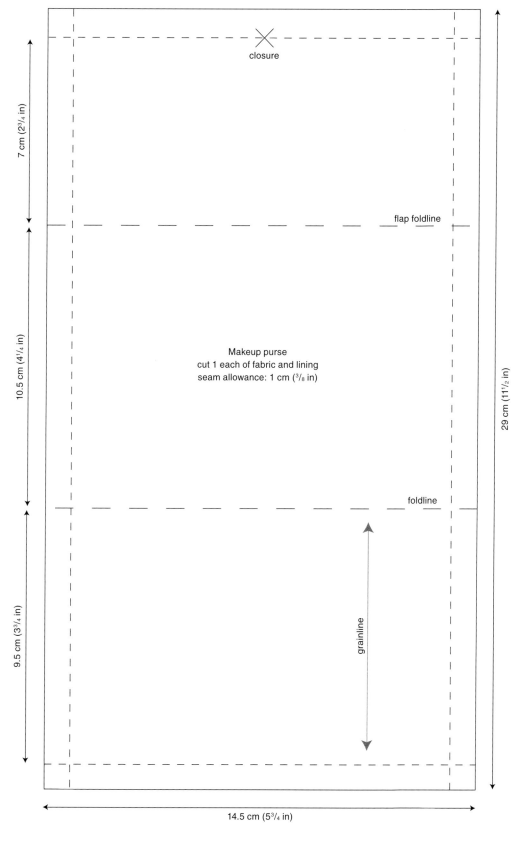

7 cm (2¹/₄ in)

closure

flap foldline

10.5 cm (4¹/₄ in)

Makeup purse
cut 1 each of fabric and lining
seam allowance: 1 cm (³/₈ in)

foldline

29 cm (11¹/₂ in)

grainline

9.5 cm (3³/₄ in)

14.5 cm (5³/₄ in)

Storing fabric

When storing fabric, whether embroidered or unworked, it is preferable wherever possible to roll rather than fold it. This is especially important if the work is going to be put away for some time; if the fabric is folded, over time the creases may become hard to remove and will also eventually weaken the fabric.

Roll the fabric with the right side inwards (if you like, roll it around the cardboard core of a roll of plastic wrap or kitchen towel for added support), and then wrap in a clean cotton cloth for extra protection. If you must fold the item — for example, if it is too large to roll — then lay a towel over the right side of the fabric and fold the two up together, as this will prevent creases. Also, make sure that the fabric is occasionally refolded along different lines.

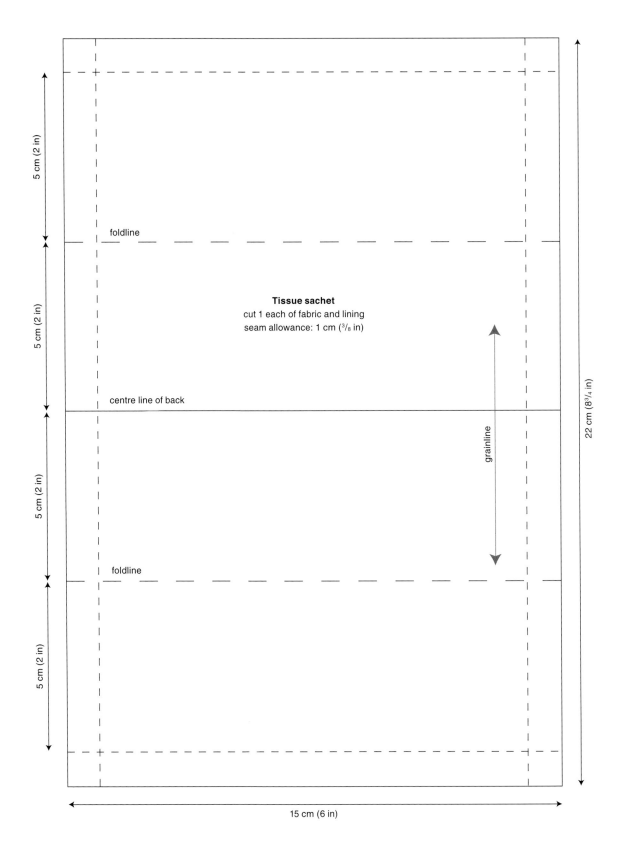

5 cm (2 in)

5 cm (2 in)

5 cm (2 in)

5 cm (2 in)

22 cm (8³/₄ in)

15 cm (6 in)

foldline

Tissue sachet
cut 1 each of fabric and lining
seam allowance: 1 cm (³/₈ in)

grainline

centre line of back

foldline

step four continued Showing one row of double hem stitching completed, the other in progress.

step five Slip stitch the lining to the evenweave fabric.

5 Finger press the seam allowances along the edges of both the linen and lining. For the makeup purse, turn under a slightly bigger hem on the lining so that it sits a millimetre or two inside the edge of the evenweave fabric when the two are placed with wrong sides together. Slip stitch the lining to the evenweave fabric around all sides and press flat from the lining side.

6 For the tissue sachet, finger press the hems at the embroidered ends only. Slip stitch the lining and the evenweave fabric together at the ends, then with right sides together, fold the ends to the middle. Pin, stitch and overlock the side seams.

7 Turn through to the right side and insert a pocket tissue pack.

8 Fold the makeup purse along the lines indicated on the pattern. The shorter end is the front flap with the embroidery on it. Press lightly from the back, using a pressing cloth to protect the fabric and embroidery. Slip stitch the side seams.

9 Attach a clear plastic press stud to the flap and the purse front to close the purse.

Hint

Silk ribbon is available from most embroidery stores in a variety of widths and colours. Its delicate sheen makes it a delight to work with. When withdrawing the threads for the ribbon insertion in this project, ensure that you withdraw enough threads for the ribbon to sit flat without bunching, but not too many, ensuring it is not held straight and secure in the weave of the fabric.

Book cover

Here is a great gift for that special someone who has everything: a lovingly embroidered slip cover for a journal, diary or sketchbook. Make it to fit a standard size, or tailor it to a particular book.

The cover can be made to look very different with just a simple change of colours, threads or fabrics. Combine a coarse hessian fabric with thick woollen threads and earthy tones, for example; or use soft linen, pearl cotton embroidery threads and pretty pastels for a traditionally feminine result.

Materials

Book to cover

Evenweave fabric for cover (the pictured example is worked on 24-count linen; see below for instructions on calculating measurements)

Fabric for lining (this can be the same as for the cover, or a contrast fabric)

DMC stranded embroidery cotton, 3371 (black-brown)

DMC stranded embroidery cotton, 3781 (dark mocha brown)

DMC stranded embroidery cotton, 3790 (ultra dark beige-grey)

DMC stranded embroidery cotton, 3782 (light mocha brown)

DMC stranded embroidery cotton, 844 (ultra dark beaver brown)

DMC stranded embroidery cotton, 310 (black)

DMC stranded embroidery cotton, 832 (golden olive)

DMC stranded embroidery cotton, 5282 (metallic gold)

DMC stranded embroidery cotton, ecru

Machine sewing thread to match fabric

Tools

Tapestry needle, No 24

General sewing supplies

Calculating measurements

Measure the height of the book; to this add 2 cm (¾ in) for seams. Measure right around the book from front cover to back; to this measurement add 12 cm (4¾ in), being 2 cm (¾ in) for seam allowances and 5 cm (2 in) at each end for facings. Cut two rectangles using these measurements, one in evenweave fabric and one in lining fabric.

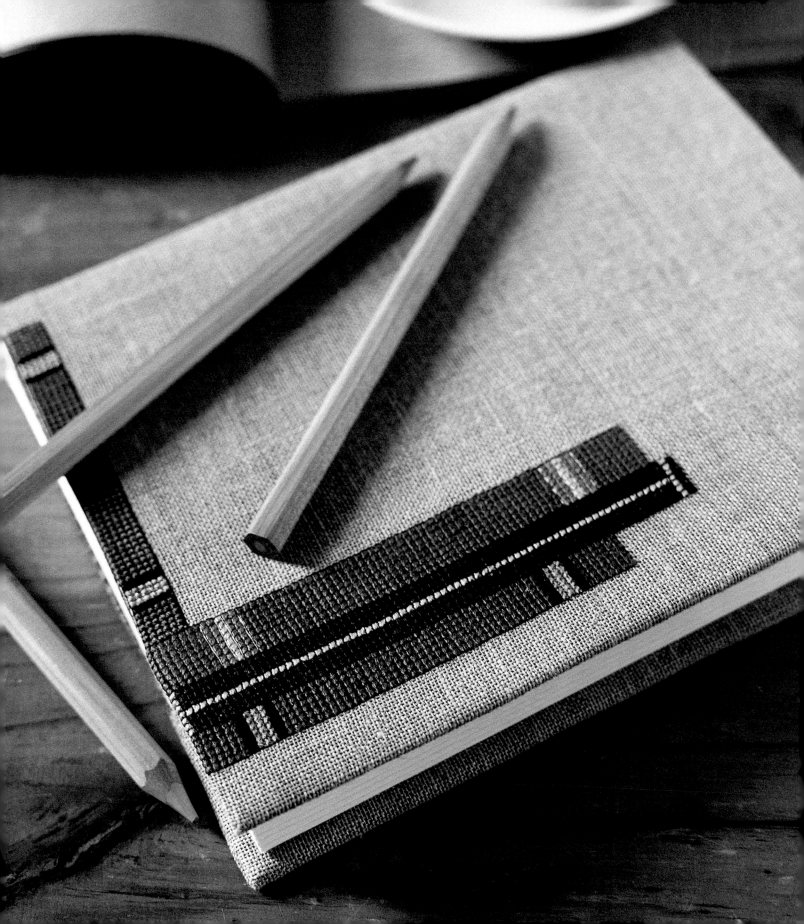

step four Place the cover and lining fabrics with right sides together and machine sew across about 15 cm (6 in) at each end of both long sides.

step four continued Once the cover is turned right side out, slip stitch the lining fabric to the cover fabric to complete the book cover.

Variation

Embroider one or more of the book motifs on a linen or Aida band to create a matching bookmark.

1 Measure the book (see page 294). On the cover fabric, draw a thread 5 cm (2 in) from each short end and 2 cm (¾ in) in from each long edge to mark the fold line for the facing.

2 Begin cross stitching 18 threads in from the right-hand drawn thread and abutting the drawn thread at the lower edge. Work the design according to the chart. Note that the book lying on its side is a repeat of the design for Book 1. Make this book shorter or longer, according to the width of the book you are covering, by adding or deleting rows of cross stitches in DMC 844 (ultra dark beaver brown) in the middle section of the embroidered book's spine.

3 With the right sides of the linen and the lining together, machine sew a 1 cm (⅜ in) seam down each short edge. Turn through and press flat. Fold back a 5 cm (2 in) facing to the wrong side and press.

4 On the long edges, fold the linen back onto itself and machine sew 1 cm (⅜ in) in from the edge for approximately 15 cm (6 in) at all four corners. Turn through to form the cover and facing.

5 Fold in the seam allowance of both cover and lining along the remaining openings. Slip stitch these openings together by hand.

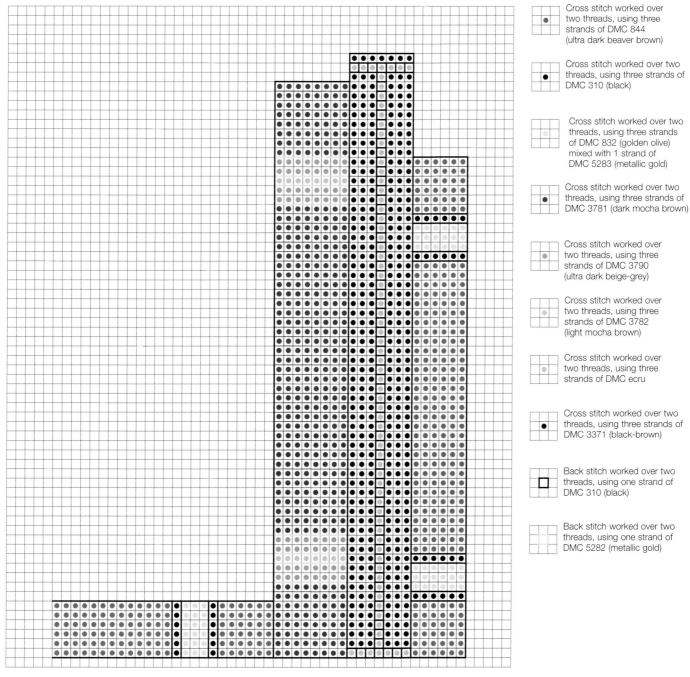

Cross stitch worked over two threads, using three strands of DMC 844 (ultra dark beaver brown)

Cross stitch worked over two threads, using three strands of DMC 310 (black)

Cross stitch worked over two threads, using three strands of DMC 832 (golden olive) mixed with 1 strand of DMC 5283 (metallic gold)

Cross stitch worked over two threads, using three strands of DMC 3781 (dark mocha brown)

Cross stitch worked over two threads, using three strands of DMC 3790 (ultra dark beige-grey)

Cross stitch worked over two threads, using three strands of DMC 3782 (light mocha brown)

Cross stitch worked over two threads, using three strands of DMC ecru

Cross stitch worked over two threads, using three strands of DMC 3371 (black-brown)

Back stitch worked over two threads, using one strand of DMC 310 (black)

Back stitch worked over two threads, using one strand of DMC 5282 (metallic gold)

Book 1 repeat   Book 3   Book 2   Book 1

Bookmarks

Embroidered bookmarks combine the pretty with the practical. Their small size makes them a quick, easy and inexpensive project. Use woven bands of evenweave fabric, as these have a flat, decorative edge finish: a hem might cause excess bulk that will ruin the binding of the book. For the same reason, do not use knots to finish your threads on the back of the fabric, but run the ends of the thread under the stitching to keep the work as flat as possible.

For each bookmark, you will need 40 cm (16 in) of banding and pearl cotton or stranded embroidery cotton (this is a useful project for using up remnants of thread from other projects). Use the fabrics and threads listed, or experiment with other combinations.

Materials
40 cm (16 in) of 5 cm (2 in) hessian band
DMC pearl cotton No 5, 304 (China red)
or
40 cm (16 in) of 5 cm (2 in) Aida band
DMC stranded embroidery thread, 839 (dark beige-brown) and 840 (medium beige-brown)
or
40 cm (16 in) of 4 cm (1½ in) linen band
DMC stranded embroidery thread, 115 (variegated garnet)

Sewing thread to match fabric (optional)

Tools
Water-soluble fabric marker
Tapestry needles

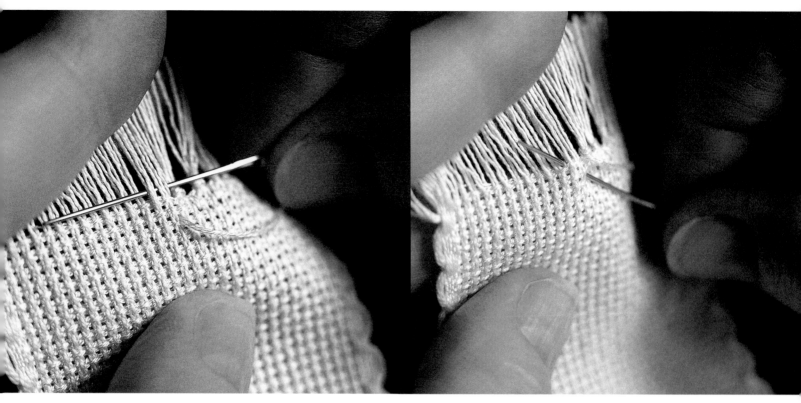

step two, hem stitch Use a matching or contrasting thread for the hem stitching, depending on the effect desired.

step two, hem stitch continued Bring the needle up after a group of threads.

Hint

A frame or hoop can still be used with pieces of fabric (such as evenweave or other bands, as in this project) that are smaller than the hoop. You will need fabric oddments of a similar weight. Cut four pieces to a size that will fit both the item to be embroidered and the frame or hoop, and baste them to each side of the embroidery fabric. Then stretch it in the hoop in the usual way.

1 Fray the bookmark for about 1 cm (⅜ in) at each end, ready to hem stitch.

2 The hem stitching (see page 142) can be done in a matching sewing thread (so it cannot be seen) or the embroidery thread that you are using for the cross stitch; or use the thread that you have withdrawn from the fabric for a slightly more visible effect than when using machine thread.

3 Using a water-soluble fabric marker, mark the placement points for the dots onto the bookmark. In the pictured examples, the dots are randomly placed. On the linen and Aida bands, the stitch groups are more

dense at one end, gradually thinning out towards the other end. On the hessian band, the stitches are evenly distributed throughout. If you prefer a more even arrangement of stitch groups, mark the dots accordingly.

HESSIAN BAND

On the hessian band, work cross stitches over four threads in pearl cotton No 5. The unevenness of the weave will cause the stitches to vary in size, giving a casual look. Work some of the stitches in two thicknesses of thread and others in a single thickness to give a varied effect.

embroidery Work groups of cross stitches over the water-soluble fabric marker dots.

These examples are worked on bands of (from left) hessian, Aida and linen, with stitches in stranded cotton or pearl cotton placed randomly.

AIDA BAND

On the Aida, work stitches over two threads using three strands of DMC stranded embroidery cotton. Two charts are given for the stitch groups; the bookmark shown in the centre of the above right photograph uses the stitch grouping shown in Chart 1. Chart 2 is given as an alternative; this design is shown in the step photograph for Step 4, above. Work some of the stitch groups in DMC 839 (dark beige-brown) and others in DMC 840 (medium beige-brown).

LINEN BAND

On the linen, work stitches over two threads using two strands of stranded

embroidery cotton, in either of the stitch patterns in Charts 1 and 2. Using a variegated cotton such as the one in the pictured example will give a gradation of colour without the need to change threads.

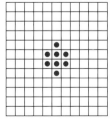

chart 1

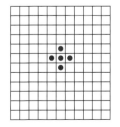

chart 2 Alternative design

Cross stitch cards

Accompanying a gift with a handmade card is
a lovely personalized touch. Blank cards are
available from craft stores, some embroidery
stores and specialty paper stores. The designs
shown are worked on evenweave fabric in a
variety of threads; you can change the type of
thread to achieve a different effect.

Secure the embroidery to the cards with fabric
adhesive or double-sided adhesive tape.

Materials

Design 1 (nappy pins)
28-count evenweave linen in ecru
DMC stranded embroidery cotton, 3799
    (very dark pewter grey)
DMC stranded embroidery cotton, 3782
    (light mocha brown)
DMC stranded embroidery cotton, 816
    (garnet)
DMC stranded embroidery cotton, 930
    (dark antique blue)

Design 2 (Aztec-style motif)
18-count evenweave linen in stone
DMC Medicis wool, 8102 (medium dark
    garnet)
DMC Medicis wool, 8306 (dark coffee brown)
DMC Medicis wool, 8307 (dark tawny)

Design 3 (floral)
28-count evenweave linen in natural
DMC broder cotton, 310 (red)

Design 4 (initial)
28-count evenweave linen in natural
The Gentle Art sampler thread, dark chocolate

Tools
Tapestry needle: No 24 for Designs 1, 3 and 4;
    No 20 for Design 2
Blank cards
Embroidery scissors
Fabric adhesive or double-sided adhesive tape
General sewing supplies

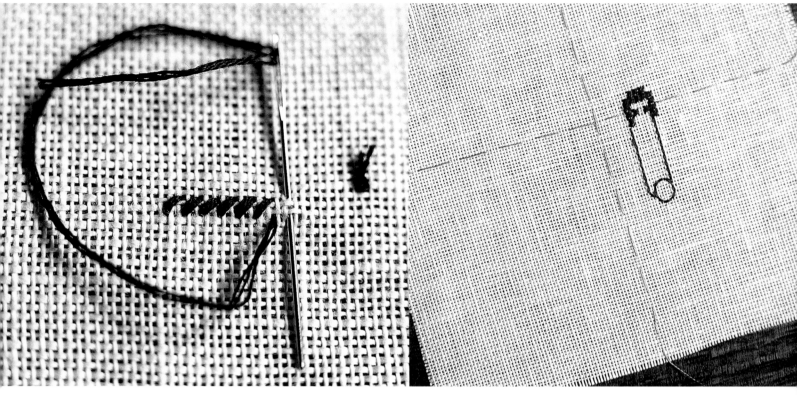

step one Work cross stitch in rows, rather than singly, wherever possible.

step two Mark the centre of the fabric with running stitch to aid in placing the embroidery accurately.

1 The cross stitches and back stitches are both worked over two threads of the fabric. Remember that it is preferable to work rows of crosses where possible, stitching a row of half crosses and then coming back to complete the crosses. Make sure all the top stitches lie in the same direction.

2 Mark the centre of the fabric in both directions with a row of running stitches in a contrasting machine thread. Match the centre of your chosen design (as marked on the charts opposite) to the intersection of the machine threads on the fabric. This allows you to centre the design neatly.

3 Following the charts, work your chosen design, extending it if desired. Start and end threads neatly on the wrong side of the fabric. If working on a pale fabric with much darker threads, ensure that the beginnings and ends of threads will not shadow through to the front of the design.

4 The finished design can be attached to the card using fabric adhesive or double-sided adhesive tape.

DESIGN 1 (NAPPY PINS)

Work the cross stitches for the pin heads in three strands of embroidery cotton, following the chart. Work the back stitch for

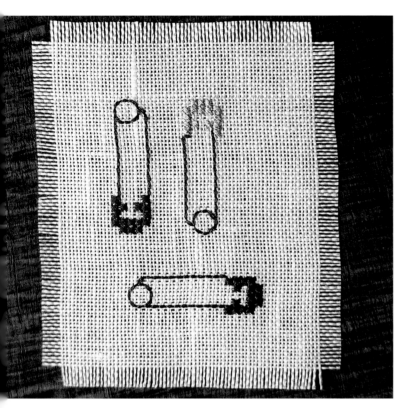

design one Work as many nappy pins as you like for this design.

Caring for work in progress

If you store your work in a wicker or cane basket, line it with woven fabric first to ensure that the ends of the strands don't catch on and pull your fabrics and threads.

Keep work in progress away away from pets and children, and always make sure your hands are clean before you begin embroidering. If you wish, apply talc to smooth your hands before working.

Avoid leaving the needle in the work, as it may rust and cause a mark that will be almost impossible to shift.

Fabric, whether worked or not, should not be stored in plastic bags, as it needs to 'breathe'.

the pin bodies using two strands of embroidery cotton in DMC 3799 (very dark pewter grey), with a No 24 tapestry needle. Work as many pins as you like.

DESIGN 2 (AZTEC-STYLE MOTIF)

Work the cross stitches in two strands of DMC Medicis wool with a No 20 tapestry needle, following the chart. This design can be repeated to create an interesting border.

DESIGN 3 (FLORAL)

Work cross stitches in one thickness of DMC broder cotton 310 (red), with a No 24 tapestry needle. Repeat the pattern as desired to create a border.

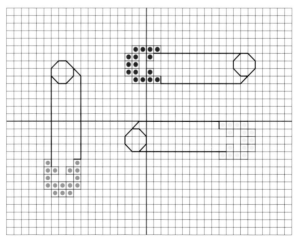

design 1 Nappy pins

Cross stitch worked over two threads, using three strands of DMC 816 (garnet)

Cross stitch worked over two threads, using three strands of DMC 3799 (very dark pewter grey)

Cross stitch worked over two threads, using three strands of DMC 3782 (light mocha brown)

Back stitch worked over two threads, using two strands of DMC 930 (dark antique blue)

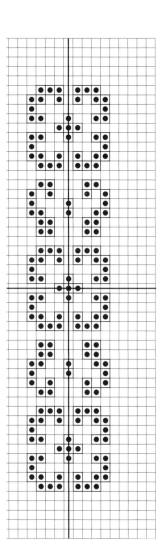

 Cross stitch worked over two threads using one thickness of DMC broder cotton 310 (red)

detail The finished Aztec-inspired motif.

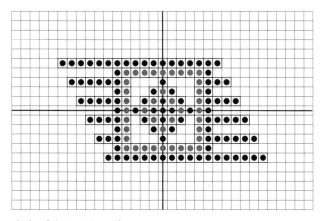

	Cross stitch worked over two threads, using two strands of DMC Medicis 8306 (dark coffee brown)

Cross stitch worked over two threads, using two strands of DMC Medicis 8306 (dark coffee brown)

Cross stitch worked over two threads, using two strands of DMC Medicis 8307 (dark tawny)

Cross stitch worked over two threads, using two strands of DMC Medicis 8102 (medium dark garnet)

design 2 Aztec-style motif

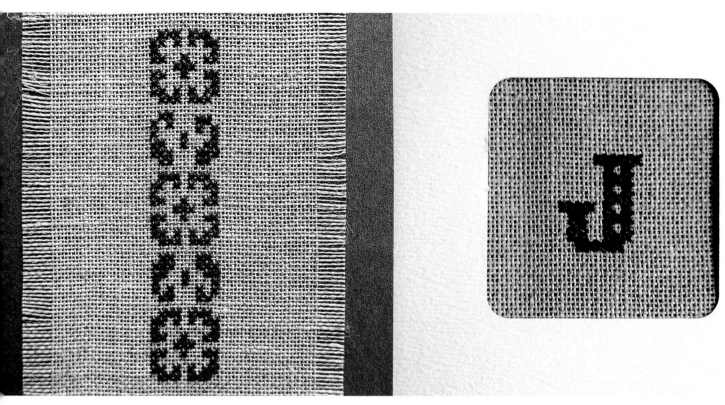

detail The finished floral motif.

detail The finished initial; the full alphabet is on page 181.

DESIGN 4 (INITIAL)

Use three strands of The Gentle Art sampler thread in dark chocolate for cross stitches, working with a No 24 tapestry needle. The design could be expanded to create several initials or an entire name, if desired. For the full alphabet, see page 181.

ASSEMBLY

When the embroidery is complete, select a blank card and trim the embroidered fabric to fit. There are several ways to attach the embroidery to a card: simply fray the edges of the fabric by drawing a few threads, and adhere the embroidery directly to the front of a plain card, or purchase a card with a ready-cut window and adhere the fabric behind the front panel so the embroidery is visible through the window. These cards usually have a flap behind the front cover to hide the back of the fabric.

Buttons

These handmade buttons, embroidered in loose cross stitches and embellished with pretty seed beads, look lovely on a simple garment. Make a set with all buttons the same, or make a mixed set for added interest. Do-it-yourself covered buttons are easy to assemble; kits for them are available from craft and fabric stores.

Materials

Fabric to cover buttons
Voile or interfacing (optional)
Do-it-yourself covered button kit
DMC pearl cotton No 5, ecru
DMC pearl cotton No 5, 840 (medium beige-brown)
Mill Hill seed beads in off-white
Machine sewing thread to match fabric

Tools

Pencil or water-soluble fabric marker
Crewel needles, various sizes
Beading needle and thread
Tack hammer (optional), for assembling buttons

step one Transfer the design onto the covering fabric.

step two Cut out circles of fabric and interfacing.

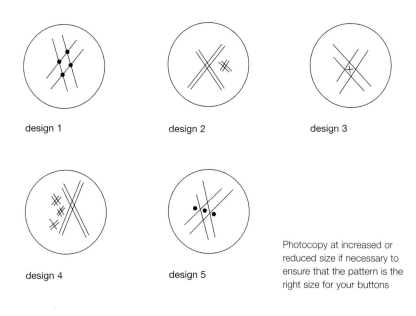

design 1

design 2

design 3

design 4

design 5

Photocopy at increased or
reduced size if necessary to
ensure that the pattern is the
right size for your buttons

1 The designs illustrated at left are stitched
on natural linen using DMC pearl cotton
No 5 in colours ecru and 840 (medium
beige-brown), adding off-white Mill Hill
seed beads last. Transfer one or more of the
designs onto your fabric using a pencil or
water-soluble fabric marker. Ensure that
you keep the entire design within a circle
the size of the buttons in your kit, and leave
enough room between each design to cut
the extra fabric required, according to the
manufacturer's instructions in the kit.

2 Cut the fabric (and voile or interfacing,
if required; see Hint, opposite) according to
the instructions provided with the button kit.

step six Work running stitch around the outer edge of the fabric circle.

step seven Gather the fabric at the back of the button and secure the thread.

3 Work loose cross stitches in pearl cotton, according to the design. If you are using more than one colour, work the darker colour first, followed by the lighter one. When starting and finishing threads, take care to do so in a manner that creates a flat result; this will ensure a better-looking button than one with lumpy knots.

4 Attach the beads as desired, using a beading needle and machine sewing thread. Beading thread can also be used.

5 Once the embroidery is complete, follow the manufacturer's instructions to make up the buttons.

6 With a needle and sewing thread, work running stitch about 3 mm (⅛ in) in from the edge of the circle of fabric. Leave the needle and thread attached to the fabric.

7 With the embroidered side of the fabric facing down, place the button in the centre of the circle. Draw up the running stitch to tightly gather the fabric at the back of the button, then secure the thread with a few back stitches. Some button kits have a backing plate: if you need to put pressure on the button to clip the pieces together, use a soft towel or a scrap of quilt batting between the button and the work surface to protect the beads.

Hint

If your fabric is lightweight or pale in colour, you may also need a layer of voile or interfacing behind it to make it opaque and to support the embroidery. If using voile or interfacing, fuse or baste the two layers together before commencing the stitching.

crochet

Introduction

The word 'crochet' is derived from the Middle French *croc* or *croche*, meaning hook, and describes a process of making fabric from thread, yarn or cord using a special type of hook. Crochet is one of the most recent textile processes. Although other woven, knitted and knotted textiles survive from early times, there are no examples of crochet as we know it today that can be dated earlier than about 1800. Other early forms of needlework produced similar results, but used quite different techniques. Crochet may have developed from tambour embroidery (in which a chain stitch was worked through fabric using a small hook) when someone realised that the chains thus formed would hold together without the background fabric.

Whatever its origins, the earliest known examples of true crochet began appearing in Europe in the early 1800s. The craft rapidly caught on, especially as a quick and easy substitute for old-style needle lace and bobbin lace designs that were much slower to produce. By the early 1840s, a huge variety of instructions for crochet was being published in England, and crochet became a thriving cottage industry in many countries. However, it was at first perceived by many as a cheap substitute for lace made by older and more expensive methods, rather than admired as a craft in its own right. This impression later lessened, in part due to the influence of Queen Victoria, who promoted the craft by buying Irish crocheted laces and even learned to crochet herself.

Even today, despite a recent resurgence in popularity, crochet is sometimes regarded as the poor relation of knitting. This is an unfortunate perception, given that crochet is easy to learn, easy and comparatively quick to do, and lends itself much better than knitting to freeform designs. Making curves and three-dimensional forms (some of them elaborate and highly sculptural), improvising shapes and working in the round are all much easier to do in crochet than in knitting.

After enormous popularity in the Victorian and Edwardian periods, crochet began to decline in the inter-war years, then to regain popularity from the 1940s onwards. In the last few years it has undergone a revival, partly due to the great variety of interesting yarns now available.

crocheted flowers Round and three-dimensional shapes such as these are easy to crochet.

Types of crochet

Some types of crochet require only a hook and yarn; in others (such as broomstick and hairpin crochet), the yarn is wound around another tool, then the crochet stitches are formed with the hook.

Broomstick crochet (also known as broomstick lace) This technique combines the use of a crochet hook and another long, slender item (traditionally a broomstick, but now more usually a thick knitting needle or a piece of craft dowel). The foundation of the piece is a chain, into which are worked loops that are then transferred to the knitting needle or dowel. Several loops are then crocheted together and slipped off the dowel, creating a soft but stable fabric.

Cro-hook This special double-ended crochet hook is used to make double-sided crochet. The hook has two ends, allowing two colours of yarn to be handled at once and freely interchanged.

Filet crochet A type of crochet consisting of filled and open meshes constructed from chain and treble crochet stitches. The way in which the filled and open meshes are arranged creates an infinity of possible patterns. It is usual for open mesh to form the background and for the pattern to be created in filled mesh. Filet crochet instructions are generally given as charts rather than words.

Hairpin crochet (also known as hairpin lace) In this technique, lace is made using a crochet hook and a small U-shaped metal loom (formerly a hairpin was used, hence the name). Yarn is wrapped around the prongs of the loom, and one crochets into the middle of the loops to create a strip of lace. The strips thus formed can then be joined to create a lightweight fabric.

Irish crochet An intricate and beautiful type of lace in which motifs are crocheted separately, laid out and tacked onto a temporary background fabric, then joined using crochet mesh. Sometimes, parts of the motifs are reinforced with cord to give extra definition. In mid-19th century Ireland, in the wake of the devastating potato famine, the craft was encouraged as a cottage industry to provide income for families that might otherwise have been destitute. Families often had their own carefully guarded designs; a unique pattern was worth more money.

Tunisian crochet (also known as Afghan crochet) In this technique, stitches are formed in two parts. Working from right to left, a loop is picked up in each stitch across the row without being worked off the hook. At the end of the row, and working from left to right, the yarn is drawn through two loops at a time, thus completing each stitch. This technique creates a dense fabric with a definite right and wrong side.

Yarns and threads

Any yarn that is suitable for knitting can be used for crochet. Yarns may be natural, synthetic or a mixture of both. Natural yarns are derived either from animals (including wool, mohair, alpaca and angora), or plants (including hemp, linen, soy silk, corn silk and bamboo). Synthetic yarns include rayon, nylon, acrylic and polyester, and are often combined with natural fibres to enhance their performance or texture. Each fibre has its own inherent characteristics, which the manufacturer may modify in various ways during processing; for example, yarns can be treated and spun to make them fluffier, denser, flatter, shinier or more twisted.

When choosing a yarn, there are several factors to consider. Beginners will find it easier to work with a smooth yarn than a highly textured one. A smooth yarn is also the best choice for an intricate pattern, as a highly textured or novelty yarn will mask the beautiful details of the piece. If you wish to use one of the many interesting textured or 'busy' yarns that are available, choose a simple stitch pattern so that the yarn itself is the focus of the finished article.

Consider also the use to which the finished item will be put. For an easy-care garment, for example, choose a machine-wash yarn; this will ensure that the garment does not felt and shrink when it is washed. Cotton also wears and washes well. Items made of delicate yarns should be gently hand-washed or, in some cases, dry-cleaned only. The ball band — the piece of paper that comes wrapped around the ball of yarn when you buy it — will tell you how the garment should be treated, as well as the composition of the yarn, the weight of the ball and the length of yarn it contains, among other things.

The terms used to describe yarns vary from country to country. The following conversion chart may be useful.

yarns and threads The term 'yarn' usually refers to thicker fibres and 'thread' to thinner ones, although the terms are sometimes interchanged. Clockwise from the top are various yarns: fine mohair, DK-weight mercerized cotton, aran-weight Tencel, aran-weight cotton, cashmere–merino mix, and alpaca. In the centre are two spools of mercerized cotton thread.

Some terms used to describe yarn refer to its content (such as wool, cashmere, cotton) and others (such as bouclé, tweed, aran) to its texture, finish and/or thickness.

Crochet uses about 30 per cent more yarn than knitting.

International yarn equivalents Note that figures given are approximate and will vary between manufacturers and individual crocheters. Tension is expressed as the number of stitches per 10 cm (4 in) over double crochet/dc (US single crochet/sc).

Weight	Australia/NZ	USA	UK and Canada	Tension	Hook
Super-fine	2 or 3-ply	Sock, fingering, baby	Lace weight, sock	21–32 sts	2.25–3.5 mm
Fine	4 or 5-ply	Sport, baby	Sport	16–20 sts	3.5–4.5 mm
Light	8-ply	Double knitting (DK), light worsted	Double knitting (DK)	12–17 sts	4.5–5.5 mm
Medium	10-ply	Worsted weight, afghan, aran	Aran	11–14 sts	5.5–6.5 mm
Bulky	12-ply	Chunky, craft, rug	Chunky	8–11 sts	6.5–9 mm
Super bulky	14-ply plus	Bulky, roving	Super chunky	5–9 sts	9 mm or larger

types of hook Fine metal hooks are used with fine cotton threads; aluminium, bamboo or plastic hooks are used with thicker yarns.

Metric	UK Yarn	UK Cotton	US Yarn	US Cotton
0.6 mm		7, 7½, 8		14
0.75 mm		6½		13
1 mm		6, 5½		11, 12
1.25 mm		4½, 5		9, 10
1.5 mm		3½, 4		7, 8
1.75 mm		2½, 3		6
2 mm	14	1½, 2		4, 5
2.25 mm	13			
2.5 mm	12	0, 1	0, 1	B, 1, 2, 3
2.75 mm				
3 mm	11	3/0, 2/0	2	C, 0
3.25 mm	10			
3.5 mm	9		3, 4	D, E
3.75 mm	–			
4 mm	8		5	F
4.5 mm	7		6	G
5 mm	6		7	
5.5 mm	5		8	H
6 mm	4		9	I
6.5 mm	3			
7 mm	2		10	J, K
8 mm	0		11, 12	L
9 mm	00		13, 15	M, N
10 mm	000		15	N, P
15 mm				P, Q

Hooks

Crochet hooks come in various sizes and materials. The thinnest hooks, used with very fine yarns, are made of steel. Larger hooks are made from aluminium, plastic or bamboo. No one material is superior to another; they are simply different, and you should use whichever material suits you better. People with arthritis, for example, may prefer plastic hooks to the colder and slightly heavier metal ones.

Crochet hook sizes are expressed differently from country to country; see the table at left. The patterns in this book give hook sizes in metric (millimetres) followed by the equivalent US and pre-metrification UK/Canadian sizes. Sometimes there will be more than one equivalent for a metric size. The hook size is often printed or stamped onto the flattened part in the middle of the hook's shaft. If not, the shaft of the hook can be inserted into the holes in a knitting-needle gauge to determine the size. Hooks vary slightly in size between manufacturers; always be guided by your tension square rather than the nominal size of the hook.

For any yarn, the size of crochet hook needed will be larger than that of the knitting needle recommended on the ball band; this is because a crochet stitch consists of three threads of fabric, unlike a knitted stitch, which comprises only two.

Other equipment

As well as hooks of various sizes, the following will be useful:

Blunt-ended wool needle Used for darning in ends of yarn and for sewing seams. Choose a needle with an eye large enough to take your chosen yarn.

Dressmaker's pins Glass-headed pins are preferable to plastic-headed ones, as they will not melt if you accidentally press them with an iron.

Knitting needle gauge Useful for measuring crochet hooks that do not have the size printed or stamped on them.

Ruler To obtain an accurate measurement when measuring a tension square, use a ruler (which is inflexible) rather than a tape measure, that may stretch or warp.

Safety pins To hold together two pieces of crochet while joining them.

Scissors A small pair with sharp points is best.

Tape measure Choose a pliable one with both metric and imperial measures.

Holding the hook and yarn

There is no one 'right' way to hold the hook or yarn; you should do so in any way that is comfortable, lets you obtain an even tension and allows the yarn to flow freely. Aim to hold the hook gently and comfortably, about a third of the way down the shaft, rather than gripping it tightly. Shown below are two common holds.

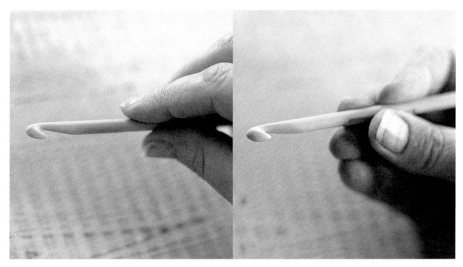

knife hold One method is to hold the hook as you would a knife.

pen hold Alternatively, hold the hook as you would a pen.

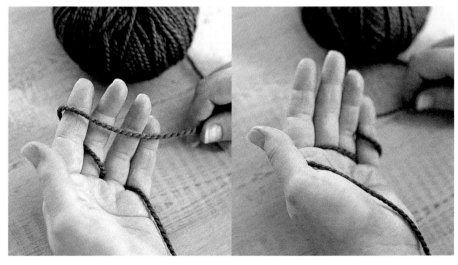

one method of holding the yarn The yarn is laced between the fingers.

alternative method The ball end of the yarn is wound around the little finger.

Holding the yarn

Holding the yarn is also a matter of personal choice and comfort. The yarn needs to flow freely and not be stretched, which may change the gauge to which it works. The way in which you hold the yarn should also be comfortable enough to be sustained through a long crocheting session; if your hands cramp up frequently, try various holds until you find one that suits you better.

Two possible methods of holding the yarn are shown below left. In the first, the yarn is run over the ring finger, under the second finger and over the index finger. In the second, the yarn is run under the middle two fingers and around the little finger.

Hints

When making loops around the hook, do so along the main part of the shaft, rather than close to the head of the hook, where the hook is narrower. If you do the latter, your stitches will be too small.

Unless otherwise instructed, the yarn is always put over the hook before being caught and pulled through. If the yarn is taken under the hook and then caught, the stitch produced will look different from that in the pattern.

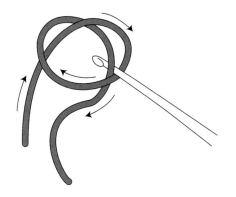

Making a slip knot

Make a loop in a length of yarn. Bring the
yarn up from back to front through the loop
and pull to tighten. You have now made
a slip knot. Place the loop on the crochet
hook. You can now begin making a crochet
chain. Remember that the slip knot is not
included when counting how many chain
stitches you have made.

The basic stitches

Crochet can be worked either flat, as shown on the following pages, or in rounds
(see page 330). When crochet is worked flat, it is turned at the end of each row;
the fabric thus produced is the same or very similar on both front and back. When
working in the round, however, the work is not turned; the same side of the work
always faces you, and the appearance of back and front will be quite different.
Usually, the flatter side is considered the 'right' side, but if you prefer the other
side, by all means use that as the front of the work.

Chain

The chain is the basis of all crochet, whether it is worked flat or in the round. The
chains worked at the start of a piece of crochet are known as foundation chain.

1 First, make a slip knot (see left) and put it onto the crochet hook.

2 Insert the hook under then over the yarn and draw the yarn through the loop
of the slip knot. You have created one chain stitch. Repeat as required.

Note When counting foundation chains, the initial slip stitch is not counted.

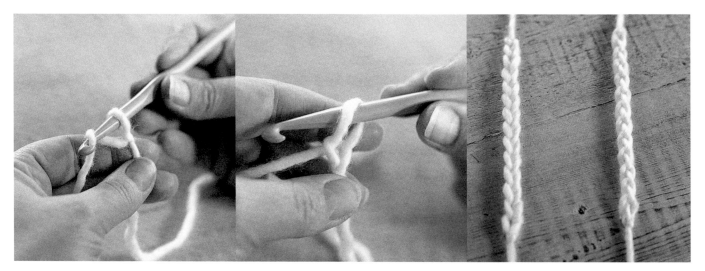

step two Insert hook under then over yarn and
draw the yarn through the loop on the hook.

the completed chain stitch Repeat Step 2
until you have the required length of chain.

back and front The front of the chain forms a
smooth series of V shapes; the back looks bumpy.

Turning chain

Chains are also used at the beginning of a row or round, to lift the hook up to the same height as the stitches that are to be worked in the next row or round. These are known as turning chain. The various crochet stitches are each of a different height, so the number of turning chain worked depends on the height of the stitch in use. You will generally need to work one chain for double crochet, two chain for half-treble crochet, three chain for treble crochet, and so on. See also Hint at right.

Chain mesh or lace

Chains are also used to make lacy patterns, or to separate one block or group of stitches from another, creating a mesh effect. To produce a series of arches, several chains are worked, then a double crochet or slip stitch is made into the row below; these steps are repeated to the end of the row.

Slip stitch

The slip stitch is essentially a chain that is worked into another stitch or another part of the fabric. It is used to join a round of crochet, and also to move the hook from one position to another, as when making motifs; it forms a barely visible link between one area and the next, particularly useful when creating lacy motifs.

Hint

When working trebles or longer stitches using yarn rather than cotton, you may find that you need one less turning chain than the pattern specifies. Work a small sample first, or experiment with your tension swatch. Should working the specified number of turning chain result in a curved edge or a small hole at the beginning of a row, try working one less turning chain to see if the effect is better.

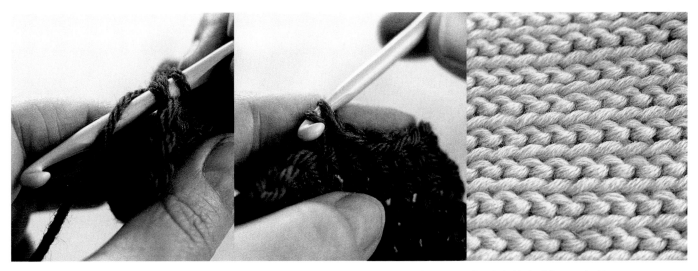

slip stitch Insert the hook into the fabric, then catch the yarn with the hook.

slip stitch, continued Draw the yarn through both the fabric and the loop on the hook.

slip stitch fabric When worked in rows or rounds, slip stitch creates a very dense fabric.

Double crochet

Double crochet (dc) — known in the United States as single crochet (sc) — produces a fabric that is firm, dense and stable, yet also flexible. When worked in rows, as shown right, a distinct horizontal pattern is created.

When working in double crochet, the number of foundation chain should equal the number of stitches required, plus one for the turning chain. Hold the chain with the smooth side facing you.

1 Insert the hook from front to back through the second chain from the hook, picking up two strands of chain. Wrap the yarn over the hook (yoh).

2 Draw the yarn through the chain to the front; there will be two loops on the hook. Wrap yarn over hook again.

3 Draw the yarn through both loops on the hook. You have now completed one double crochet stitch. One loop will remain on the hook.

4 Repeat Steps 1 to 3 to the end of the row, working one double crochet into each chain. At the end of the row, turn and work 1 turning chain; this counts as one stitch, so the first double crochet of the second row is worked into the second stitch of the previous row.

5 When working back along the row, insert the hook under both loops of each stitch in the previous row.

step one Insert the hook into the second chain from the hook, then wrap the yarn over the hook.

step two Draw the yarn through the chain (two loops on hook). Wrap the yarn over the hook again.

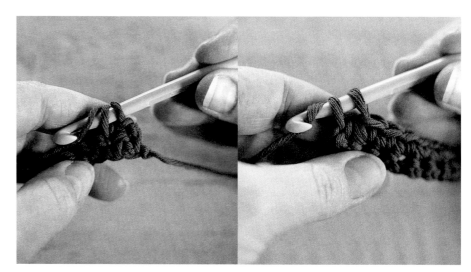

start of second row Turn, work 1 turning chain, insert hook in second stitch of previous row.

last stitch of a row This is worked into the turning chain at the start of the previous row.

Half treble crochet

Half treble crochet (htr) — known in the United States as half double crochet (hdc) — produces a fabric that is flexible, yet less dense than double crochet. When working in half treble crochet, the number of foundation chain should equal the number of stitches required, plus two for the turning chain. Hold the chain with the smooth side facing you.

1 Wrap the yarn over the hook and insert the hook into the third chain from the hook, picking up two strands of chain. Wrap the yarn over the hook.

2 Draw the yarn through the chain to the front; there will be three loops on the hook. Wrap the yarn over the hook again.

3 Draw the yarn through all three loops on the hook. You have now completed one half treble crochet. One loop will remain on the hook.

4 Repeat Steps 1 to 3 to the end of the row, working one half treble crochet into each chain. At the end of the row, turn and work two turning chain; these count as one stitch, so the first half treble crochet of the second row is worked into the second stitch of the previous row.

5 When working back along the row, insert the hook under both loops of each stitch in the previous row.

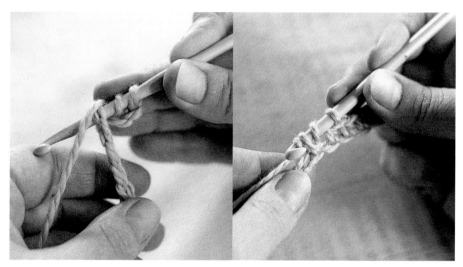

step one Wrap the yarn over the hook and insert it into the third chain from the hook.

step two Draw yarn through chain (three loops on hook), then wrap the yarn over the hook again.

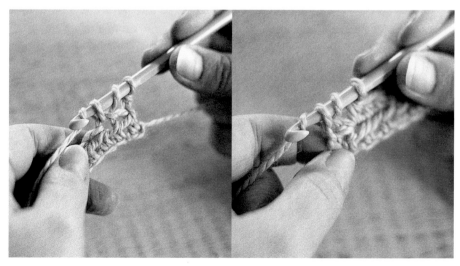

start of second row Work 2 turning chain, yarn over hook, insert hook into second stitch.

last stitch of a row This is worked into the top of the turning chain at the start of the previous row.

Treble crochet

Treble crochet (tr) —known in the United States as double crochet (dc) — produces a flexible, slightly open fabric. When working in treble crochet, the number of foundation chain should equal the number of stitches required, plus three for the turning chain. Hold the chain with the smooth side facing you.

1 Wrap the yarn over the hook and insert the hook into the fourth chain from the hook, picking up two strands of chain. Wrap the yarn over the hook.

2 Draw the yarn through the chain to the front; there will be three loops on the hook. Wrap the yarn over the hook again.

3 Draw the yarn through two loops on the hook. Wrap the yarn over the hook again and then draw it through two more loops. You have now completed one treble crochet stitch. One loop will remain on the hook.

4 Repeat Steps 1 to 3 to the end of the row, working one treble crochet into each chain. At the end of the row, turn and work three turning chain; these count as one stitch, so the first treble crochet of the second row is worked into the second stitch of the previous row.

5 When working back along the row, insert the hook under both loops of each stitch in the previous row.

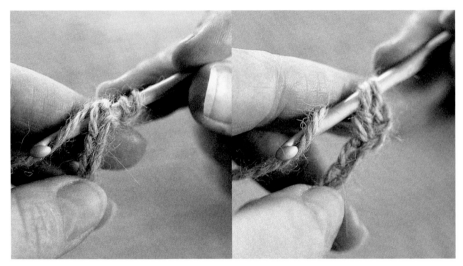

step one Wrap yarn over hook, insert it in third chain from hook, and wrap yarn over hook again.

step two Draw yarn though chain, yarn over hook, draw yarn through two loops on hook, yarn over hook.

end of first row At the end of the row, work three turning chain.

end of subsequent rows Work the last stitch of a row into the top of the turning chain.

Double treble

Double treble crochet (dtr) — known in the United States as treble crochet (tr) — is usually used in combination with other stitches rather than to form a fabric on its own.

When working in double treble crochet, the number of foundation chain should equal the number of stitches required, plus four for the turning chain.

1 Wrap the yarn over the hook twice and insert the hook into the fifth chain from the hook, picking up two strands of chain. Wrap the yarn over the hook.

2 Draw the yarn through the chain to the front; there will be four loops on the hook. Wrap the yarn over the hook again.

3 Draw the yarn through two loops on the hook, *wrap yarn over hook and draw it through two more loops.* Repeat from * to * once. You have now completed one double treble stitch. One loop remains on the hook.

4 Repeat Steps 1 to 3 to the end of the row, working one double treble crochet into each chain. At the end of the row, turn and work four turning chain; these count as one stitch, so the first double treble of the second row is worked into the second stitch of the previous row. Work the last stitch of each row into the the top of the turning chain of the previous row.

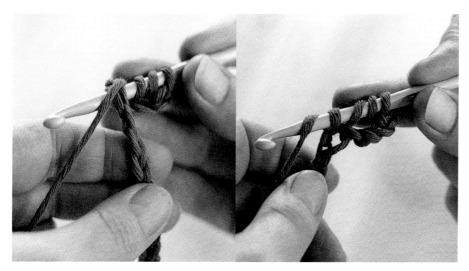

step one Yarn over hook twice, insert hook into fifth chain from hook, yarn over hook.

step two Draw the yarn through the chain to the front. Wrap yarn over hook.

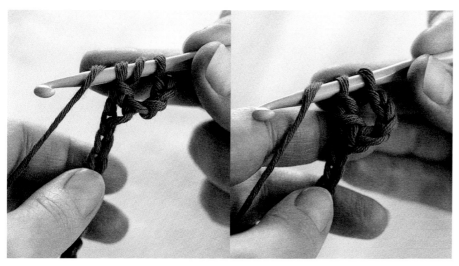

step three Yoh and draw through two loops on hook. Repeat once.

step three, continued Yoh and draw through two loops on hook.

Triple treble

Triple treble crochet (trtr) is known in the United States as double treble crochet (dtr). When working in triple treble crochet, the number of foundation chain should equal the number of stitches required, plus five for the turning chain.

1 Wrap the yarn over the hook three times, then insert the hook into the sixth chain from the hook. Draw the yarn through the chain to the front.

2 *Yarn over hook, draw through two loops on hook*, repeat from * to * until only one loop remains on hook.

3 At the beginning of each row, turn, then work five turning chain. At the end of each row, work the last stitch into the top of the turning chain at the beginning of the previous row.

2 *Yarn over hook, draw through two loops on hook*, repeat from * to * until only one loop remains on the hook.

3 At the beginning of each row, turn, then work six turning chain. At the end of each row, work the last stitch into the top of the turning chain at the beginning of the previous row.

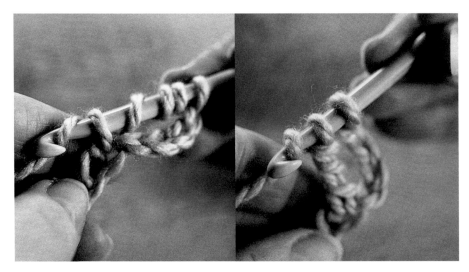

triple treble, step one Yoh three times, insert hook into sixth chain, draw yarn through.

triple treble, step two (Yoh, draw through two loops on hook) until only one loop remains.

Quadruple treble

Quadruple treble crochet (qdtr) is known in the United States as triple treble crochet (trtr). When working in quadruple treble crochet, the number of foundation chain should equal the number of stitches required, plus six for the turning chain.

1 Wrap the yarn over the hook four times, then insert the hook into the seventh chain from the hook. Draw the yarn through the chain to the front of the work.

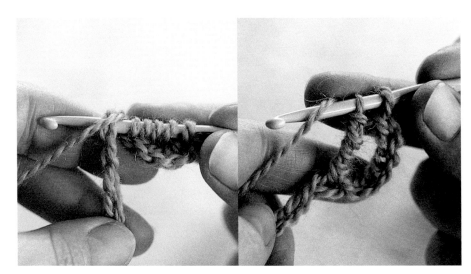

quadruple treble, step one Yoh four times, insert hook into seventh chain, draw yarn through.

quadruple treble, step two (Yoh, draw through two loops on hook) until only one loop remains.

Working groups of stitches

Working a number of stitches together produces a group (also known as a cluster). Groups can be utliized with any of the longer stitches (half treble crochet and up). They can be worked all in one type of stitch, or in a combination.

Each stitch of the group is worked until two loops remain on the hook (rather than the usual one loop). The last step of the last stitch of each group is to draw the yarn through all the loops on the hook, thus gathering the tops of all the stitches together.

Groups can be worked into a chain loop or chain space (as shown in blue yarn in the photographs at left), or into a single stitch. Alternatively, each successive stitch of the group can be worked into a separate stitch of the previous row (as shown in pink yarn). Groups are usually separated from each other with a number of chain, as shown.

1 Using the required stitch type, work a stitch until two loops remain on the hook. Repeat until you have worked the required number of stitches for that group.

At the end of this step, there should be one more loop on the hook than there are stitches in the group (for example, if working a group of four stitches as at left, you will end up with five loops on the hook).

2 Wrap the yarn over the hook and draw the yarn through all the loops on the hook. You have now completed one group.

3 Work the required number of chains to separate the group from the next.

4 Repeat Steps 1 to 3 as required.

working into a chain loop Here, each group consists of four treble crochet stitches.

last step of last stitch yoh and draw the yarn through all the loops on the hook.

working into successive stitches Work one stitch into each stitch of the previous row.

Increases

To make an internal increase along a row, work to where the increase is required, then work two or more stitches into the same stitch. To shape garment edges neatly, this method is used one stitch in from the edge at the beginning or end of a row. At the beginning of a row, work the first stitch, then work the increase in the next stitch. At the end of the row, work until two stitches remain, work the increase in the second-last stitch, then work the last stitch.

To make an external increase at the start of a row, work the required number of chains at the end of the previous row (remember to include the turning chain), then turn and work along the row as usual. At the end of a row, leave the last few stitches unworked. Remove the hook, join a length of yarn to the last stitch of the row, and work the required number of extra chains (remember to include the turning chain). Fasten off. Insert the hook back into the row, complete the row, then work the extra stitches along the chain.

Shaping techniques

A piece of crochet is shaped by increasing or decreasing. Increases are made by working two or more stitches into the same stitch of the previous row. Decreases are made by skipping stitches, or by working two or more stitches together. These shapings are described as 'internal' when made along a row, and 'external' when made at the beginning or end of a row. Each method produces a different effect.

internal increase along a row Work two or more stitches into the same stitch.

internal increase at edge of crochet Work the increase one stitch in from the edge.

external increase at start of row Work extra chain at end of previous row, turn, then work along row.

external increase at row end, step one Join in yarn and work required number of extra chains.

external increase at row end, step two Reinsert hook into row and work to end of chain.

Decreases

To decrease, skip one or more stitches when working across the previous row (which creates a small hole in the fabric), or work two or more stitches together. To do this, work to where the decrease is required, then work a partial stitch by working it until two loops remain on the hook. Work another partial stitch until a total of three loops remain on the hook. Wrap the yarn over the hook and draw it through all three loops on the hook. You have now decreased one stitch. To decrease two stitches at once, work three partial stitches (four loops will remain on the hook), then wrap the yarn over the hook and draw it through all four loops.

To work an external decrease at the start of a row, simply slip stitch across the number of stitches to be decreased. Work the turning chain, then continue across the row. For an external decrease at the end of a row, stop several stitches before the end of the row, then turn, work the turning chain and continue back across the row.

internal decrease along a row, method one
Skip one or more stitches in the previous row.

internal decrease along a row, method two
Work two or more stitches together.

external decrease at start of row Slip stitch across the required number of stitches.

external decrease at start of row, step two Work the turning chain, then continue across the row.

external decrease at end of row Stop several stitches before end of previous row, then turn.

Making and working into a ring

To make a ring, work the specified number of chain, then insert the hook into the first chain that you made and join with a slip stitch. Wrap the yarn over the hook and draw it through both the chain and the loop on the hook. You have now created a ring of chains. This becomes the centre of your crochet and is what you will work into to create the first round.

To commence the first round, make the appropriate number of turning chain. Insert the hook from front to back into the ring (not into the chain) and work the number of stitches specified in the pattern. At the end of the round, join the round by working a slip stitch into the top of the starting chain that you made at the beginning of the round.

At the end of the last row of the shape or motif, join the round with a slip stitch. Cut the yarn, leaving a tail, then draw the tail of yarn through the loop left on the hook. Pull the yarn firmly to fasten off.

Working in rounds

Crochet can easily be worked in the round to create many different shapes and motifs, both simple and elaborate. All pieces worked in the round begin with a short length of chain joined to form a ring. Successive rounds are formed from combinations of stitches and chain spaces or chain loops. The piece is worked in rounds rather than back-and-forth rows, and is never turned; the right side always faces you.

joining chain to form a ring Make a slip stitch into the first chain that you made.

working first round Work all the stitches of the first round into the centre of the ring.

end of first round Join round with a slip stitch into top of first stitch (or into the turning chain).

second round Chain loops form the foundation for the third and final round.

finished motif A simple but effective openwork flower in crisp aran-weight cotton.

Measuring tension (gauge)

Tension, or gauge, refers to the number of stitches and rows to 2.5 cm (1 in) over the crocheted fabric. Every crochet pattern will specify a gauge; always pay attention to this, as the gauge determines the size of the finished item. Every person crochets at a different tension; some people crochet loosely and others tightly. Tension may not be crucial in, say, a scarf or cushion, but it is crucial in a garment that is meant to fit precisely. It is vital to check your tension before beginning a garment. In your eagerness to get started on a project it is tempting to skip this step, but crocheting a tension swatch may prevent the disappointment, and the waste of time and money, of a garment that does not fit.

Crocheting a tension square

The first step in every crochet project should be a tension square. Use the specified hook size and the yarn that you intend to use, whether it is the yarn recommended in the pattern or a replacement. Make a crochet chain about 15 cm (6 in) long, then work in the specified stitch until the piece is at least 15 cm (6 in) long. If the pattern is constructed from motifs, you will need to make one whole motif as instructed, then measure its diameter.

Fasten off the yarn and, if appropriate, block (see page 335) or lightly press the tension square. Insert a pin a few stitches in (do not measure from the sides, as the side edge is always slightly distorted). Avoid stretching the tension square. Measure precisely 10 cm (4 in) from the pin and place another pin at that point as a marker. Do the same vertically, placing the first pin a few rows in from the edge. Count how many stitches and rows there are between the pins; this is your tension.

If the counts are correct, go ahead and start crocheting the item. If you have more stitches than the specified tension, you are working too tightly, and your garment will be too short and too narrow. Make another tension square with a slightly larger hook, and measure again. If you have fewer stitches than specified, you are working too loosely, and your garment will be too long and too wide. Make another tension square with a slightly smaller hook, and measure again. If necessary, repeat this process more than once, until the tension is correct.

Save your tension square and use it to test how well the yarn washes and whether it can be pressed. Pin the ball band to the square, and note on the ball band if you changed the hook size to obtain the correct tension. You now have a reference for the yarn used, and for how the crocheted fabric looks and feels.

tension squares These two tension squares were crocheted by the same person, in the same 8-ply (DK) yarn, but with different-sized crochet hooks. The purple square was made using a 4.5 mm crochet hook and the blue one with a 5 mm hook. The size difference is clear even over such a small sample; over a large item or a garment, the consequences of using the incorrect tension can be ruinous.

measuring a tension square Using pins, and an inflexible ruler rather than a tape measure, mark two points precisely 10 cm (4 in) apart and count the number of stitches between the pins.

Reading diagrams

The written pattern for the motif shown below reads as follows:

Make 5ch, join with ss to form a ring.

Round 1: 1ch, 8dc into ring, ss into ch at beg of rnd.

Round 2: 3ch, (ss into next dc, 3ch), rep to end, ss into 1st ch sp at beg of rnd.

Round 3: 2ch (counts as 1htr), (2tr, 1htr) into same ch sp as ss, *(1htr, 2tr, 1htr) into next ch sp*, rep from * to * to end, ss into base of 2ch at beg of rnd.

Floral motif This motif can be made by following either the instructions above or the diagram below.

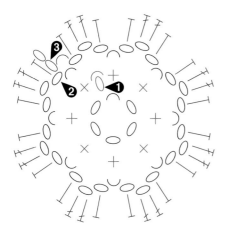

diagram of motif See opposite for a key to the symbols used.

Working from a pattern

Crochet patterns can be either written in words or represented by symbols. A beginner may feel safer using a written pattern. However, as you become more adept at crochet, or when tackling large or complicated motifs, working from a diagram may be preferable. A diagram is a visual representation of the motif or pattern, with the symbols used replicating the stitches; as such, the diagram will show how the motif or pattern should look in a way that words cannot.

The pattern will tell you which yarn and hook size to use, the tension required and the size of the finished item. For a garment with more than one size, instructions for the smallest size are given first and those for larger sizes in parentheses.

Before you begin crocheting, it is vital to work a tension square (see page 331). You should also read through the pattern and make sure you understand all the abbreviations used. If the pattern uses an unfamiliar stitch, practise the stitch on a small test swatch first; it is less time consuming and frustrating to have to pull back and redo a small piece than a large one. If using a multi-size pattern, read right through the pattern and highlight the figures that relate to the size you are making.

Differences in terminology

Different regions use different terms for crochet; confusingly, sometimes the same term is used for a different stitch. The following chart may help. When choosing a pattern, first determine where it was published (this will be stated on the pattern) and then adjust the instructions if needed. Any differences in terminology will be of little concern if you are working from a diagram rather than a written pattern.

Australia/New Zealand/UK	United States
slip stitch	slip stitch
double crochet (dc)	single crochet (sc)
half treble (htr)	half double crochet (hdc)
treble (tr)	double crochet (dc)
double treble crochet (dtr)	treble crochet (tr)
triple treble crochet (trtr)	double treble crochet (dtr)
quadruple treble (qdtr)	treble treble (trtr) or long treble (ltr)
tension	gauge

Symbols

⬭ chain

⌒ slip stitch

+ double crochet

┬ half treble

Ŧ treble

Ŧ double treble

Ŧ triple treble

Ŧ quadruple treble

⋏ tr2tog

⋏ tr3tog

⋎ inc 1tr

⌒⌒ 2 half-treble group

⋔ 3 half-treble group

⋔ 4 half-treble group

⋔ 3 treble group

⋔ 3 double-treble group

⋔ 3 triple-treble group

⋔ 3 quadruple-treble group

● bead

⬥ beaded chain

⬦ beaded double crochet

⬭ bouclé loop stitch

⬭ solomon's knot

▸2 number of row/round showing direction in which you work from one row or round to the next

Abbreviations

Abbreviations are used extensively in crochet patterns to save space. Not all publications will use the same abbreviation for the same term, so read through the pattern to familiarize yourself with what each abbreviation means. Be aware that terminology differs between regions; for example, what is known as dc (double crochet) in Australia, New Zealand and the United Kingdom is called sc (single crochet) in the United States. This book uses the Australian, New Zealand and United Kingdom terminology. See opposite for some common US equivalents.

3tr group three-treble group (three incomplete treble stitches worked into one stitch before the yarn is drawn through all remaining loops on hook)

4tr group four-treble group (four incomplete treble stitches worked into one stitch before the yarn is drawn through all remaining loops on hook)

alt alternate

b/ch beaded chain

b/dc beaded double crochet

beg begin/beginning

bet between

blk block

ch chain

ch loop chain loop

ch sp chain space

cl cluster

cm centimetre(s)

col(s) colour(s)

cont continue

dc double crochet (US single crochet/sc)

dc2tog decrease 1 dc over 2 sts

dc3tog decrease 1 dc over 3 sts

dec decrease/decreasing

DK double knitting

dtr double treble

dtr group double treble group

g gram(s)

gr group

htr half treble

htr group half treble group

in inch(es)

inc increase/increasing

include include/including

lp(s) loop(s)

MC Main Colour

mm millimetre

pc picot

patt pattern

prev previous

qdtr quadruple treble

qdtr group quadruple treble group

rem remain(s)/remaining

rep repeat(s)/repeated

rnd round

RS right side(s) of work

sp(s) spaces(s)

ss slip stitch

st(s) stitch(es)

tog together

tr treble

tr group treble group

tr2tog decrease 1 tr over 2 sts

tr3tog decrease 1 tr over 3 sts

trtr triple treble

WS wrong side(s) of work

yoh yarn over hook

Finishing techniques

Crocheted pieces may be joined with sewn or crocheted seams. Each has its advantages and disadvantages, so choose the most appropriate seam for the item you are making. The pattern will generally tell you which type of seam is preferred. Sewn seams are less visible than crocheted seams, but they stretch more; they are generally best avoided in any crocheted piece that has a tendency to drop.

Oversewn seam

This method produces a very flat seam. Place the two pieces to be joined on a flat surface, with right sides up and edges aligned. Insert a large, blunt-ended needle through corresponding stitches in both pieces. The seam can be sewn through both loops of the stitch, or the back loop only.

Backstitch seam

This method produces a strong but non-elastic seam. Hold the two pieces to be joined with right sides facing. Using a large blunt-ended needle, secure the yarn by passing it around the end of the seam twice. On the next stitch, pass the needle around the back of the work and through the second stitch to the front. Pass the needle one stitch to the right, then through the fabric from the front to the back. Bring it out two stitches along and repeat for the length of the seam. (Note that stitches on the back of the fabric travel forwards and those on the front of the fabric travel backwards.)

Woven seam

Lay the pieces flat, right sides up and edges aligned. Start at the bottom and work in a ladder fashion (first from left to right, then right to left), passing the yarn through the loops of corresponding stitches. Pull the yarn tight every 2.5 cm (1 in) or so.

oversewn seam, step one Sew through loops of corresponding stitches on each piece.

oversewn seam, step two The finished seam is flat but slightly visible.

backstitch seam A backstitch seam is very sturdy, but less flexible than a crocheted seam.

woven seam When stitched in the same colour as the garment, a woven seam is almost invisible.

Crocheted seams

A crocheted seam is more visible than a sewn one, but will have a similar degree of elasticity to the rest of the item.

Crocheted seams can be worked with the right sides or the wrong sides of the pieces together, depending on the effect you wish to create. If worked with the wrong sides together, the finished seam will be visible on the right side of the item. A visible seam can be a feature on, for example, a cushion or rug (especially if worked in a contrasting colour), but may be undesirable on the outside of a garment. If in doubt, try out both methods to see which you prefer.

Double crochet seam

Hold the pieces together, having the edges even. Join in the yarn. Inserting the hook through both loops of both corresponding stitches on each side, work in double crochet for the length of the seam. If joining rows of motifs, as for a rug, join all the motifs in one direction first, then work the seam in the other direction.

Slip stitch seam

For a slightly less raised seam (not pictured), join the two pieces with slip stitch rather than double crochet.

double crochet seam, step one Work double crochet through both loops of each stitch.

double crochet seam Double crochet produces a strong, visible, raised seam.

Blocking and pressing

Blocking and pressing are methods of shaping a finished piece of crochet. They are not always necessary; check the pattern instructions, and also the yarn's ball band. Blocking and pressing are often required for crocheted lace or motifs, as they improve stitch definition and give a better shape. The extra effort required to block and press a piece is small, and will give your work a professional-looking finish.

Blocking should be done before sewing seams. To block, lay a clean, colourfast towel or sheet on a padded surface such as carpet. Lay the item to be blocked on top of this and pin it out to size, easing and gently stretching where necessary and making sure the sides and ends are completely straight.

For natural fibres such as wool or cotton, set the iron on a steam setting and hold the iron about 2.5 cm (1 in) above the farbric and allow the steam to penetrate for several seconds. Work in sections, without allowing the iron to touch the crochet. Allow to dry before removing the pins.

Pieces made from synthetic yarns should not be pressed; they will go limp, or in some cases melt. Instead, pin as described above, then spray lightly with cold water and leave to dry completely before removing the pins.

When the pins are removed, a blocked piece should be flat, be the correct size, and have clearly defined stitches.

Hints

It is important, when working an edging, to space the stitches evenly so that the edge of the crocheted piece remains flat. When working an edging on a solid fabric, such as one made entirely of double crochet or treble crochet, simply work one edging stitch into each stitch along the top and bottom edges of the fabric. When working along the side edges of such fabric, or on a lacy or openwork fabric, you may need to experiment with the spacing of the edging stitches; working too few stitches will draw in the edge of the fabric, and too many stitches will produce a wavy edge.

At the end of the final row or round of any piece of crochet, cut the yarn, leaving a tail of 10–15 cm (4–6 in) — or longer if you are intending to use the tail for seaming — then draw the tail of yarn through the loop left on the hook. Pull the yarn firmly to fasten off.

Edgings

Adding an edging to your work can make all the difference to the finished item. There are many different types of edgings. As well as being decorative, edgings also act as a binding on a crocheted fabric (such as along the edge of a rug), stabilize the edge of a lacy or open fabric, or reinforce the neck, hem or armhole edge of a garment. Some edgings are worked separately, then sewn onto a woven fabric. All of the following are worked directly into the edge of a crocheted fabric, with the right side of the fabric facing you.

Double crochet edging

This is the simplest type of edging, in which one or more rows or rounds of double crochet are worked along the edge of a finished piece of crochet. When edging, for example, a rug, you might choose to work several rounds of double crochet to give a wider edging. Space the stitches evenly along the edge. When working around corners, make 3 dc into the same stitch.

Scallop edging

Also known as a shell edging, this edging should be worked over a multiple of 6 stitches. With right side of work facing, join in the yarn. *Miss 2 sts, 5tr in next st, miss 2 sts, 1ss in next st*, repeat from * to * end. Fasten off.

double crochet edging A simple edging that can be worked in one or more rounds.

scallop edging *5tr into 3rd st from hook, 1ss into 3rd st from hook*, rep from * to * to end.

crab stitch edging Crab stitch is worked as for double crochet, but backwards, from left to right.

Crab stitch edging

Crab stitch is simply a double crochet stitch worked backwards, from left to right. It is a strong, fairly rigid edging that lacks the chain-edge look of other crochet stitches, instead forming little bumps along the edge of the fabric.

With the right side of the work facing you, and keeping the yarn to the left, insert the hook into the next stitch and wrap the yarn over the hook. Draw the loop through the stitch so that there are two loops on the hook. Wrap the yarn over the hook again and draw it through both loops on the hook. One crab stitch has now been formed. Continue in this manner from left to right along the entire edge.

Picot edging

This delicate edging features small protruding loops of yarn. It can be worked directly into the edge of the fabric, or into a previous row of double crochet.

With right side of work facing, join in yarn. *1dc into next st, 3ch, 1dc into same st as previous dc, 1dc into next st*, repeat from * to * to end. Fasten off. (The distance between the picots can be altered by working more dc between them.)

Wavy edging

With right side of work facing, join in the yarn. *1dc, 1htr, 1tr, 1dtr, 1tr, 1htr*, rep from * to * until 1 st remains, 1dc. Fasten off.

Crocheted cords

Crocheted cords can be used as straps for bags, ties to secure garments, or as braids to be attached to a crocheted or sewn item. All crocheted cords will stretch; if you wish to prevent this, sew a piece of woven ribbon to the back of the crocheted cord.

The most basic crocheted cord is simply a length of crocheted chain. Other types are:

Single slip stitch cord Make a foundation chain of the required length, then work a row of slip stitches along one side of the chain.

Double slip stitch cord Make a foundation chain of the required length, then work a row of slip stitches along the first side of the chain. Work 1 turning ch, then another row of slip stitches along the second side.

Double crochet cord Make a foundation chain of the required length, then work a row of double crochet along the first side of the chain. Work 1 turning chain, then another row of double crochet along the second side.

picot edging *1dc into next st, 3ch, 1dc into same st as prev dc, 1dc into next st*, rep to end.

wavy edging Stitches of differing height are worked along the edge, creating a wavy effect.

cords From left: single slip stitch cord; double slip stitch cord; double crochet cord.

Bedlinen trim

Lie in luxury with lovely cotton sheets trimmed with lacy squares of silk yarn. Colour coordinate the crocheted trim with your bedroom décor. The quantity specified will make a trim for a queen-sized sheet and two standard pillowcases. If you want to make a trim for smaller or larger sheets, measure across the top of the sheet and divide by 9 cm (3½ in) —the width of the squares — to determine the number of squares required.

Do make sure that the yarn you choose is colourfast and machine washable, as you will need to wash the sheets and pillowcases with the trim still attached.

Materials:
Four 50 g (1¾ oz) balls Debbie Bliss Spun Silk
   3-ply yarn
1 flat queen-size bedsheet, 2 standard
   pillowcases

Tools
3 mm (US 2/UK 11) crochet hook

Tension
Each motif is approximately 9 cm (3½ in)
   square

Abbreviations
ch: chain
dc: double crochet
dtr: double treble
htr: half treble
rnd: round
ss: slip stitch
tr: treble

first square motif The second and subsequent motifs are worked in a similar manner, but joined through the picots of the previous motif.

round 2 Work half-treble groups into the spaces of the previous row.

FIRST SQUARE MOTIF

Make 6ch, join with ss to form a ring.

Round 1 4ch, *1tr into ring, 1ch*, rep from * to * 10 times, 1ss into 3rd of 4ch at beg of rnd.

Round 2 2ch, 3htr group in next ch, 2ch, 4htr group in next ch, 3ch, **1dtr in next tr, 3ch, *4htr group in next ch, 2ch*, rep from * to * once, 4htr group in next ch, 3ch**, rep from ** to ** twice, 1dtr in next ch, 3ch, 4htr group in next ch, 2ch, 1ss in top of 2ch at beg of rnd.

Round 3 1ch, *1dc in htr group, 5-ch picot in same dc, 2ch, 5tr into 3-ch loop, 1ch, 1dtr in next dtr, 3-ch picot in dtr just formed, 1ch, 5tr into next 3-ch loop, 2ch*,

round 3 Join subsequent squares at the picots of the previous square.

Hints

Be careful not to distort the squares during pressing.

Mercerized cotton is a good alternative to silk: it is less expensive and more resistant to wear.

Always measure sheets before you start work, as many brands differ in size. This pattern is based on a width of 180 cm (71 in) for a queen sheet.

The number of repeats is based on a square which measures 9 cm (3½ in) across (picot to picot) when pressed. Use this measurement to work out how many squares to make should you wish to make the trim for a larger or smaller item.

rep from * to * three times, 1ss into dc at beg of rnd. Fasten off; finish ends into piece.

SUBSEQUENT SQUARE MOTIFS

Make 6ch, join with ss to form a ring.
Rounds 1 and 2 As for Rows 1 and 2 of first square motif.
Round 3 1ch, *1dc in htr group, 5-ch picot in same dc, 2ch, 5tr into 3-ch loop, 1ch, 1dtr in next dtr, 3-ch picot in dtr just formed, 1ch, 5tr into next 3-ch loop, 2ch*, rep from * to * once; 1dc in htr group, 5-ch picot in same dc, 2ch, 5tr into 3-ch loop, 1ch, 1dtr in next dtr, 1ch, 1ss through corner picot of first square, 1ch, 1ss in beginning of picot, 1ch, 5tr into 3-ch loop, 2ch, 1dc in central htr group, 2ch, 1ss through centre picot of first square, 2ch, 1ss in beginning of picot, 2ch, 5tr into 3-ch loop, 1ch, 1dtr in next dtr, 1ch, 1ss through corner picot of first square, 1ch, 1ss in beginning of picot, 1ch, 5tr into 3-ch loop, 2ch, 1ss in first htr group. Fasten off.

Repeat subsequent square motif to make a strip of six squares for each pillowcase and a strip of 20 squares for a queen-size sheet. Finish ends into work.

Carefully press the finished strips on the wrong side, then stitch onto the bedlinen.

Lampshade

Taking inspiration from the floral prints of Liberty fabrics, this lampshade uses pastel colours and pretty motifs to complement most styles of décor.

Be sure to use materials and yarns in your lampshade that will withstand the heat of the electric globe. Always use flame-retardant spray to treat the yarn, and always use natural fibres for both the yarn and the fabric to cover the lampshade. Man-made fibres may melt from the heat of the lamp.

Materials
50 g (1¾ oz) Debbie Bliss Spun Silk 3-ply yarn in each of Colours 1 and 2
50 g (1¾ oz) TLC Cara Mia 4-ply angora blend yarn (Colour 3)
1 cylindrical lampshade, 33 cm (13 in) long x 46 cm (18 in) circumference)
35 cm (14 in) of fabric at least 50 cm (20 in) wide, to cover the lampshade

Tools
3 mm (US 2/UK 11) crochet hook
Low-tack adhesive tape
Adhesive spray
Fabric adhesive
Flame-retardant spray

Size
To fit cylindrical lampshade, 33 cm (13 in) long x 46 cm (18 in) circumference

Tension
Tension is not crucial for this project; the small silk flowers are approximately 2.5 cm (1 in) in diameter and the large silk flowers 3 cm (1¼ in) in diameter

Abbreviations
ch: chain
dc: double crochet
htr: half treble
ss: slip stitch

flower 1 Make 15 flowers in the silk yarn.

loop Create a large loop in chains and double crochet; this will be used to secure the flowers and vines to the inside top edge of the lampshade.

Hints

Different yarns can be used for each of the flowers to give more colour and texture variation.

Variations in yarn thickness will result in different-sized flowers.

FLOWER 1 Make 15

Using 3-ply yarn in Colour 1, make 4ch, join with ss to form a ring.

Round 1 Make 1ch, 9dc into ring, 1ss into ch at beg of rnd.

Round 2 *2ch, 2htr group into next dc, 2ch, 1ss into next dc*, rep from * to * 4 times to make five petals. Fasten off.

FLOWER 2 Make 15

Using 3-ply yarn in Colour 2, make 4ch, join with ss to form a ring.

Round 1 *2ch, 2htr group into ring, 2ch, 1ss into ring*, rep from * to * 4 times to make five petals. Fasten off.

FLOWER 3 Make 15

Using 4-ply yarn in Colour 3, make 4ch, join with ss to form a ring.

Round 1 *2ch, 2htr group into ring, 2ch, 1ss into ring*, rep from * to * 4 times to make five petals. Fasten off.

You should now have a total of 45 flowers. Finish ends into flowers and press carefully.

ASSEMBLING THE LAMPSHADE

Spray the lampshade with adhesive spray, then attach the fabric.

Loop Using 4-ply yarn in Colour 3, make 89ch, join with ss to make a large ring, ensuring that the ring is not twisted.

vines Attach the flowers to crocheted chains through the back of the flowers to make the vines.

flowers Join the vines and flowers to the loop using slip stitch.

Loop, Round 1 Miss 1ch, 1dc in each ch to end, 1ss into 1st ch of rnd.

Loop, Round 2 Miss 1ch, 1ch, 1dc into each dc to end, 1ss into 1st dc of rnd, fasten off. Finish ends into loop.

Vines, Row 1 1ch, 1ss into the centre back of a flower, 1ch, 1ss into the other side of the centre back of the same flower; 10ch, 1ss into the centre back of a second flower, 1ch, 1ss into the other side of the centre back of the same flower; 15ch, 1ss into the centre back of a third flower, 1ch, 1ss into the other side of the centre back of the same flower; 20ch, 1ss into the centre back of a fourth flower; 1ch, 1ss into the other side of the centre back of the same flower.

Attach to the crochet loop using ss, fasten off and finish ends into vine. Repeat 3 times to give four vines, fixed onto the loop 90 degrees apart.

Flowers Tape the loop temporarily to the inside top edge of the lampshade. Incorporate the remaining flowers randomly around the shade, using the same technique as that used to create the vines and varying the number of chains used between each flower, as required. Increase the density of flowers towards the bottom edge of the shade. Fasten off; finish ends into the vines.

Finishing Fix top loop inside top edge of the lampshade using fabric adhesive. Spray entire lampshade with flame-retardant spray.

Hint

Incorporating more flowers will give a more interesting and decorative look; however, adding more flowers will reduce the amount of light that comes through the shade.

Beaded choker and cuff

This delicate choker and cuff set, encrusted with pearly beads and crystals, will add the perfect finish to a chic evening ensemble. Made in white or off-white, as here, it would be a lovely adornment for a bridal outfit.

Fine rayon yarn has a lustre that complements the beads, giving an elegant touch. Substitute silk or silk/rayon blends for a different look.

Materials
50 g (1¾ oz) ball Sullivans Royal Rayon 3-ply crochet yarn (one ball of yarn is enough to make both the choker and the cuff)
286 assorted small beads (choker)
147 assorted small beads (cuff)
Four 6 mm (¼ in) pearl buttons (two each for choker and cuff)

Tools
1 mm (US 11 or 12/UK 6 or 5½) crochet hook

Size
Choker: 32 x 5 cm (12¾ x 2 in), not including beaded loops
Cuff: 17 x 5 cm (6½ x 2 in), not including beaded loops

Tension
1 row qdtr and 3 rows dc in patt across 21ch = 5 cm (2 in) wide x 3 cm (1¼ in) deep

Abbreviations
b/ch: beaded chain
b/dc: beaded double crochet
ch: chain
dc: double crochet
qdtr: quadruple treble
ss: slip stitch

Choker

BEADED CROCHET

String 220 beads onto the yarn. Make 21ch.

Row 1 Miss 1ch, 1dc in next of next 20ch, turn.

Rows 2–4 As for Row 1.

Row 5 Make 1ch, miss 1dc, *1dc in next dc, 1b/dc in next dc*, rep from * to * to end, turn.

Row 6 Make 1ch, miss 1dc, 1dc in each of next 20dc, turn.

Row 7 As for Row 5.

Row 8 Make 5ch, *1qdtr in 1st dc, 1ch, miss 1dc, 1qdtr in next dc, 1ch*, rep from * to * to end, turn.

Repeat Rows 5–8 another 9 times.

Repeat Rows 5–6.

Repeat Row 1 twice.

Next row: Make button loops Make 1ch, miss 1dc, 1dc in each of next 5dc, 12ch, 1dc in each of next 10dc, 12ch, 1dc in each of next 5ch, cut off yarn. Finish ends into work.

FINISHING

1 Sew the buttons onto the other end of the choker, aligning them opposite the button loops, to create fastenings.

2 String 30 beads onto the yarn. Join the yarn to the choker (at beginning of work) using 1ss. *(3ch, 1b/ch) 3 times, 3ch, then use 1ss to attach work between the first and second rows of quadruple treble*, rep from * to * to end [10 loops]. Finish ends into work.

3 String 36 beads onto the yarn. Join the yarn to the centre of the first loop that you made in step 2, using 1ss. *(3ch, 1b/ch) 4 times, 3ch, then use 1ss to attach work to centre of the next loop of the previous row*, rep from * to * to end [9 loops]. Finish ends into work.

Cuff

BEADED CROCHET

String 120 beads onto the yarn. Make 21ch.

Row 1 Miss 1ch, 1dc in each of next 20ch, turn.

Rows 2–4 As for Row 1.

beaded yarn Thread beads onto the yarn before beginning the crochet.

Row 5 Make 1ch, miss 1dc, *1dc in next dc, 1b/dc in next dc*, rep from * to * to end, turn.

Row 6 Make 1ch, miss 1dc, 1dc in each of next 20dc, turn.

Row 7 As for Row 6.

Row 8 Make 5ch, *1qdtr in 1st dc, 1ch, miss 1dc, 1qdtr in next dc, 1ch*, rep from * to * to end, turn.

Repeat Rows 5–8 another 4 times.

Repeat Rows 5–6.

Repeat Row 1 twice.

Row 29: Make button loops Make 1ch, miss 1dc, 1dc in each of next 5dc, 12ch, 1dc in each of next 10dc, 12ch, 1dc in each of next 5ch, cut off yarn. Finish ends into work.

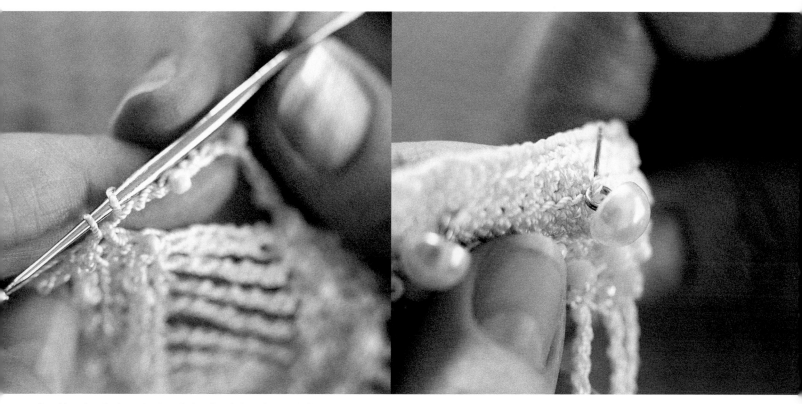

crochet Move beads along the thread when beaded stitches are indicated.

choker, finishing, step 1 Sew buttons onto one end of the choker, aligning them opposite the button loops.

FINISHING

1 Sew the buttons onto the other end of the cuff, aligning them opposite the button loops, to create fastenings.

2 String 15 beads onto the yarn. Join the yarn to the cuff (at beginning of work) using 1ss. *(3ch, 1b/ch) 3 times, 3ch, then use 1ss to fix work between first and second rows of quadruple trebles*, rep from * to * to end [5 loops]. Finish ends into work.

3 String 12 beads onto the yarn. Join the yarn to the centre of the first loop you made in step 2, using 1ss. *(3ch, 1b/ch) 3 times, 3ch, then use 1ss to fix work to centre of the second loop of the previous row*, rep from * to * to end [4 loops]. Finish ends into work.

Hints

To make the cuff or choker larger, add repeats of Rows 5 to 8.
To make the cuff or choker smaller, remove repeats of Rows 5 to 8.

Steps 2 and 3 of Finishing (the beaded loop sections) can be omitted to give a simpler effect.

To use smaller beads which will not thread onto the yarn, thread the beads onto a nylon filament (invisible thread) and crochet this alongside the main yarn.

Any smooth 3-ply yarn can be used for these designs. To use a textured yarn, thread the beads onto a filament and crochet alongside the main yarn. Lurex thread can also be crocheted alongside the main yarn to give a different look.

Beaded bracelet and pendant

Encrusted with a selection of iridescent beads,

the silky rayon yarns of these accessories will

complement a glamorous outfit. Choose beads

in a variety of shades and colours, but keep

them within the same tonal range to ensure that

the pieces will look rich but not fussy.

Materials
50 g (1¾ oz) Sullivans Royal Rayon 3-ply
   crochet yarn (silk yarn may be substituted)
198 assorted small beads (bracelet)
509 assorted small beads (pendant)
1 small button or flat bead, about 1 cm (½ in)
   diameter, for fastening (bracelet)

Tools
1 mm (US 11 or 12/UK 6 or 5½) crochet hook
Sewing needle

Size
Bracelet approximately 21 cm (8¼ in) long, to
   fit small to medium wrist (to adjust for a large
   wrist, use a slightly larger crochet hook)
Pendant 7 x 4 cm (2¾ x 1½ in), excluding
   fringe; chain 100 cm (39 in) long

Tension
30 beaded chain (b/ch) to 10 cm (4 in)

Abbreviations
b/ch: beaded chain
b/dc: beaded double crochet
ch: chain
dc: double crochet

bracelet String beads onto the yarn before commencing the crochet.

finishing the bracelet Sew the button or flat bead onto the end of the bracelet to create the fastening.

Bracelet

WRIST LOOP

String 160 beads onto the yarn. Make 80 b/ch.
Row 1 1ch, *1b/dc in next st, make 3 b/ch, miss 3b/dc*, rep to end, 1dc in last st. Fasten off and cut yarn, leaving about (15 cm (6 in) to attach finger loop.

FINGER LOOP

String 38 beads onto the yarn at the end of the bracelet. Using a sewing needle, fix the other end of the beaded yarn onto the end of the bracelet to create a finger loop. Small beads of similar size such as seed beads are best for the finger loop, and 38 should make a loop big enough to fit over a medium-sized middle finger.

FINISHING

Sew the button or flat bead onto the other end of the bracelet. The button should fasten through the loops in the bracelet chain. Finish ends into work.

Pendant

ORNAMENT

String 112 beads onto the yarn. Make 16ch.
Row 1 Make 1ch, 1b/dc in each st to end, turn.

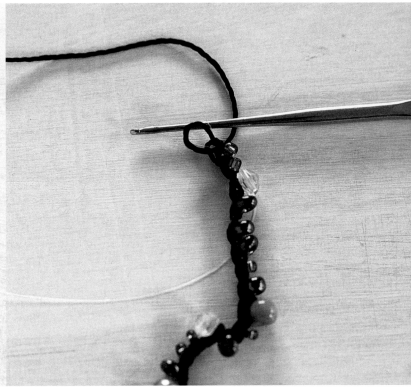

pendant ornament A variety of similarly toned beads are worked into the ornament.

pendant chain A single strand of beaded chain stitch can be made to any length desired.

Row 2 Make 1ch, 1dc in each st to end, turn.

Repeat Rows 1 and 2 another 5 times each.

Next row Repeat Row 1. Finish the ends into work.

FRINGING

String 13 beads onto the yarn and make 13b/ch, to give a short beaded chain. Repeat to make seven chains of varying lengths between 13 and 16b/ch. Using a sewing needle, sew the chains onto the bottom row of the ornament. Finish ends into work.

NECK CHAIN

String 300 beads onto the yarn. Leaving a tail of yarn about 15 cm (6 in) long, make 300b/ch to make a long chain. (The number of beaded chain can be adjusted for a longer or shorter chain; remember to adjust the number of beads also). Fasten off, leaving a tail of yarn about 15 cm (6 in) long. Using the tails of yarn, stitch the ends of the neck chain to the top corners of the pendant.

Hints

To make the bracelet larger or smaller, add or remove beaded chain, allowing four beads per centimetre (½ in).

Any smooth 3-ply yarn can be used for this design. To use a textured yarn, thread the beads onto a nylon filament (invisible thread) and crochet this alongside the main yarn. Lurex can also be crocheted alongside the main yarn to give a different look.

knitting

Introduction

The past few seasons have seen a revival in the art of hand knitting. Many new knitters are discovering the pleasures and therapeutic benefits of this traditional craft. In an increasingly frenetic, mechanized, technology-driven world, many people are attracted to pursuits that are just the opposite. Many knitters find that their craft becomes an opportunity for some time out; a chance to create, reflect and relax. The meditative rhythm of knitting provides a counterpoint to the busy pace of everyday life and an opportunity to connect with tradition and your own creativity.

Although commercially knitted garments are often much cheaper than those you knit yourself, there is no comparison in quality, or in the satisfaction of having made a unique garment. Think of knitting as an investment; the time and money you spend are well recompensed with a beautiful hand-knitted item that you can use, admire and love for years to come. A sweater or rug seems all the more cosy if you have knitted it yourself, or if it has been knitted for you by a loved one.

Although knitting isn't reliant on technology, there are certain aspects of technology that can make knitting simpler and more accessible. Many knitters' websites and chat rooms exist; these can be a valuable source of advice, help and free patterns. Internet mail order is a boon for finding yarns — including elusive, speciality and hand-spun yarns that may be difficult to find in stores — and for knitters in isolated places.

Many keen knitters have several projects on the go at the one time: perhaps a simple item such as a garter-stitch scarf to knit in front of the television; a plain sweater that requires a little more attention; and a challenge knit, such as an intricate lace or aran item, that requires patience, concentration and preferably solitude.

This section offers the basic techniques to make and finish a garment. Don't be daunted if you are a novice knitter. A ball of yarn and a pair of knitting needles are all you require to start knitting. You don't necessarily need a lot of skill or time; simple knits in chunky, quick-to-work yarns can be just as satisfying to make as a complex pattern. As your skills advance and you gain confidence, you can expand your collection of equipment and experiment with different yarns and stitch patterns.

plaited scarf Three strands of knitted fabric in a chunky velvet-look yarn are braided together.

A brief history of knitting

The origins of knitting are obscure. Fabrics of similar appearance to knitting, but made using a different technique, date back to the fifth century BC. The oldest surviving pieces of true knitting are from Egypt and can be roughly dated to between 1000 and 1400 AD. The first references to true knitting in Europe are from the early 14th century. The first knitting trade guild was established in Paris in 1527, and the trade remained male dominated for centuries to come.

Britain had a thriving cottage industry in knitting, especially of stockings, in the 14th and 15th centuries. On various groups of Scottish islands in the 17th and 18th centuries, whole families were involved in the making of knitted garments. Distinctive regional variations in knitting styles developed, among them fair isle patterns and shetland lace in Scotland, and richly cabled and textured aran designs in Ireland. Knitted sweaters were essential to the fishing communities of these islands, as the natural oils in the wool provided some degree of weather proofing. The designs were sometimes specific to a particular family, enabling the remains of lost seamen to be identified by the sweater they were wearing.

The first knitting machine, designed to make stockings, was invented in Nottingham, England, in 1589 by William Lee, a clergyman. Later, the industrial revolution made it possible to spin yarn of uniform consistency and also enabled the mass production of knitted cloth. Women came to be employed in factories rather than at home spinning and knitting their own garments; this, and the availability of cheaper mass-produced knitted goods, led to a decline in hand knitting. The skill was practised mainly by women, and as a hobby, not a way of life.

In more recent times, knitting's popularity has fluctuated. In the 1940s, wartime austerity made it a necessity; in the 1950s and 60s, it was fashionable again; and by the 1980s, it had declined worldwide.

However, since the turn of this century, knitting has been on the rise again. Technology and industry, the very factors that contributed to its earlier decline, are now partly responsible for the renewed popularity of knitting. The multitude of fancy, exotic, multicoloured and highly textured yarns that are now manufactured have attracted many new knitters to the pleasures of this traditional yet timeless craft.

mitre throw A mixture of plain and novelty yarns are combined in this rug.

Yarns

The choice of yarn is most important. Every type of yarn has distinct properties; different yarns knitted to the same pattern can produce vastly different effects, so you need to match the yarn to the project. For example, for a hard-wearing sweater that can be machine washed, a specially treated wool is the best choice. A baby's garment is better made in cotton, which can stand up to repeated washing and is also cool, so the baby won't overheat.

If your local craft or specialist yarn store doesn't stock the yarn you want, or can't order it in for you, internet mail order is a convenient way of finding and ordering yarns that might otherwise be unobtainable. The freight fees are generally modest, and it's worth the extra expense to get just the right yarn.

Knitting is usually done with commercial yarns, but any continuous piece of material can be knitted, including strips of plastic or fabric (whether knitted or woven), ribbon, tape and wire.

smooth yarns in wool or wool blends
Clockwise from top: plain 8-ply (DK) pure wool; plain 8-ply (DK) pure wool; 8-ply (DK) tweed pure wool; 10-ply (worsted/aran weight) pure wool; flecked 8-ply (DK) pure wool; (centre) variegated acrylic/wool mix.

Yarn types

When choosing yarn, you need to consider its content and thickness (or ply) and how the manufacturer has treated the fibre. Yarns may be natural, synthetic or a mixture of both. Natural yarns are obtained either from animals or plants. Yarns of animal origin include wool, from sheep; cashmere and mohair, from goats; angora, from angora rabbits; and alpaca, from a relative of the llama. Plant-derived yarns include cotton, linen and hemp. Synthetic yarns, such as acrylic, polyester and nylon, are often mixed with natural yarns to improve their texture and performance.

Yarns can also be treated and spun to make them hairier, heavier, denser, more twisted, fluffier, flatter or knobblier. Some ways in which manufacturers treat yarns to change their intrinsic characteristics are by giving a shrink-resist treatment to wool to make it machine washable, and mercerizing cotton to give it a lustre.

Some terms used to describe yarn (such as silk, cotton, cashmere) refer to the yarn's content; others (such as aran, tweed, bouclé) to its texture, appearance and/or thickness.

Smooth, plain yarns are best for fancy patterns such as cables and lace, as these yarns enable the beauty and intricacy of the stitches to be easily seen. Fashion or novelty yarns are best used with simple garter stitch or stocking stitch designs; the lovely details of more complicated patterns will be lost in these busy yarns.

yarns in other fibres and finishes Clockwise from top: Mohair; slubby pure wool; wool/silk/angora mix; variegated bouclé mohair; alpaca/silk/polyamide mix.

When starting out, you may be tempted by the intriguing textures, bright colour mixtures or sensual feel of novelty yarns, but it's best to practise on smooth, plain yarns, which are easiest to knit with. Choose pale or mid-toned yarns; these show stitch details better than dark yarns, which is especially useful if you're practising more complicated stitch textures or patterns.

Reading a ball band

On the paper band around the ball of yarn is printed useful information such as the manufacturer and composition of the yarn, the recommended needle size to use, the recommended gauge (tension) that the wool should knit up to, the weight of the ball, care instructions, and the shade and dye lot. All balls for the same garment should come from the same dye lot. Different dye lots can vary in tone; a variation that is undetectable between individual balls can be quite noticeable in the finished garment. If you are forced to mix dye lots, you can make the transition between the two less obvious by alternating two rows of one dye lot with two rows of the other throughout the garment.

Yarn weights

Yarns come in many thicknesses, from thread-like yarns used for traditional lace to super-chunky yarns that knit up thickly (and gratifyingly quickly). Not all countries use the same terms for types and weights of yarn. Also, some weights of yarn are very popular in some countries and little used in others. The following table lists some of the most popular weights of yarn and their names in different parts of the world, and how many stitches they yield per 10 cm (4 in) when knitted on the recommended needle size.

novelty yarns Clockwise from top: hairy yarn in acrylic–polyamide mix; chunky velvet-look yarn in exoline; tufted yarn in polyester–polyamide mix; velvet ribbon yarn in nylon–acrylic mix; silky-look 'eyelash' yarn in polyester.

International yarn equivalents (note that figures given are approximate and will vary between manufacturers)

Australia/NZ	USA	UK and Canada	Tension (gauge) per 10 cm (4 in)	Needle
5-ply	Sport/Baby	Baby	24 sts	3.75 mm (US 5/UK 9)
8-ply	Double knitting (DK)	Double knitting (DK)	22 sts	4 mm (US 6/UK 8)
10-ply	Worsted weight	Aran	18–20 sts	5 mm (US 8/UK 6)
12-ply	Chunky	Chunky	14–18 sts	5 or 5.5 mm (US 8 or 9/UK 6 or 5)
Novelty	Bulky	Bulky	9–12 sts	8 mm (US 11/UK 0) or up

Equipment

Knitting needles

Knitting needles may be either straight (two or more separate needles) or circular (two needles joined by a length of round plastic or nylon). Needles may be made from various materials, including aluminium, wood, bamboo and plastic.

A piece of knitted fabric can be made either flat or in the round. For example, if making a sweater using flat knitting, the back and front pieces are made separately then joined up the sides. If making a sweater in the round, all the stitches for both the back and the front are cast on at the same time and the body of the sweater is knitted in one piece, in what is effectively a spiral. This eliminates side seams. To do flat knitting, you can use either straight or circular needles; for circular knitting, you will need circular needles and/or a set of double-pointed needles.

Circular needles come in various lengths; if knitting in the round, choose a length that is shorter than the circumference of the piece you are knitting. For example, you cannot knit a piece with a 50 cm (20 in) circumference on 60 cm (24 in) needles, as the knitting will be stretched.

Circular needles are particularly useful when knitting large items, such as shawls or rugs; the length of the needle easily accommodates a large numbers of stitches, and the weight of the garment stays centred over your lap rather than awkwardly weighing down one end of the needle, as is the case with straight needles.

Double-pointed needles come in sets of four or five needles about 20 cm (8 in) in length. The stitches are cast on as normal then divided roughly equally between three or four needles. The last needle in the set is then used to knit off the stitches. Double-pointed needles are useful when knitting parts of garments that may be too narrow for circular needles, such as the collars of sweaters.

Cable needles are short needles used to hold stitches while making a cable. They may be straight, or kinked in the middle to prevent the stitches from slipping off.

Needle sizes

There is no universal guide for knitting needle sizes; they are expressed differently from country to country. Sizes many also vary slightly from one manufacturer to the next. The patterns in this book give needle sizes in metric (millimetres), followed by the equivalent US and UK/Canadian sizes. For conversions, see the chart at left.

Needle size conversion chart

Metric (mm)	US	UK/Canada
2	0	14
2.25	1	13
2.75	2	12
3	–	11
3.25	3	10
3.5	4	–
3.75	5	9
4	6	8
4.5	7	7
5	8	6
5.5	9	5
6	10	4
6.5	10½	3
7	–	2
7.5	–	1
8	11	0
9	13	00
10	15	000
12	17	–
15–16	19	–
19	35	–
25	50	–

Accessories

The following handy tools may be purchased at craft or yarn stores, or improvised.

Crochet hooks These are useful for picking up dropped stitches or for casting off. The crochet hook does not have to be the same size as the needle you are using for the work; it can be a little smaller or larger without affecting the fabric too much.

Metal ruler Used for checking tension; more accurate than a cloth tape measure.

Needle gauge Used for checking the size of knitting needles; some also have metric and imperial measurements marked on the sides, for measuring tension squares.

Pins For marking out tension squares, pinning garments into shape before blocking or pressing, and pinning knitted pieces together before sewing up.

Row counter A cylindrical gadget that fits on the end of the needle; it has numbered tumblers that can be turned at the end of each row to record how many rows you have done. Useful, but not essential; you can improvise with pen and paper.

Stitch holders Made of metal and resembling large safety pins, these come in various sizes and are used to hold stitches that will be picked up again later, for example at a neck edge. For small numbers of stitches, you can improvise with safety pins.

Stitch markers Small plastic rings slipped onto the needle to mark the start of a pattern repeat or, in circular knitting, the start of a row; you can improvise with small loops of contrasting yarn (see at right).

Tape measure For measuring garment pieces.

Wool needle For sewing up seams and darning in ends of yarn on finished pieces; it should have a blunt end so as not to split the strands of yarn.

Using stitch markers

Commercially produced stitch markers are small plastic rings of varying diameters, to fit different-sized needles (see the centre photograph below). Alternatively, you can make your own; using short lengths of contrast-coloured yarn, make a small slip knot in each and slip one loop onto the needle where required. As you come to each marker on successive rows, simply slip it off the left needle and onto the right.

When casting on a lot of stitches, you may find it useful to put a marker after every 20 stitches to assist in counting.

Markers can also help you keep track of pattern repeats, for example in lace, aran or other complex patterns. Place a marker at the start of each pattern repeat; then, if you make a mistake, it will be easier to trace where it occurred.

If working in the round on circular or double-pointed needles, slip on a marker to show where each new round begins.

needles (from top right) Double-pointed, straight, circular, and cable needles (straight and kinked).

accessories (from top left) Wool needle, crochet hook, stitch markers, row counter, pins.

accessories (from top) Tape measure, ruler; needle gauge, safety pin, stitch holders, scissors.

Casting on

Casting on is the term given to making the first row of stitches; these form the foundation of your knitting. There are several methods of casting on. The following are two of the most versatile. The golden rule of casting on is to do so loosely; even if you think your cast-on is too loose, it probably isn't.

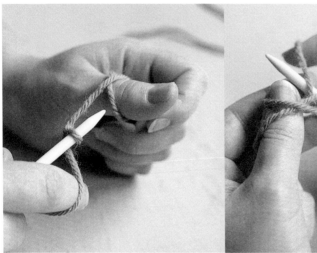

step four Insert the point of the right needle into the loop around your thumb.

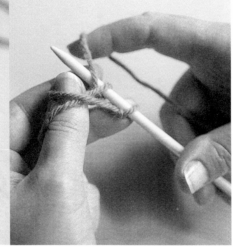

step five Wrap the ball end of yarn around the needle.

step five continued Pull the ball end of yarn through the thumb loop to make a stitch.

step six Pull on the ball end of the yarn until the loop is firm but not tight.

Thumb method

This gives a very flexible edge and is especially good for rib edges of garments and for garter stitch fabric.

1 Start with a length of yarn measuring a little more than three times the width of the edge to be cast on. Make a slip knot (see opposite) at this point.

2 Transfer the slip knot to a knitting needle. Draw it up until it is close to the needle, but not tight; you should be able to easily insert a second needle into the loop.

3 With the tail end of the yarn, make a clockwise loop around your thumb.

4 Insert the point of the right needle from front to back into the thumb loop.

5 Wrap the ball end of yarn around the needle and pull this loop through the thumb loop. You have now cast on a stitch.

6 Pull on the ball end of yarn until the stitch is firm, but not tight; you should be able to easily insert a second needle into the loop.

7 Repeat Steps 3–6 until you have cast on the required number of stitches. (Remember that the loop of the slip knot counts as one stitch.)

Cable method

Also known as the two-needle method, this gives a smooth edge and is particularly compatible with stocking stitch. It is not as flexible as the thumb method, so tension it loosely if it is to become the bottom, neck or sleeve edge of a garment.

1 Leaving a tail of yarn about 15 cm (6 in) long, make a slipknot on the left needle.

2 Holding the other needle in your right hand, insert its point from left to right into the loop of the slip knot.

3 Hook the yarn around the tip of the right-hand needle and pull it through the loop of the slip knot.

4 Put the loop just made onto the left-hand needle. You have now cast on a stitch. *Gently* pull the ball end of the yarn to secure the loop. If a needle will not pass easily through the loop with almost no resistance, the loop is too tight.

5 Insert the right-hand needle between the previous loop and the loop you just made. Hook the yarn around the tip of the right-hand needle and draw it through. Place the loop just made onto the left-hand needle and gently tighten.

6 Repeat Step 5 until you have the required number of stitches. (The slip loop counts as one stitch.)

Making a slip knot

Make a loop in a piece of yarn. Bring the yarn up from back to front through the loop and pull to tighten. You have now made a slipknot. Place the loop on the knitting needle or crochet hook. You can now begin casting on or making a crochet chain. Remember that the loop of the slipknot counts as the first cast-on or chain stitch.

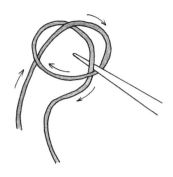

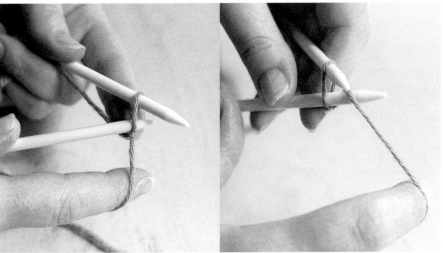

step two Insert the point of the right needle into the loop of the slip knot.

step three Hook the yarn around the tip of the right needle and pull the yarn through.

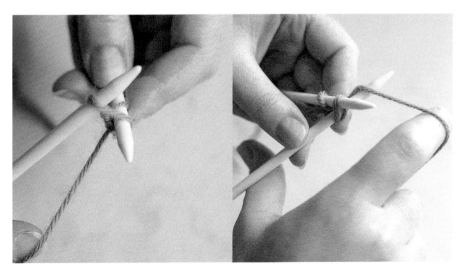

step four Put the loop just made onto the left needle and gently tighten.

step five Insert the tip of the right needle between the two loops and draw the yarn through.

The basic stitches

Knitting has just two basic stitches, the knit stitch and the purl stitch. Many different stitch patterns, including textures, cables, twists, bobbles and ribs, can be made from these alone.

Garter stitch

If you knit every row, the resulting fabric is known as garter stitch (above). It has a ridged appearance, and both sides of the fabric are identical. The fabric lies flat, without curling up at the edges.

Hint

If you look closely at the stitches on a knitting needle, you will see that they do not lie at right angles to the needle. Instead, the front 'leg' of the stitch lies slightly to the right and the back leg slightly to the left. Keep this in mind, especially if knitting a stitch that you have picked up; if you knit into the back (left leg) rather than the front (right leg) of the stitch, you will twist the stitch and it will look different to all the other stitches in the row.

The knit stitch

1 Insert the point of the right needle from left to right through the front of the first stitch on the left needle.

2 Wrap the yarn around the tip of the right needle.

3 With the tip of the right needle, draw the yarn through the stitch on the left needle.

4 Slip the original stitch off the left needle. You have now made a knit stitch.

5 Repeat Steps 1–4 until you reach the end of the row. To start the next row, you need to turn to the work. To do this, transfer the needle in your right hand, with the work on it, to the left hand; the empty needle is held in the right hand. You are now ready to begin knitting the second row.

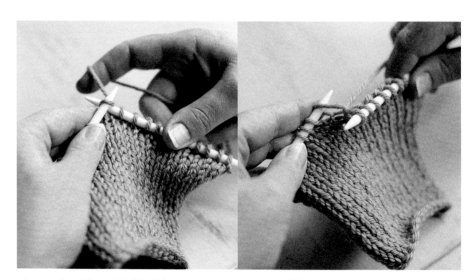

step one Insert the point of the right needle through the stitch on the left needle.

step three With the tip of the right needle, draw the yarn through the stitch on the left needle.

The purl stitch

The purl stitch is, in effect, the reverse of the knit stitch.

1 Insert the point of the right needle from right to left into the front of the first stitch on the left needle.

2 Wrap the yarn around the tip of the right needle.

3 With the tip of the right needle, draw the yarn through the stitch on the left needle.

4 Slip the original stitch off the left needle. You have now made a purl stitch.

5 Repeat Steps 1–4 until you reach the end of the row, then turn the work and begin the next row.

Stocking stitch (stockinette)

If you knit and purl alternate rows, the resulting fabric is known as stocking stitch, or stockinette. One side of the fabric is smooth, with stitches looking like little Vs. The other side is knobbly and looks similar to garter stitch. Usually the smooth side is used as the right side. If the knobbly side is used, the fabric is known as reverse stocking stitch. The difference in using reverse stocking stitch rather than garter stitch when you want a knobbly look on the right side is that reverse stocking stitch fabric is thinner than garter stitch fabric, giving a less bulky garment.

If you purl every row, you get garter stitch, but as purl stitch is slower to make than knit stitch, there is no advantage to making a garter-stitch fabric by purling.

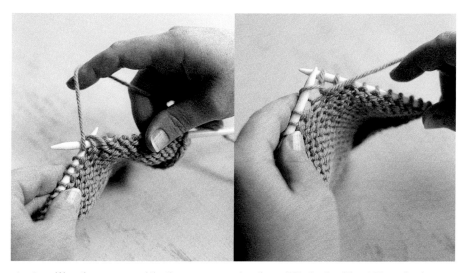

step two Wrap the yarn around the tip of the right needle.

step three With the tip of the right needle, draw the yarn through the stitch on the left needle.

Increasing

Increasing and decreasing are ways of shaping the fabric. There are several methods of increasing; the following are two of the most useful. Increasing is usually, but not always, done on a right-side row. It may be done at the edge or in the body of the piece of knitted fabric.

knit fabric, step one Knit a stitch as usual, but do not slip the stitch off the left needle.

knit fabric, step two Knit into back of same stitch, then slip the stitch off the left needle.

purl fabric, step one Purl a stitch as usual, but do not slip the stitch off the left needle.

purl fabric, step two Purl into back of same stitch, then slip the stitch off the left needle.

Working into both the back and front of the same stitch produces a neat but slightly visible increase. This increase can be done on either knit or purl fabric. Both versions are shown here. This increase is usually abbreviated simply as inc, but you may also see it as kfb (knit into front and back) or pfb (purl into front and back).

INC ON KNIT FABRIC

1 Knit a stitch as usual, but do not slip the stitch off the left needle.

2 Insert the tip of the right needle into the back of the same stitch, from front to back and right to left. (You may need to wriggle the needle about a little to enlarge the loop, especially if your tension is tight.) Knit the stitch, then slip the stitch off the left needle. You have now made an extra knit stitch.

INC ON PURL FABRIC

1 Purl a stitch as usual, but do not slip the stitch off the left needle.

2 Insert the tip of the right needle into the back of the same stitch, from back to front and left to right. Knit the stitch, then slip the stitch off the left needle. You have now made an extra purl stitch.

Making a stitch (M1)

Another method of increasing is by working into the running stitch — that is, the thread that lies between two stitches. Working into the back of the stitch (rather than the front, as is usual) twists the stitch and prevents a hole from forming, making the increase almost invisible. This is particularly useful if you need to increase in the body of the garment. This increase is usually abbreviated as M1 (make a stitch), and can be done on either knit or purl fabric; both versions are shown here.

M1 ON KNIT FABRIC

1 With the tip of the left needle, pick up the loop that lies between the first stitch on that needle and the first stitch on the right needle. Make sure that the front of the loop slopes to the right.

2 Knit into the back of the loop. You have now made an extra knit stitch.

M1 ON PURL FABRIC

1 With the tip of the left needle, pick up the loop that lies between the first stitch on that needle and the first stitch on the right needle. Make sure that the front of the loop slopes to the right.

2 Purl into the back of the loop. You have now made an extra purl stitch.

knit fabric, step one With tip of left needle, pick up the loop lying between the two stitches.

knit fabric, step two Knit into the back of the loop that you have just picked up.

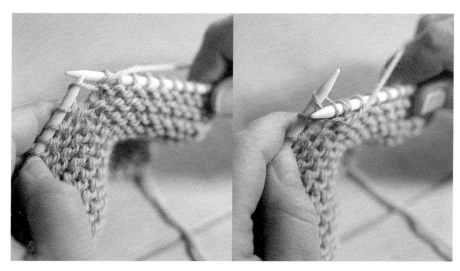

purl fabric, step one With tip of left needle, pick up the loop lying between the two stitches.

purl fabric, step two Purl into the back of the loop that you have just picked up.

Decreasing

By working one or more stitches together, thus decreasing the number of stitches in a row, you can shape a knitted piece. Decreasing may be done at either the edge or in the body of the knitting, and on both knit and purl fabric.

Hints

The number of normal rows worked between one decrease row and the next determines how steep the angle of the decrease will be. Decreasing every row produces a steep angle; decreasing less often, for example every fourth or sixth row, produces a shallower angle.

Perfecting your decreases

The most rudimentary decrease is made by working together the first or last two stitches in a row. However, a much neater look is achieved by making 'fully fashioned' decreases; these are worked a consistent number of stitches (usually two or three) in from each end of the knitting.

To make the decreases at each end mirror each other, you will need to make one of them slope to the right and the other to the left. To make a right-sloping decrease, work two stitches together through the front of the stitch as explained at right. To make a left-sloping decrease, work two stitches together through the back of the stitch.

Working in this way emphasizes the way the knitting is shaped, or 'fashioned'. It results in a decorative effect at the decreased edge, and will add a professional touch to your knitting.

KNITTING TWO STITCHES TOGETHER (ABBREVIATED AS K2TOG)

Insert the tip of the right needle into the first two stitches on the left needle, from left to right and front to back as normal. Pass the yarn around the right needle and knit a stitch, slipping both original stitches off the left needle. You have now decreased by one stitch. (It is usual to decrease by one stitch at a time, but sometimes you may be instructed to k3tog, thus decreasing two stitches.)

PURLING TWO STITCHES TOGETHER (ABBREVIATED AS P2TOG)

Insert the tip of the right needle into the first two stitches on the left needle, from right to left and back to front as normal. Pass the yarn around the right needle and purl a stitch, slipping both original stitches off the left needle. You have now decreased by one stitch. (It is usual to decrease by one stitch at a time, but sometimes you may be instructed to p3tog, thus decreasing two stitches.)

k2tog Two stitches are knitted together, then the original stitch is slipped off the left needle.

p2tog Two stitches are purled together, then the original stitch is slipped off the left needle.

Casting (binding) off

Casting (or binding) off is how you finish a piece of knitting. It can be done either knitwise or purlwise, and is usually done on the right side of the fabric. Unless otherwise specified, casting off should be done in pattern; that is, each knit stitch should be cast off knitwise and each purl stitch purlwise.

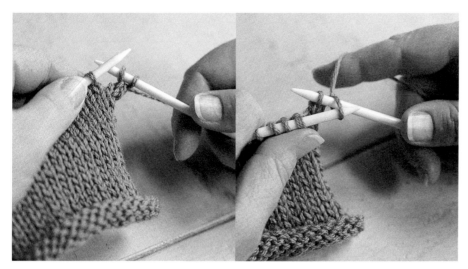

casting off knitwise, step one Loosely knit two stitches as normal.

casting off knitwise, step two Lift the first stitch on the right needle over the second and off the needle.

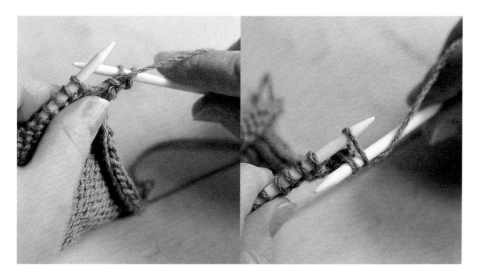

casting off purlwise, step one Loosely purl two stitches as normal.

casting off purlwise, step two Lift the first stitch on the right needle over the second and off the needle.

When casting off, do so loosely; an otherwise beautifully knitted piece can be ruined by a too-tight cast-off, especially at the neck, cuff or lower edge of a garment. If unsure, cast off a few stitches and then stretch the fabric; the cast-off edge should stretch almost as much as the rest of the fabric.

CASTING OFF KNITWISE

1 Knit two stitches as normal.

2 From the front of the work, insert the tip of the left needle into the first stitch on the right needle and lift this stitch over the second stitch and off the needle. You have now cast off one stitch knitwise.

3 Knit another stitch and then repeat Step 2. Continue in this manner until one stitch remains on the left needle. Remove the needle, bring the end of the yarn through the last stitch and pull firmly to fasten. The cast-off is now complete.

CASTING OFF PURLWISE

1 Purl two stitches as normal.

2 From the back of the work, insert the tip of the left needle into the first stitch on the right needle and lift this stitch over the second stitch and off the needle. You have now cast off one stitch purlwise.

3 Purl another stitch and then repeat Step 2. Continue until one stitch remains, then fasten off.

Using graphs or charts

In a chart or graph, each stitch is represented by a single square, and the symbol within that square indicates what you do with that stitch; for example, knit, purl, increase, decrease or cable.

Some symbols go across more than one square of the chart; for example, an instruction to make a 6-stitch cable may be represented by two diagonal lines each crossing three squares (which represent the three stitches in each 'leg' of the cable).

Charts are read from the bottom up, starting at the first row, and from right to left on odd-numbered (right-side) rows, and from left to right on even-numbered (wrong-side) rows. Charts show the pattern as it appears from the right side of the work, so you need to work out what stitch to make on wrong-side rows to get the correct effect on the right side. For example, a stitch marked as knit on the chart will need to be knitted on a right-side row but purled on a wrong-side row.

This diagram shows a pattern in chart form, followed by the same pattern in written form.

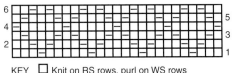

KEY ☐ Knit on RS rows, purl on WS rows
☐ Purl on RS rows, knit on WS rows

Row 1 (RS): k3, p1, (k5, p1) to last 3 sts, k3.
Row 2: p2, k1, p1, k1, (p3, k1, p1, k1) to last 2 sts, p2.
Row 3: k1, p1, (k3, p1, k1, p1) to last 5 sts, k3, p1, k1.
Row 4: k1, (p5, k1) to end.
Row 5: As row 3.
Row 6: as row 2.
Rep these 6 rows.

Working from a pattern

Patterns come in both written and chart (or graph) formats. When starting out, you will probably find it easiest to work from a written pattern, but once you come to attempt more complicated patterns, you may prefer to work from charts. One advantage of a chart is that it is a visual representation of the pattern, so it will give you an idea of how the pattern will look in a way that written instructions cannot.

It's a good idea to make a photocopy of the pattern on which you can mark off every row as you finish it. This way, if you have to put the knitting away, you are less likely to lose your place in the pattern. On this copy also write any changes you've made to the pattern, and any notes of things you need to remember. If the pattern gives instructions for several different sizes, you will find it useful to circle or highlight the instructions pertaining to the size you are making.

A pattern should give the finished size of the item; if for a sweater, it should give measurements for the chest, length and sleeve seams. If the pattern has both imperial and metric measurements, use one or the other; never mix them up. Many patterns are written for several sizes. Instructions for the smallest size are given first, then for the remaining sizes in parentheses. If only one instruction or figure is given, it pertains to all the sizes. The pattern should also tell you the equipment and amounts of yarn required and the tension (gauge) (see page 372).

Knitting instructions are generally given in abbreviated form to save space. The pattern will explain what each abbreviation means and, where appropriate, how you make that stitch or perform that technique.

When a sequence of stitches is repeated, this is indicated with asterisks or parentheses. For example, '*p3, k3, rep from * to end' means to purl three stitches, then knit three stitches, then repeat that sequence to the end of the row. This instruction could also be written '(p3, k3), rep to end'.

When there are decreases or increases, a figure or figures will often be given in square brackets — for example [56 sts] — to indicate how many stitches you should have at the end of that row or section of knitting.

Read the pattern completely before beginning, to make sure you understand all the abbreviations. Look up any unfamiliar terms or stitches. If attempting a stitch pattern for the first time, work a sample swatch to familiarize yourself with the sequence before beginning the garment itself. It is less frustrating to have to re-do a small swatch than part of a large garment. If you cannot understand part of a pattern, don't assume that the pattern is wrong or that you are stupid; some sections of a pattern may only become clear once you are actually knitting them.

Abbreviations

The following are the most common abbreviations used in knitting. Abbreviations that are specific to a particular pattern are explained on the pattern page.

alt alternate

beg begin/beginning

C1, C2, C3 etc contrast colour 1, 2, 3 etc (when there are several contrast colours)

C4B make 4-stitch right-twisting cable: slip 2 sts onto cable needle, hold cable needle at back of work, k2 from left needle, k2 from cable needle

C4F make 4-stitch left-twisting cable: slip 2 sts onto cable needle, hold cable needle at front of work, k2 from left needle, k2 from cable needle

C6B make 6-stitch right-twisting cable: slip 3 sts onto cable needle, hold cable needle at back of work, k3 from left needle, k3 from cable needle

C6F make 6-stitch left-twisting cable: slip 3 sts onto cable needle, hold cable needle at front of work, k3 from left needle, k3 from cable needle

CC contrast colour (when there is only one contrast colour)

CO cast on (see also 'end cast-on')

col(s) colour(s)

cont continue

dec decrease/decreasing

double rib 1 row of knit 2, purl 2, alternating with 1 row of purl 2, knit 2, continued to form pattern

dpn(s) double-pointed needle(s)

end cast-on a cast-on performed in the middle of a row: wrap the yarn around your left thumb, then insert the tip of the right needle into the thumb loop and transfer it to the right needle (see photograph on page 82). This casts on one stitch. Rep as needed.

foll follows/following

garter st garter stitch

in inch(es)

inc increase/increasing; or, increase by working into the front and back of the same stitch

k knit

kfb increase by one stitch, by knitting into front and back of same stitch

knitwise inserting needle into next stitch as for a knit stitch (that is, from left to right and front to back)

k1b knit into the next stitch one row below, slipping st above off left needle (to create fisherman's rib pattern)

k2tog knit 2 stitches together to decrease number of stitches by one

k3tog knit 3 stitches together to decrease number of stitches by two

m1 make one (increase) by picking up the loop between two stitches and working into the back of it

MC Main Colour

p purl

patt pattern

pfb increase by one stitch, by purling into front and back of same stitch

prev previous

psso pass slipped stitch over previous stitch

purlwise inserting needle into next stitch as for a purl stitch (that is, from right to left and back to front)

rem remain(s)/remaining

rep repeat(ed)

rev St st reverse stocking stitch: one row knit, one row purl, as for stocking stitch, but with the reverse (purl) side of the fabric used as the right side of the work

RS right side(s)

sl 1 slip 1 stitch onto other needle without working it

st(s) stitch(es)

st holder stitch holder

St st stocking stitch/stockinette: one row knit, one row purl, continued to form pattern

tbl through back loop

tog together

WS wrong side(s)

yrn take yarn around needle to create new stitch

Crochet abbreviations

ch chain

dc double crochet (US single crochet/sc)

sl st slip stitch

Tension (gauge)

Tension, or gauge, refers to the number of stitches and rows per 2.5 cm (1 in) of the knitted fabric. Every knitting pattern will tell you what gauge should be used; it is vital to pay attention to this, as the gauge determines what size the finished garment will be. Every knitter knits at a different tension; some people knit loosely and others tightly. A slight difference in tension may not be crucial in an item such as a scarf, but it can ruin a garment such as a sweater that needs to fit precisely.

As well as determining the fit of a garment, an even tension produces a neat, even fabric. If you are a beginner, you may find that your tension varies from stitch to stitch and row to row at first. This is frustrating, but persevere; as you grow accustomed to the feel of the needles and yarn, and develop a smooth, rhythmic action, the fabric that you produce will become neater and more even.

Even if you think that you knit at a standard tension, always check your tension before beginning a garment. The half-hour or so that this takes is a worthwhile investment of time, as it will prevent the disappointment, and the waste of time and money, of a garment that does not fit.

The two tension swatches pictured opposite were knitted by the same person from the same wool, one of them on 4 mm (US 6/UK 8) needles and the other on 5 mm (US 8/UK 6) needles. The difference in needle size results in a noticeable variation in the size of the swatches.

Knitting a tension square

Before you being to knit a garment, you will need to check your tension by knitting a tension square. To do this, cast on using the size of needles specified and the yarn that you intend to use, whether the specified yarn or a substitute. Cast on until you have enough stitches so that they measure about 15 cm (6 in) when spread, without stretching, along the needle. Work in stocking stitch, or the stitch specified in the pattern, for at least 15 cm (6 in).

Cast off and (if appropriate for the yarn) lightly press the tension square. Insert a pin a few stitches in (do not measure from the sides, as the side edge is always slightly distorted). Measure precisely 10 cm (4 in) from the pin and place another pin at that point as a marker. Do the same vertically, placing the first pin a few rows in from the cast-on or cast-off edge. Count how many stitches and rows there are between the pins; this is your tension.

Hint

Save your tension square; it may come in handy later for testing how well the yarn washes, and whether it can tolerate being pressed. It is better to risk ruining a tension square than a finished garment.

Pin the ball band to the tension square so that you have a reference of the yarn used and how it knits up.

If the counts are correct, go ahead and start knitting the garment. If you have more stitches than the specified tension, you are knitting too tightly, and your garment will be too short and too narrow. Make another tension square with slightly larger needles, and measure again. If you have fewer stitches than specified, you are knitting too loosely, and your garment will be too long and too wide. Make another tension square with slightly smaller needles, and measure again.

If necessary, repeat this process more than once, until the tension is correct. This may seem tedious, but it will save disappointment, time and money in the long run.

Substituting yarns

In general, it is best to buy the exact yarn specified in the pattern, as the pattern has been designed for that yarn and other yarns may give different results. However, if you can't find (or don't like) the specified yarn, you will need to find another yarn of similar composition, properties and texture to the specified yarn. Check the thickness; the substitute yarn should be the same thickness as the specified yarn so that it will knit up to the same gauge. You can check the required gauge by looking at the ball band.

To work out how many balls to buy, it is more accurate to go by the length of yarn in the ball than by the ball's weight. For example, if the pattern specifies 13 balls of a yarn that contains 120 metres or yards per ball, you require 1560 metres or yards of yarn. If your intended substitute yarn measures 95 metres or yards per ball, divide 1560 by 95; the result is 16.4, meaning you will need to buy 17 balls of the substitute yarn.

Whether you are using the specified yarn or a substitute, it is always advisable to buy an extra ball just in case, as quantities of yarn used vary between knitters. Always knit a tension swatch before starting your garment, so that you can adjust the needle size if necessary.

Note that even when you find a substitute yarn that knits up to the same tension, the knitted fabric that it produces may not have the same appearance as that of the recommended yarn. This is due to differences in, for example, the way the yarn is spun or finished. If possible, buy just one ball of the substitute yarn to start with and knit a sample swatch to see if you are happy with the look of the yarn.

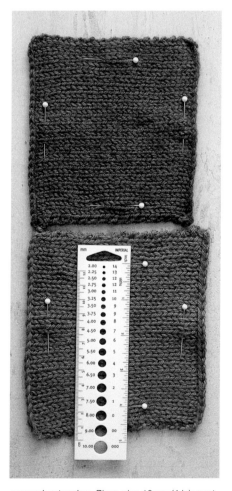

measuring tension Place pins 10 cm (4 in) apart and count the stitches and rows between them.

Beaded jewellery

The technique of incorporating beads into the structure of knitted cloth is hundreds of years old, and dates back to the early traditions of knitting. The basic principle of bead knitting is very simple, but the technique can sometimes take a little time to perfect. Use a variety of sizes so the beads will fit together like a random jigsaw puzzle. Use a yarn appropriate to the size of the beads; small beads will not work with thick yarn. Fine yarn such as beading thread or buttonhole thread is excellent. Most buttonhole thread will knit on 2½–3 mm needles and is available in a range of colours. Some manufacturers make linen and lurex threads, which can be fun to use.

Jewellery findings such as earring hooks, parrot clasps, crimps, jump rings and brooch clasps are available in various sizes and finishes from most craft suppliers or beading stores.

Materials for Pendant
108 glass beads in assorted sizes
Buttonhole thread
1 parrot clasp
4 crimps
2 closed jump rings

Tools for Pendant
2½–3 mm (US 2/UK 12 or 11) needles
Crimping pliers
Darning needle

Materials for Brooch
102 glass beads of assorted sizes
Buttonhole thread
1 bar-style brooch pin, 2½ cm (1 in) long

Tools for Brooch
2½–3 mm (US 2/UK 12 or 11) needles
Darning needle

Materials for Earrings
48 glass beads of assorted sizes (choose even numbers of each bead, so that the earrings will be identical)
1 set earring hooks
Buttonhole thread

Tools for earrings
2½–3 mm (US 2/UK 12 or 11) needles
Darning needle

Size
Earrings approx 4 cm (1½ in) long
Brooch approx 6½ cm (2½ in) long
Necklace approx 27 cm (10½ in)

Tension
Tension is not critical for these items

Pendant

Thread 48 beads onto the yarn. CO 5 sts.

Row 1 Knit.

Row 2 Slip first stitch, place 1 bead against knitting and k second st, k third st, place 1 bead against knitting and k fourth st, k fifth st.

Row 3 As for Row 2.

Row 4 Slip first st, k second st, place 1 bead against knitting and k third stitch, k fourth st, place 1 bead against knitting and k fifth st.

Row 5 As for Row 4.

Repeat Rows 2–5 until all beads have been incorporated.

Cast off, leaving a 15 cm (6 in) tail. Stitch the tails of the yarn into the fabric of the pendant to conceal them and cut them off close to the knitted fabric.

Cut a piece of yarn approx 1 m (3 ft) long and double it over. Feed the folded end into the needle and pass it through the fabric at the top of the pendant. You should have a small loop on one side and two ends of yarn on the other. Pull the ends of yarn through the loop and pull tight. Thread one large bead on one end of yarn and two small beads on the other, then push them down towards the pendant, securing them loosely in place with a knot. Rep until you have incorporated 10 medium or large beads and 20 small beads, and tied 10 knots (approx 1 cm/½ in apart). Thread two crimps onto the yarn, followed by a jump ring. Thread the yarn back through the crimps and pull the yarn through to give the desired length from the pendant (21 cm/8¼ in will give a classic 43 cm/17 in necklace).

Then, using the crimping pliers, squeeze the crimps flat (not too tightly, or you will cut the yarn). Trim off the ends.

Repeat the process with the remaining beads to create the other side of the necklace, up to the point where you have incorporated the remaining beads and have tied 10 knots. Thread two crimps onto the yarn, followed by a jump ring and a parrot clasp. Thread yarn back through the crimps and pull yarn through to give the same length as the other side of the pendant. Squeeze crimps flat and trim ends of yarn.

Brooch

Thread 102 beads onto the yarn, alternating sizes. CO 13 sts.

Row 1 Knit.

Row 2 Slip first stitch, (place bead against knitting and k 1 st, k next st) to end.

Row 3 Knit.

Row 4 Slip 1 st, (k 1 st, place bead against knitting and k next st) to end.

Row 5 Knit.

Repeat Rows 2–5 until all 102 beads are incorporated.

Knit 6 more rows.

Cast off in single rib. Cut off the yarn, leaving a 25 cm (9 in) tail. Use this tail of yarn to stitch the flat (cast-off) end of the brooch fabric around the bar of the brooch pin (this will become the top of the brooch). Secure it tightly through the holes in the bar so that it will not slide around. When the pin is secure, trim off the end of the yarn. Stitch the tail of yarn at the lower (cast-on) edge into the fabric of the brooch to conceal it and cut off the end close to the knitting.

Earrings

Make 2 the same.

Divide the beads into 2 piles, splitting different beads evenly between the piles to give matching earrings.

For the first earring, thread 1 pile of 24 beads onto the yarn, alternating sizes; thread the larger ones first, so they end up at the bottom of the earring, then medium, and finally small beads.

CO 4 sts, leaving a 15 cm (6 in) tail.

Row 1 Knit.

Row 2 Slip the first st from the left needle onto the right needle without knitting it. Draw up 1 bead, place it against the knitting and k the second st. K the third st, then place 1 bead against the knitting and k the fourth st.

Row 3 As for Row 2.

Row 4 Slip first st, k second st, place bead against knitting and k third st, k fourth st.

Row 5 As for Row 4.

Repeat rows 2–5 until all 24 beads have been used.

Cast off, then cut yarn, leaving a tail of about 25 cm (9 in). Thread this tail of yarn into the darning needle and stitch it firmly through the bottom of the earring hook. Then darn the remaining yarn into the fabric of the earring and cut off the end close to the earring.

Take the bottom tail of yarn (at the cast-on edge) and stitch it into the fabric of the earring to conceal it, then cut off the end close to the earring.

earring This shows the cast-off end attached to the earring hook

back of brooch This shows the brooch pin attached to the flat (cast-off) end of the knitted fabric

index

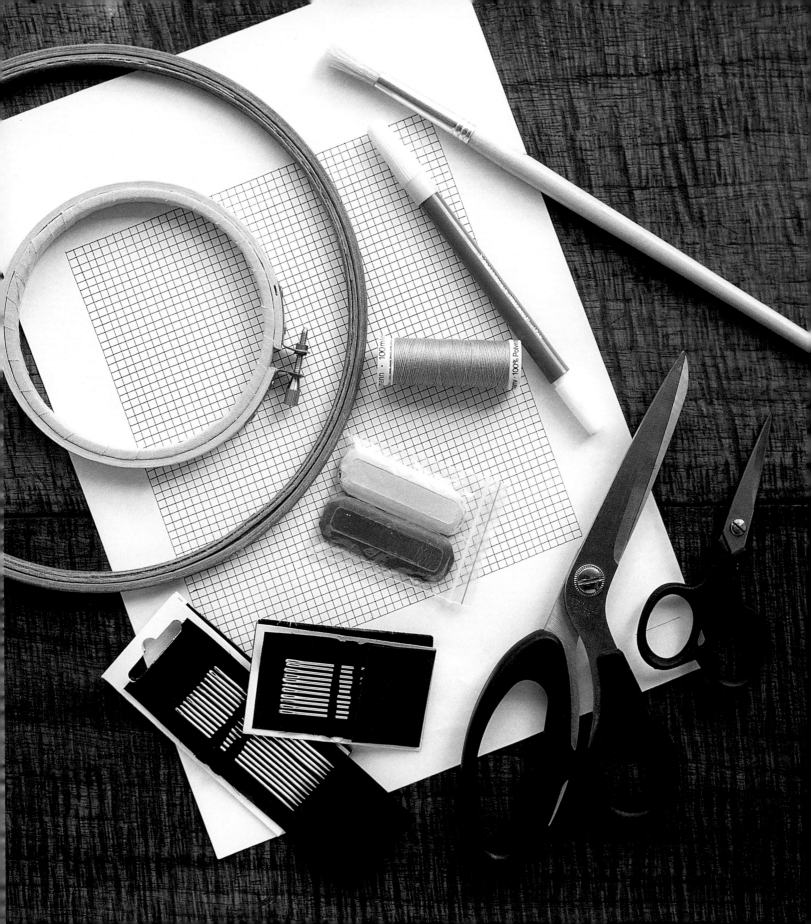